Blueprint for Success
Implementing MTSS in Your School District

Anthony Fitzpatrick Ed.D.

Copyright © 2025 MTSS Leadership Network

All rights reserved.

No part of this book may be reproduced or transmitted in any form or by any means, electronic or mechanical, including photocopying, recording, or by any information storage and retrieval system, without permission in writing from the publisher.

ISBN-13: 978-0-9864377-1-7
Published in the United States of America
MTSS Leadership Network

DEDICATION

To the unwavering educators, visionary leaders, and dedicated support staff who tirelessly strive to unlock every student's potential. Your passion, resilience, and commitment to fostering inclusive and equitable learning environments inspire this work. May this blueprint empower you to continue making a profound difference in the lives of countless children and shape the future of education with compassion and excellence.

To my family, who have supported me through this journey and my career in education.

Table of Contents

DEDICATION 3

Chapter 1: Understanding MTSS 14

1.1 What is MTSS? 14
Definition and Key Components 14
Core Components of MTSS 15
Rationale and Benefits 15
MTSS vs. Traditional Intervention Models 17
Concluding Thoughts for Section 1.1 20

1.2 The MTSS Framework & Its Tiers 20
Tier 1: Universal Supports 20
Tier 2: Targeted/Small Group Interventions 21
Tier 3: Intensive/Individualized Interventions 22
Connecting the Tiers: A Continuum of Support 23
Practical Tips for Implementation 24
Conclusion of Section 1.2 25

1.3 Foundations of Effective MTSS 25
A Systems Approach to Education 25
Team-Based Leadership and Collaboration 26
The Importance of Equity and Inclusivity 27
Reflection & Planning 28

1.4 Reflection & Planning 29
Self-Assessment: Current Understanding and Existing Systems 29
Identifying Key Challenges and Opportunities 30
Action Steps for Reflection and Planning 30
Looking Ahead 31

Chapter 2: Laying the Foundation for MTSS Success 32

2.1 Establishing a Vision and Setting Goals 32
Crafting a Mission Statement Aligned with MTSS Principles 32
Setting SMART Goals for Student Outcomes 33
Aligning MTSS with District/School Strategic Plans 34
Reflection & Planning 34

2.2 Building Leadership Teams ... 35
Roles and Responsibilities (District vs. School-Level) ... 35
Creating Cross-Functional and Interdisciplinary Teams ... 37
Scheduling Effective Team Meetings ... 37
Reflection & Planning ... 38

2.3 Developing Policies and Procedures ... 39
Data Privacy, Access, and Sharing Policies ... 39
Universal Screening and Progress Monitoring Protocols ... 40
Referral and Exit Criteria for Each Tier ... 42
Reflection & Planning ... 43

2.4 Reflection & Planning ... 44
Reflection on Vision and Goals (Section 2.1) ... 44
Reflection on Leadership Structures (Section 2.2) ... 45
Reflection on Policies and Procedures (Section 2.3) ... 45
Action Steps for Cohesive MTSS Implementation ... 46
Moving Forward ... 48

Chapter 3: Data-Driven Decision-Making ... 49

3.1 The Role of Data in MTSS ... 49
Why Data Matters in MTSS ... 50
Using Data to Identify Needs, Monitor Progress, and Evaluate Outcomes 50
Connecting MTSS Data to Broader School/District Systems ... 52
Practical Tips for Data-Driven Success ... 54
Looking Ahead ... 55

3.2 Universal Screening and Assessment ... 55
Selecting Screening Tools for Academic, Behavior, and SEL Needs ... 55
Implementing Efficient Screening Practices ... 56
Interpreting Screening Results ... 57
Reflection & Planning ... 57

3.3 Progress Monitoring ... 58
Setting Benchmarks and Tracking Growth ... 58
Tools and Techniques for Progress Monitoring ... 59
Analyzing Data to Adjust Interventions ... 59
Reflection & Planning ... 60

3.4 Reflection & Planning ... 60

Creating or Refining Your Data Cycle (Plan-Do-Study-Act) 61

Identifying Trends and Prioritizing Intervention Areas 62

Reflection & Planning 63

Chapter 4: Tier 1 – Universal Supports 65

4.1 Core Instructional Practices 65

Evidence-Based Curriculum and Instructional Strategies 66

Culturally Responsive Teaching and Learning 66

Instructional Differentiation to Meet Diverse Needs 68

Reflection & Planning 69

4.2 Schoolwide Positive Behavior Supports 69

Establishing Clear Expectations and Consistent Routines 70

Positive Reinforcement Systems (PBIS Alignment) 71

Classroom Management Strategies 72

Reflection & Planning 73

4.3 Social-Emotional and Mental Health Promotion 73

Universal SEL Curriculum and Practices 74

Building Trauma-Informed and Restorative Classroom Environments   75

Family and Community Engagement for SEL 76

Reflection & Planning 76

4.4 Reflection & Planning 77

Reflecting on Academic Core (Sections 4.1 & 4.2) 77

Reflecting on SEL and Mental Health (Section 4.3) 78

Assessing Overall Tier 1 Fidelity 78

Action Steps for Strengthening Tier 1 79

Looking Ahead 80

Chapter 5: Tier 2 – Targeted/Small Group Interventions 81

5.1 Identifying Students for Tier 2 Supports 81

Data-Driven Criteria for Entry 82

Collaboration Between Teachers, Counselors, and Support Staff 82

Preventing Over-Identification and Bias 83

Reflection & Planning 84

Small-Group Instruction Models 85

Use of Evidence-Based Intervention Programs 86

    Co-Teaching and Push-In/Pull-Out Services 87

    Reflection & Planning 88

5.3 Behavioral and SEL Interventions 89

    Small-Group Counseling and Skill-Building Sessions 89

    Check-In/Check-Out (CICO) Systems 90

    Mentoring and Peer Support Programs 90

    Monitoring and Communication 92

    Reflection & Planning 93

5.4 Monitoring and Communication 94

    Tracking Progress in Tier 2 and Adjusting Strategies 94

    Engaging Families and Caregivers in Tier 2 Support 95

    Decision Points: When to Transition Students or Escalate to Tier 3 95

    Reflection & Planning 96

5.5 Reflection & Planning 97

    Reflecting on Tier 2 Implementation 97

    Ensuring Sustainability and Fidelity 97

    Connecting Tier 2 with Tier 1 and Tier 3 98

    Action Steps and Future Directions 99

    Moving Forward 99

Chapter 6: Tier 3 – Intensive/Individualized Interventions 100

6.1 Criteria for Tier 3 Support 100

    Using Data to Determine the Need for High-Intensity Interventions ... 101

    Aligning with Special Education Evaluations (When Appropriate) 101

    Key Considerations for Determining Tier 3 Eligibility 103

    Reflection & Planning 103

6.2 Designing Individualized Interventions 104

    Developing Personalized Support Plans (IEPs, 504 Plans, or Other Plans) 104

    Intervention Techniques for Severe Academic, Behavioral, or SEL Needs 106

    Collaboration with Specialists (School Psychologists, Social Workers, etc.) 107

    Reflection & Planning 108

6.3 Ongoing Evaluation and Adjustment 109

    Frequent Data Collection and Review 109

    Communicating Progress with Stakeholders 110

    Making Decisions About Next Steps 110

Reflection & Planning 111

6.4 Reflection & Planning 112

Ensuring Capacity for Intensive Services 113

Resource Allocation for Students with Significant Needs.......................113

Next Steps for Your Tier 3 Journey 114

Reflection & Planning 115

Chapter 7: Integrating SEL and Equity Across All Tiers 116

7.1 Why SEL and Equity Must Be Embedded 116

Impact of SEL on Academic and Behavioral Outcomes 117

Addressing Disproportionality and Opportunity Gaps 117

Shared Goals of SEL and Equity within MTSS..................................118

Concluding Thoughts for Section 7.1 118

7.2 Building a Culturally Responsive MTSS...119

Cultural Competence in Curriculum, Instruction, and Assessment......119

Family and Community Engagement from a Strengths-Based Perspective 120

From Universal to Intensive SEL Supports...120

Reflection & Planning 121

7.3 Sustaining SEL and Equity Across Every Tier 122

Tier 1: Universal Culture of Equity and SEL..................................122

Tier 2: Targeted, Culturally Responsive SEL Supports...........................123

Tier 3: Intensive, Individualized Support with Cultural Competence..124

Maintaining Momentum Through Professional Development and Data 124

Reflection & Planning 125

7.4 Reflection & Planning 127

Reflecting on Your SEL and Equity Integration...128

Action Steps for Embedding SEL and Equity in MTSS................................128

Resources and Tools for Sustaining Progress...129

Looking Ahead...130

Chapter 8: Professional Development and Stakeholder Engagement....131

8.1 Building Staff Capacity 131

Designing Effective MTSS-Focused PD Cycles...131

Coaching and Peer Observation Models..132

Ongoing Training in Data Literacy and Intervention Strategies............133

Reflection & Planning 133

8.2 Engaging Families and Community 134
Strategies for Family Outreach, Education, and Participation 134
Partnering with Community Organizations and Mental Health Providers 135
Fostering Collaborative Culture 135
Reflection & Planning 136

8.3 Fostering a Collaborative Culture 137
Cross-Disciplinary Collaboration (General Ed, Special Ed, Administration) 137
Teacher Leadership and Shared Responsibility 138
Shared Responsibility for Student Success 138
Reflection & Planning 139

8.4 Reflection & Planning 139
Reflecting on Chapter 8 140
Action Steps for Comprehensive Professional Learning 140
Strategies for Effective Stakeholder Communication 141
Reflection & Planning 142

Chapter 9: Technology, Tools, and Resources 143

9.1 Leveraging EdTech in MTSS 143
Digital Platforms for Screening, Progress Monitoring, and Data Analysis 143
Online Intervention Tools and Personalized Learning Software 144
Practical Tips for Successful EdTech Integration 145
Reflection & Planning 146

9.2 Efficient Documentation and Reporting 147
Templates and Checklists for Tracking Student Interventions 147
Using Dashboards and Data Visualization to Drive Decisions 148
Enhancing Communication and Transparency 149
Reflection & Planning 150

9.3 Curating High-Quality Resources 150
Identifying and Vetting Evidence-Based Programs 151
Resource Hubs, Toolkits, and Communities of Practice 152
Cultivating an Ongoing Resource Culture 153
Reflection & Planning 154

9.4 Reflection & Planning 154
Reflecting on Sections 9.1–9.3 154

Technology and Resource Audit 155
Making Data-Driven Refinements 156
Fostering a Future-Focused Mindset 156
Conclusion of Chapter 9 157

Chapter 10: Continuous Improvement and Sustainability 158

10.1 Developing a Continuous Improvement Mindset 158
Plan-Do-Study-Act (PDSA) Cycles for MTSS Teams 159
Iterative Goal-Setting and Adjustment 160
Examples of PDSA in Action 161
Reflection & Planning 162

10.2 Scaling MTSS Across the District 162
Phased Implementation Strategies for Multiple Sites 162
Maintaining Fidelity at Scale 164
Sharing Success Stories and Lessons Learned 164
Reflection & Planning 165

10.3 Funding and Resource Management 165
Budgeting for MTSS (Local, State, and Federal Funding Sources) 166
Grant Writing and Community Partnerships 166
Maintaining Fidelity Over Time 167
Reflection & Planning 168

10.4 Reflection & Planning – Next Steps for Your MTSS Journey 168
Sustainability Checklist: From Pilot to District-Wide Adoption 168
A Roadmap for Long-Term Success 169
Celebrating Milestones and Looking Ahead 170
Conclusion of Chapter 10 170

Chapter 11: Case Studies and Success Stories 172

11.1 Real-World Examples of MTSS Implementation 172
Elementary School Success Story 172
Secondary School Success Story 173
District-Wide Transformation 173
Reflection & Planning 174

11.2 Lessons Learned and Common Pitfalls 175
Pitfall 1: Inconsistent Application of Tiers and Interventions 175

- Pitfall 2: Data Overload or Underuse 175
- Pitfall 3: Lack of Fidelity and Follow-Through 176
- Pitfall 4: Insufficient Collaboration and Stakeholder Engagement 176
- Pitfall 5: Ignoring Cultural Responsiveness and Equity 177
- Additional Pitfalls and Considerations 177
- Reflection & Planning 177

11.3 Reflection & Planning – Applying Lessons Across Contexts 178
- 1. Tailoring Lessons to Your School's Demographics and Needs 178
- 2. Building on Strategies That Yield "Quick Wins" 179
- 3. Evolving with Your Changing Student Population 179
- 4. Sustaining Momentum Through Reflection and Collaboration 180
- Reflection & Planning 180

Chapter 12: Your MTSS Blueprint in Action 182

12.1 Creating Your Personalized MTSS Roadmap 182
- 1. Pulling Together Reflection and Planning Components 182
- 2. Implementation Timeline and Checkpoints 183
- 3. Structures and Checkpoints for Accountability 184
- 4. Sustaining Progress and Celebrating Wins 184
- Reflection & Planning 185

12.2 Establishing Accountability Measures 185
- 1. Setting Up Review Processes and Feedback Loops 186
- 2. Celebrating Quick Wins and Milestones 186
- 3. Sustaining Accountability Over Time 187
- Reflection & Planning 188

12.3 Final Thoughts and Future Directions 188
- 1. Evolving Research and Emerging Trends in MTSS 188
- 2. Long-Term Vision for Your School/District 189
- 3. Next Steps for Your MTSS Journey 190
- Reflection & Planning 190

12.4 Integrating Continuous Feedback and Iterative Refinement 191
- 1. Establishing Feedback Mechanisms 191
- 2. Analyzing and Acting on Feedback 193
- 3. Fostering a Culture of Adaptability and Continuous Improvement . 193
- 4. Sustaining Momentum Through Innovation 194

 Reflection & Planning 195
Glossary of Key Terms..**196**
References **200**
About the Author **201**

Chapter 1: Understanding MTSS

1.1 What is MTSS?

A Multi-Tiered System of Supports (MTSS) is a systematic framework designed to provide high-quality, evidence-based instruction and interventions tailored to meet the varying academic, social-emotional, and behavioral needs of all students (McIntosh & Goodman, 2016). By integrating practices such as Response to Intervention (RTI) for academics and Positive Behavioral Interventions and Supports (PBIS) for behavior, MTSS ensures that districts and schools proactively identify student needs, monitor progress, and deliver supports at increasing levels of intensity.

Definition and Key Components

1. **Data-Driven Decision-Making:**
   MTSS relies on the ongoing collection and analysis of data—ranging from universal screening results to frequent progress monitoring—to make informed decisions about student placement and interventions (Burns & Gibbons, 2012). These data points help educators quickly identify students who may need additional or more intensive supports.
2. **Tiered Levels of Support:**
   MTSS organizes support into tiers. At **Tier 1**, all students receive high-quality instruction, universal behavioral expectations, and core social-emotional learning (SEL) supports. **Tier 2** provides targeted, small-group interventions for those who require additional help. **Tier 3** offers intensive, individualized interventions for students with the most significant needs (Fuchs, Fuchs, & Vaughn, 2014).
3. **Collaboration and Leadership:**
   Effective MTSS implementation depends on coordinated efforts among administrators, teachers, school psychologists, counselors, and other stakeholders (McIntosh & Goodman, 2016). Leadership teams work together to establish goals, analyze data, and monitor fidelity of implementation.
4. **Continuous Improvement:**
   MTSS is not a one-time initiative; instead, it is a continuous process of evaluating outcomes, adjusting interventions, and refining the system to best meet student needs (Buffum, Mattos, & Weber, 2010). Schools engage in iterative cycles of planning, implementation, and review to sustain and improve the quality of supports.

Core Components of MTSS

A successful MTSS framework relies on the integration of academic, behavioral, and SEL supports tailored to meet the diverse needs of all students. The structured tiers ensure that interventions are both scalable and specific, providing the right level of support at the right time.

To better understand the multifaceted nature of MTSS, it is essential to examine its core components across the three tiers. The following table provides a detailed breakdown of the academic, behavioral, and SEL supports integral to each tier of the MTSS framework.

Core Components of MTSS

Tier	Academic Supports	Behavioral Supports	SEL Supports
Tier 1	- High-quality core instruction - Differentiated teaching - Universal screening	- School-wide Positive Behavioral Interventions and Supports (PBIS) - Clear behavior expectations - Universal social norms	- School-wide SEL programs - Classroom-based SEL activities - Emotional regulation strategies
Tier 2	- Small-group tutoring - Targeted skill-building - Progress monitoring	- Targeted behavior interventions - Check-in/ Check-out systems - Social skills training	- Small-group SEL sessions - Peer mentoring programs - Enhanced emotional support
Tier 3	- One-on-one tutoring - Intensive skill acquisition - Individualized education plans (IEPs)	- Intensive behavior therapy - Functional Behavioral Assessments (FBAs) - Personalized behavior plans	- Individual counseling - Crisis intervention - Specialized SEL support

Rationale and Benefits

1. **Academic Gains:**
   When all students receive consistent, evidence-based instruction, the majority can succeed without additional supports. Those who need more help are quickly identified and receive interventions targeted to their specific academic challenges (Fuchs et al., 2014). This early identification and support reduce learning gaps and help prevent chronic academic failure.

2. **Positive Behavioral Outcomes:**
   By establishing clear expectations, providing systematic behavior supports, and using data to identify students who need additional social or behavioral interventions, MTSS can foster a positive school climate (Sugai & Horner, 2009). Schools often see reductions in office discipline referrals, suspensions, and expulsions when MTSS is implemented with fidelity.

3. **Social-Emotional Development:**
   MTSS frameworks increasingly integrate social-emotional learning components to promote self-awareness, relationship skills, and responsible decision-making (Greenberg et al., 2017). Fostering SEL within MTSS supports the "whole child" and reduces the likelihood of academic or behavioral issues escalating over time.

4. **Equitable Access:**
   By universally screening all students, schools are more likely to identify needs that might otherwise go unnoticed—especially in historically underserved populations. MTSS helps ensure that every student has access to the supports necessary for success, regardless of background or ability level (McIntosh & Goodman, 2016).

Beyond the structured supports, MTSS offers a range of benefits that enhance the educational experience for all stakeholders. By fostering a collaborative and data-driven environment, MTSS ensures that every student receives the support they need to succeed academically, behaviorally, and socially.

Benefits of Implementing MTSS

Stakeholder	Benefit	Explanation
Students	- Personalized Support	Tailored interventions address individual academic, behavioral, and SEL needs.
	- Improved Academic Outcomes	Enhanced instruction and targeted interventions lead to better learning results.
	- Enhanced Social-Emotional Skills	SEL programs foster emotional regulation, empathy, and relationship-building.
Teachers	- Structured Frameworks	Clear guidelines and tiered supports streamline instructional planning.
	- Data-Driven Decision Making	Access to comprehensive data aids in identifying and addressing student needs.
	- Professional Growth	Ongoing training and collaboration opportunities enhance teaching skills.
Schools	- Positive School Climate	PBIS and SEL initiatives create a supportive and inclusive environment.
	- Reduced Disparities	Equitable practices ensure all student groups receive appropriate support.
	- Increased Collaboration	MTSS fosters teamwork among educators, counselors, and administrators.

MTSS vs. Traditional Intervention Models

MTSS distinguishes itself from older or more fragmented intervention models in several ways:

- **Proactive vs. Reactive:** Traditional intervention models often wait for students to fail before providing help. MTSS uses universal screening to proactively identify needs and provide supports before large gaps develop (Fuchs et al., 2014).
- **Integrated Framework vs. Separate Silos:** Under MTSS, academic, behavioral, and social-emotional supports operate under one overarching system. In many traditional models, these domains function separately, making it more difficult to coordinate efforts (Sugai & Horner, 2009).

- **Tiered Continuum vs. Isolated Strategies:** Rather than offering a single intervention for students who struggle, MTSS provides multiple levels of increasingly intensive support tailored to each student's need (Burns & Gibbons, 2012).
- **Ongoing Data Use vs. One-Time Placement:** Traditional models may rely on a single test or teacher referral to identify struggling students. MTSS emphasizes regular progress monitoring to ensure interventions are effective and that students receive timely support or escalation to a higher tier when needed (Buffum et al., 2010).

Unlike traditional support systems, MTSS provides a proactive and holistic framework to meet the needs of all students. Figure 1.3 compares the two approaches, highlighting the strengths of MTSS in addressing both prevention and intervention.

Figure 1.3 MTSS vs. Traditional Support Systems

Comparison Categories	MTSS	Traditional Support Systems
Framework Structure	Integrated, multi-tiered system encompassing academic, behavioral, and SEL supports.	Often siloed approaches focusing primarily on academic or behavioral issues separately.
Support Levels	Three-tiered continuum (universal, targeted, intensive).	Less defined tiers, often reactive and individualized without a structured progression.
Data Utilization	Proactive, data-driven decision-making with regular monitoring and adjustments.	Limited data use, primarily used for identification rather than ongoing monitoring.
Scope of Support	Holistic approach addressing academic, behavioral, and social-emotional needs.	Narrow focus, typically addressing academic or behavioral needs in isolation.
Equity and Inclusivity	Emphasis on equitable practices and culturally responsive interventions.	May lack a focus on equity, potentially leading to disproportionality in support distribution.
Collaboration and Teamwork	High level of collaboration among educators, specialists, and families.	Limited collaboration, often with isolated roles and responsibilities.
Continuous Improvement	Ongoing reflection, feedback, and iterative refinements.	Reactive adjustments, less emphasis on continuous improvement.

Concluding Thoughts for Section 1.1

MTSS represents a fundamental shift from waiting for students to struggle to a system of early identification and responsive intervention. By integrating academic, behavioral, and social-emotional supports into a cohesive continuum, MTSS provides a clear path to help every student achieve success. The following sections will further explore how to build a solid MTSS foundation, how to effectively use data to guide decisions, and how to implement evidence-based interventions that support all learners.

1.2 The MTSS Framework & Its Tiers

A Multi-Tiered System of Supports (MTSS) provides a layered or tiered approach to meeting the needs of all students. In a well-implemented MTSS framework, each tier builds upon the previous one, offering increasingly intensive levels of support for students who need them (McIntosh & Goodman, 2016). While the specific design of tiers may vary by district or state, the general structure includes three levels of support: **Tier 1 (Universal Supports)**, **Tier 2 (Targeted/Small Group Interventions)**, and **Tier 3 (Intensive/Individualized Interventions)**.

Tier 1: Universal Supports

High-Quality Core Instruction and Curriculum

At the foundation of MTSS is **Tier 1**, which provides **all** students with access to high-quality, research-based instruction. This includes:

- Curriculum that is aligned to state standards and grounded in evidence-based practices.
- Culturally responsive teaching strategies that acknowledge and leverage students' diverse backgrounds (Gay, 2018).
- Clear, consistent behavioral expectations and social-emotional learning opportunities for all students (Greenberg et al., 2017).

When designed effectively, Tier 1 instruction meets the needs of the majority of students (i.e., approximately 80% to 85% of the student population), minimizing the number of students who will require more intensive interventions (Sugai & Horner, 2009).

Universal Screening and Assessment

Tier 1 supports also involve **universal screening**—the practice of assessing every student in key academic areas (e.g., reading, math) and behavioral or social-emotional competencies (McIntosh & Goodman, 2016). The goal is to identify early any students who might be at risk for academic or behavioral difficulties. These screenings typically occur multiple times a year to track student progress and ensure that the majority of learners are responding positively to Tier 1 instruction.

Schoolwide Positive Behavior Interventions and Supports

In addition to academic instruction, Tier 1 includes establishing a schoolwide system of positive behavioral supports. This might involve:

- Teaching and modeling expected behaviors.
- Recognizing students who meet or exceed these expectations.
- Maintaining consistent routines and procedures throughout the building (Sugai & Horner, 2009).

Such universal behavioral supports help foster a safe, structured, and supportive environment that is conducive to learning.

Tier 2: Targeted/Small Group Interventions

Despite high-quality universal supports, some students will require additional help. **Tier 2** interventions are:

- **Targeted**: Focused on a specific skill gap or behavioral need.
- **Small Group**: Delivered to small groups of students with similar needs.

Academic Interventions

In academics, Tier 2 might involve small-group reading interventions for students who have been flagged by universal screening as having foundational reading gaps. These sessions could occur outside of core instruction (e.g., in a resource period) or through differentiated instructional blocks within the classroom (Fuchs, Fuchs, & Vaughn, 2014).

- Use of evidence-based programs and materials (e.g., structured literacy interventions for reading, strategy-focused interventions for math).
- Regular progress monitoring (every two weeks or monthly) to assess growth and determine if additional supports are required.

Behavioral and Social-Emotional Interventions

Students who exhibit mild to moderate behavioral or social-emotional needs may benefit from small-group interventions such as:

- Social skills training groups (e.g., practicing communication and conflict resolution).
- Check-In/Check-Out (CICO) systems, where a student receives daily feedback and positive reinforcement from a mentor or teacher (McIntosh & Goodman, 2016).
- Short-term counseling or skills groups targeting specific needs like anxiety, peer relationships, or self-regulation.

Tier 2 interventions should be time-bound and measurable. If students demonstrate adequate improvement, they can return to receiving only Tier 1 supports. If they do not respond to Tier 2 strategies, they may need to move on to Tier 3 for more individualized help (Fuchs et al., 2014).

Tier 3: Intensive/Individualized Interventions

Tier 3 offers the highest level of support within an MTSS framework, providing **individualized** interventions for students with significant academic, behavioral, or social-emotional challenges.

Individualized Academic Support

Students in Tier 3 often have more pronounced gaps in foundational skills or may not have responded adequately to Tier 2 interventions. Tier 3 supports:

- Are **highly intensive**—often delivered one-on-one or in very small groups of two to three students.
- Are **driven by diagnostic assessments**, which provide detailed information about skill deficits (Burns & Gibbons, 2012).
- Involve **frequent progress monitoring**—often weekly—to ensure that interventions are tailored and adjusted based on real-time data.

Many students receiving Tier 3 supports will also be evaluated for, or may already have, Individualized Education Programs (IEPs) under the Individuals with Disabilities Education Act (IDEA). However, it is important to note that not all students in Tier 3 will qualify for special education services. The MTSS process helps teams make informed decisions about the necessity of more formalized special education evaluations.

Intensive Behavioral and SEL Supports

Students with severe or chronic behavioral issues or significant social-emotional challenges may require individualized plans that go beyond small-group interventions. Tier 3 supports can include:

- Functional Behavioral Assessments (FBA) and Behavior Intervention Plans (BIP) designed to address the specific triggers and functions of a student's behavior (Sugai & Horner, 2009).
- Wraparound services involving counselors, social workers, mental health professionals, and community resources.
- Highly specialized or trauma-informed strategies tailored to the student's context (Greenberg et al., 2017).

Connecting the Tiers: A Continuum of Support

MTSS views these tiers as **a continuum**, where students can move between tiers as their needs change. A student might briefly receive Tier 2 reading support and then return to Tier 1 after demonstrating sufficient progress. Conversely, some students may need more comprehensive, individualized support for an extended period (Fuchs et al., 2014).

1. **Early and Ongoing Identification**: Frequent universal screening and progress monitoring ensure students do not slip through the cracks.
2. **Fluid Movement Between Tiers**: A student's supports should adjust based on reliable, ongoing data—rather than staying static for an arbitrary time frame.
3. **Collaboration and Communication**: Successful tier transitions often depend on strong communication among classroom teachers, intervention specialists, administrators, and families (McIntosh & Goodman, 2016).

Figure 1.2 MTSS Framework

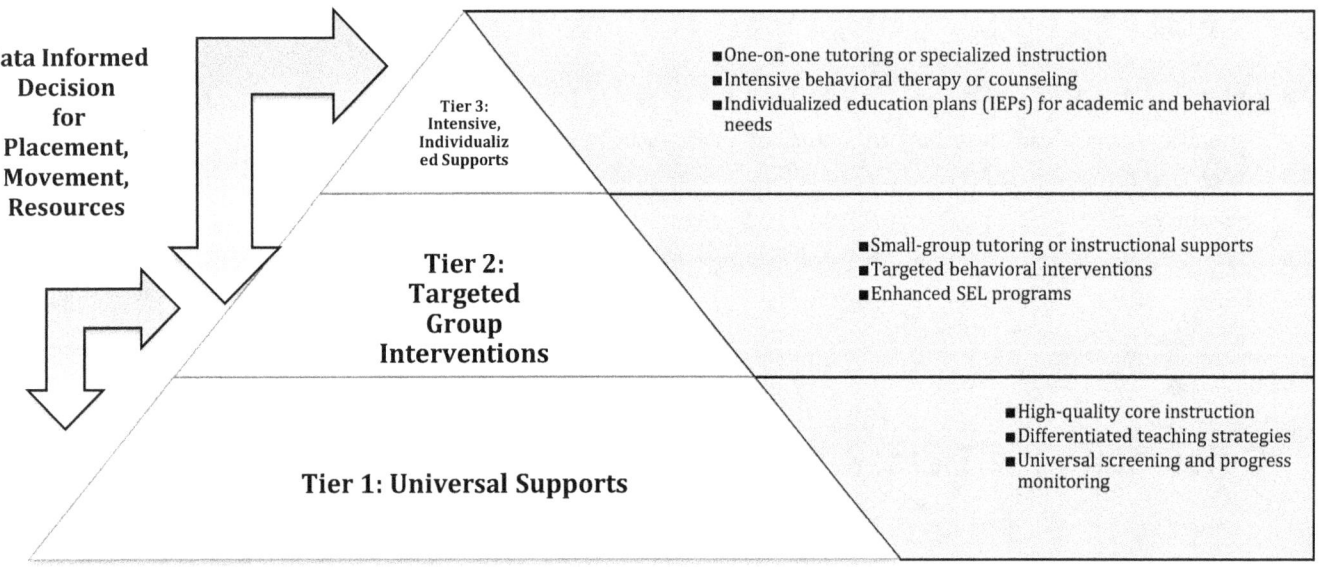

Practical Tips for Implementation

1. **Establish Clear Entry and Exit Criteria**
   - Define data-based thresholds for moving a student from Tier 1 to Tier 2 or from Tier 2 to Tier 3.
   - Create school- or district-wide guidelines to maintain consistency and clarity among staff (Buffum, Mattos, & Weber, 2010).
2. **Ensure Fidelity of Each Tier**
   - Provide professional development for staff on how to effectively implement Tier 1 strategies (e.g., differentiated instruction, classroom management).
   - Use intervention integrity checklists or fidelity check-ins for Tier 2 and Tier 3 programs to ensure that supports are delivered as intended (Burns & Gibbons, 2012).
3. **Monitor Data Consistently**
   - Adopt a user-friendly data management system so that educators can easily track student progress.
   - Meet regularly (e.g., monthly) to review progress monitoring data and adjust interventions as necessary (Fuchs et al., 2014).
4. **Communicate with Families**
   - Share screening results, progress monitoring data, and intervention plans with families.
   - Collaborate with parents or guardians to reinforce learning, behavior, or social-emotional strategies at home (Sugai & Horner, 2009).

Conclusion of Section 1.2

The three-tiered structure at the heart of MTSS ensures a well-organized approach to supporting every learner. By providing increasingly intensive interventions aligned to students' academic, behavioral, and social-emotional needs, schools create an environment where each student can thrive. In the next sections, we will delve deeper into establishing a solid foundation for MTSS success, including leadership team development, goal-setting, and the policies and procedures essential to maintaining a robust multi-tiered framework.

1.3 Foundations of Effective MTSS

Implementing a Multi-Tiered System of Supports (MTSS) requires more than just adding a new set of programs or interventions. It demands a holistic, **systems-level approach** that brings together leadership, collaboration, and equity as core principles (McIntosh & Goodman, 2016). These foundational elements serve as the bedrock on which all MTSS practices are built, ensuring coherence, consistency, and sustainability over the long term.

A Systems Approach to Education

A "systems approach" looks at education as an interconnected network of stakeholders, practices, and policies. Rather than focusing on isolated interventions, MTSS emphasizes alignment and coordination across **all** levels—from the district office to the classroom (Fullan, 2014).

1. **Coordinated Policies and Procedures**
   - District-level guidelines (e.g., universal screening protocols, data-sharing agreements) provide a clear blueprint for schools to follow.
   - School-level teams adapt these guidelines to meet local needs while maintaining fidelity to district and state regulations.
2. **Cross-Functional Intersections**
   - MTSS merges academic, social-emotional, and behavioral supports in one framework. This promotes cohesive planning, where, for example, social-emotional learning (SEL) strategies are integrated into academic instruction (Greenberg et al., 2017).

- Community partnerships (e.g., mental health agencies, after-school programs) can align with the school's MTSS vision to ensure that students' needs are met both inside and outside the classroom.

3. **Continuous Improvement Culture**
    - Data-driven decision-making is a hallmark of MTSS. Schools routinely review student performance data and implementation fidelity metrics (Burns & Gibbons, 2012).
    - This cycle of planning, action, and evaluation encourages an adaptable system that can respond quickly to new challenges or emerging student needs.

A systems approach ensures that each school or district component—the people, processes, and policies—operates in harmony rather than isolation, thus maximizing the impact on student outcomes (Fullan, 2014).

Figure 1.3 The Evolution of MTSS

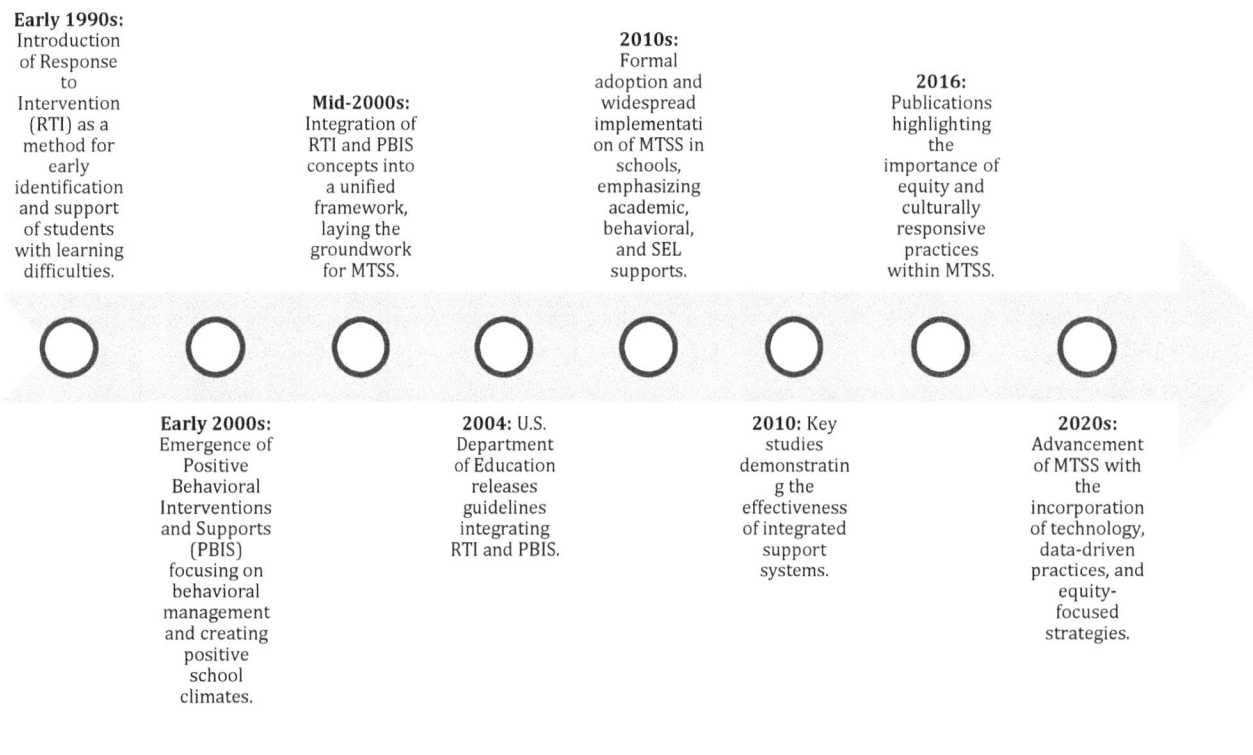

Team-Based Leadership and Collaboration

At its core, MTSS implementation is a **collective effort**. While a principal or district leader may serve as the driving force, success hinges on effective teamwork that shares responsibility and builds capacity across the organization (Spillane, 2006).

1. **Leadership Structures**
   - **District Leadership Teams (DLT):** These groups typically include district administrators, curriculum directors, special education directors, and other key stakeholders. They set the overall MTSS vision and policy framework.
   - **School-Based MTSS Teams:** Composed of principals, teachers, school psychologists, counselors, and instructional coaches, these teams implement the district's MTSS framework at the building level. They analyze data, plan interventions, and monitor fidelity.
   - **Grade-Level or Department Teams:** Smaller teams dedicated to shared student groups or subject areas. They often serve as the frontline for identifying at-risk students and delivering tiered supports.
2. **Collaboration and Shared Expertise**
   - **Regular Meeting Cycles:** Teams should convene routinely (e.g., weekly, biweekly) to review data, refine interventions, and discuss implementation challenges (McIntosh & Goodman, 2016).
   - **Professional Learning Communities (PLCs):** Collaboration within PLCs fosters peer learning, encourages sharing of best practices, and helps educators refine instructional strategies (DuFour & Fullan, 2013).
   - **Distributed Leadership:** Rather than relying on a single "expert," MTSS teams tap into the diverse strengths of staff—making use of counselors' expertise in SEL, special educators' knowledge of differentiation, and teachers' insights into student learning styles (Spillane, 2006).
3. **Building Collective Efficacy**
   - Collective efficacy, or the shared belief that educators can positively affect student outcomes, has been shown to significantly impact student achievement (Donohoo, Hattie, & Eells, 2018).
   - By involving all stakeholders in decision-making and celebrating incremental successes, school leaders can build a culture where every staff member feels responsible and empowered to support students.

The Importance of Equity and Inclusivity

An essential goal of MTSS is to ensure **all** students, regardless of background or ability level, have access to the supports they need. This emphasis on equity is woven into every tier and practice within the system (McIntosh & Goodman, 2016).

1. **Culturally Responsive Practices**
   - Culturally responsive teaching tailors instructional materials and strategies to students' backgrounds, interests, and experiences (Gay, 2018).

- Incorporating students' cultural and linguistic heritage in curricula ensures that Tier 1 supports reach—and resonate with—a diverse student body.
2. **Identifying and Addressing Disproportionality**
    - Data systems within MTSS should track not only overall performance but also disaggregate results by race, gender, language status, and other relevant factors (Fergus, 2017).
    - If certain groups are overrepresented in Tier 2 or Tier 3, teams should investigate possible root causes, such as implicit bias in referrals or a mismatch between curriculum and student needs (Skiba et al., 2011).
3. **Inclusive Practices for Students with Disabilities**
    - Although MTSS is not synonymous with special education, it creates a framework where students with disabilities can receive supports within the general education setting, as appropriate.
    - Collaboration between general and special educators, along with proper differentiation in Tier 1 and targeted interventions in Tier 2 and Tier 3, helps schools move closer to a truly inclusive model (Fuchs, Fuchs, & Vaughn, 2014).

By weaving equity and inclusivity into the very fabric of MTSS, schools can proactively identify and support students who have historically been marginalized or underserved (McIntosh & Goodman, 2016).

Reflection & Planning

Before moving on to subsequent chapters, it's valuable to assess **your** current foundation. Consider the following reflection prompts and planning exercises:

1. **Self-Assessment: Current Systems**
    - Does your school or district have a clear, consistent process for identifying students who need additional supports?
    - How well do existing academic, behavioral, and SEL initiatives align under one unified framework?
2. **Identifying Key Challenges and Opportunities**
    - What are the biggest barriers to effective collaboration (e.g., scheduling, competing initiatives, staff buy-in)?
    - What resources—human, financial, community-based—can be leveraged or reallocated to strengthen your MTSS framework?
3. **Team Readiness and Capacity**
    - Who are the key players at the district, school, and grade/department levels?
    - How can leadership roles be distributed to capitalize on each stakeholder's expertise?

By systematically evaluating these elements—systems approach, leadership and collaboration structures, and equity considerations—schools can establish a **solid MTSS foundation**. This groundwork will guide the successful implementation and scaling of the tiered supports described in the chapters ahead.

1.4 Reflection & Planning

Effective implementation of a Multi-Tiered System of Supports (MTSS) begins with a clear understanding of your current practices, system structures, and school or district culture (McIntosh & Goodman, 2016). This section provides guiding questions and planning prompts to help you reflect on what you have learned in Chapters 1.1 to 1.3, assess your organization's readiness, and map out initial steps toward a cohesive MTSS framework.

Self-Assessment: Current Understanding and Existing Systems

1. **General MTSS Awareness**
    - How familiar are you and your staff with the core principles of MTSS (e.g., tiered supports, data-based decision-making)?
    - In what ways are you already addressing academic, behavioral, and social-emotional needs in a coordinated manner?
2. **Policies and Procedures**
    - Do you have a district- or school-wide universal screening process? If so, how is the data used?
    - Are there clear procedures for moving students between Tier 1, Tier 2, and Tier 3 based on their response to intervention or support?
3. **Collaboration and Leadership**
    - Do you have established MTSS or RTI teams? If so, who serves on these teams, and how do they communicate with each other?
    - What role do administrators, teachers, and support staff currently play in the decision-making process for student interventions?
4. **Equity and Inclusivity**
    - How are diverse cultural and linguistic needs addressed in your core instruction and interventions?
    - Are there student groups (e.g., English learners, students with disabilities) who are disproportionately referred for more intensive supports?

Reflecting on these questions will help you identify where your system is already strong and where there may be gaps or inconsistencies that require attention (Burns & Gibbons, 2012).

Identifying Key Challenges and Opportunities

After examining your current state, clarify the challenges and opportunities that will shape your MTSS implementation journey:

1. **Challenges**
   - **Infrastructure or Resource Limitations:** Do you have enough time, personnel, and material resources to implement MTSS with fidelity (Buffum, Mattos, & Weber, 2010)?
   - **Professional Learning Gaps:** Are staff members equipped with the necessary skills to deliver tiered interventions, use data effectively, and collaborate across roles?
   - **Resistance to Change:** How might historical practices or established routines pose barriers to adopting a unified MTSS framework (Fullan, 2014)?
2. **Opportunities**
   - **Existing Initiatives:** Are there current programs—e.g., PBIS, SEL curricula, or departmental PLCs—that could be integrated into your MTSS approach?
   - **Community Partnerships:** Could local agencies, mental health providers, or after-school programs support your students' academic, behavioral, or social-emotional needs?
   - **Leadership Commitment:** In what ways can district or school leaders champion the process, secure funding, and model the collaborative mindset essential for MTSS success (Spillane, 2006)?

By naming your most pressing challenges and leveraging your greatest opportunities, you create a realistic roadmap that frames your next steps in MTSS planning and implementation.

Action Steps for Reflection and Planning

Below are suggested actions to guide your reflection and planning process:

1. **Assemble or Strengthen an MTSS Leadership Team**
   - Identify key stakeholders to serve on the team (e.g., administrators, general educators, special educators, counselors, psychologists, family representatives).
   - Establish a regular meeting schedule dedicated to data review, strategic planning, and monitoring fidelity of MTSS practices (McIntosh & Goodman, 2016).
2. **Conduct a Needs Assessment**
   - Review existing data sources (e.g., screening results, discipline referrals, attendance records) to gauge current student outcomes.
   - Use a "gap analysis" to compare desired MTSS practices (Chapter 1.2 and 1.3) with your current reality (Burns & Gibbons, 2012).
3. **Create an Initial Implementation Timeline**

- Outline short-term goals (e.g., create a district MTSS handbook, begin universal screening) and long-term objectives (e.g., reduce academic achievement gaps by a defined percentage).
- Designate who will lead each task, what resources are needed, and how you will measure progress (Buffum et al., 2010).

4. **Prepare for Professional Development**
   - Identify areas in which staff need further training (e.g., culturally responsive teaching, behavior intervention strategies, assessment literacy).
   - Plan ongoing professional development sessions and coaching support to build and maintain staff capacity (Donohoo, Hattie, & Eells, 2018).

5. **Engage Families and Communities**
   - Develop communication strategies to educate families about the MTSS model, clarify how they can be involved, and share updates on student progress.
   - Explore partnerships with community organizations that can offer supplementary programs or resources (McIntosh & Goodman, 2016).

Looking Ahead

The insights you gain from this reflection and planning process form the foundation for the work ahead. By pinpointing strengths, gaps, and clear next steps, you will be better positioned to move into the deeper components of MTSS—starting with **Chapter 2**, where we will discuss how to lay a strong organizational foundation, build leadership teams, and set measurable goals that align with your MTSS vision.

Chapter 2: Laying the Foundation for MTSS Success

2.1 Establishing a Vision and Setting Goals

An effective Multi-Tiered System of Supports (MTSS) begins with a **clear vision**—one that articulates why your organization is embracing MTSS and how it will improve outcomes for all students. This guiding vision drives decision-making, ensures alignment among initiatives, and fosters a sense of shared purpose among stakeholders (Fullan, 2014). When a district or school develops a strong vision statement aligned with MTSS principles, it lays the groundwork for strategic planning, resource allocation, and continuous improvement.

Crafting a Mission Statement Aligned with MTSS Principles

1. **Focus on the Whole Child**
   - A truly holistic mission highlights academic, behavioral, and social-emotional growth.
   - Emphasizing equity and inclusivity within the statement communicates that every student's needs will be addressed (McIntosh & Goodman, 2016).
2. **Clarity and Brevity**
   - Effective mission statements are concise yet powerful—easily understood by staff, students, families, and community partners (Bryk et al., 2010).
   - Use accessible language that resonates with diverse stakeholders.
3. **Reflecting Local Context**
   - While drawing upon established MTSS frameworks, ensure that your unique school or district context (e.g., student demographics, community resources) shapes the mission.
   - Include language that demonstrates cultural responsiveness and a commitment to addressing any achievement or opportunity gaps (Gay, 2018).

MTSS integrates academic, behavioral, and social-emotional supports into a comprehensive framework, ensuring every student receives holistic and equitable assistance. Figure 2.1 illustrates how these domains interconnect to support the whole child.

Figure 2.1 Integration of Academic, Behavioral, and SEL Supports

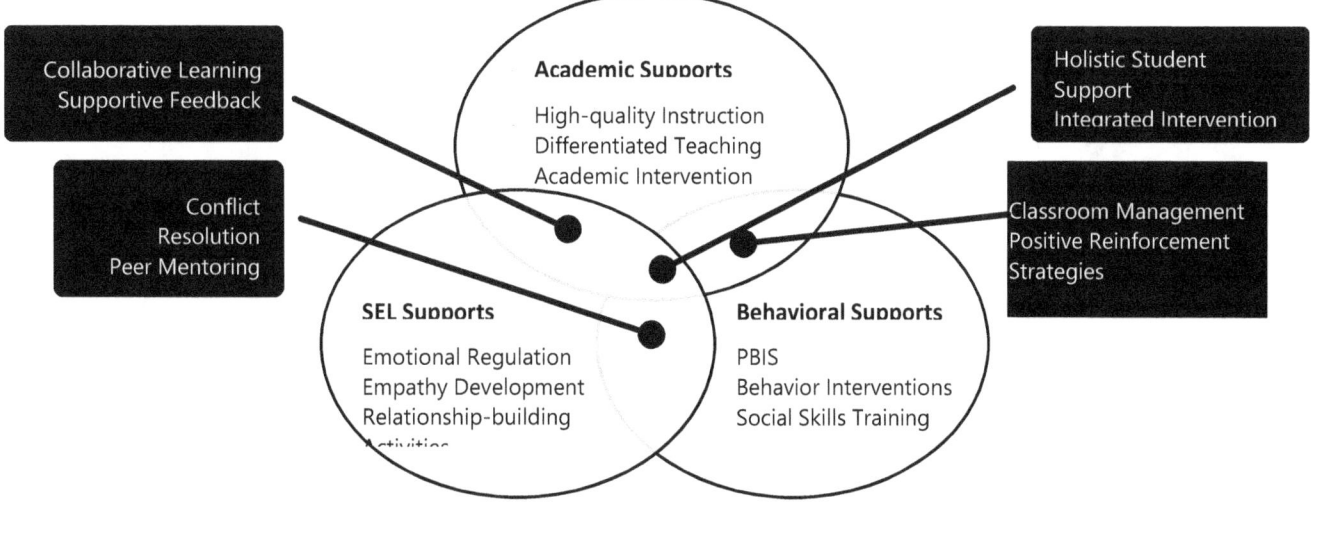

Setting SMART Goals for Student Outcomes

Once the vision is clear, the next step is establishing **SMART** goals—Specific, Measurable, Achievable, Relevant, and Time-Bound (Doran, 1981). Goals guide the strategic implementation of MTSS and provide benchmarks for tracking progress.

1. **Specific**
    - Instead of broad aims like "improve reading scores," set concrete objectives: "Increase the percentage of third-grade students reading at or above grade level from 70% to 80% within one academic year."
2. **Measurable**
    - Goals should be tied to quantifiable indicators—e.g., benchmark assessment data, behavior referral counts, SEL survey results—so progress is clear and actionable (Buffum, Mattos, & Weber, 2010).
3. **Achievable**
    - Assess your school's baseline data and set targets that are ambitious but feasible. Unrealistic goals may erode stakeholder confidence.
4. **Relevant**

- Align goals with your MTSS vision and existing district priorities. For instance, if SEL is a district-wide focus, include a goal such as "Reduce the number of reported peer conflict incidents by 25% through consistent Tier 1 SEL implementation."

5. **Time-Bound**
    - Each goal needs a definitive timeframe, whether it's a quarter, semester, or full academic year. This creates urgency and a built-in review point for evaluating effectiveness (Doran, 1981).

Aligning MTSS with District/School Strategic Plans

To maximize impact, the MTSS framework should be woven into **every** level of planning—district, school, department, and classroom. Consider the following strategies:

1. **Embed MTSS in the Comprehensive Improvement Plan**
    - Highlight MTSS as a central strategy in district or school improvement documents, ensuring that leadership teams frequently revisit and update related action items (Fullan, 2014).
    - Align resources—financial, human, and material—to directly support MTSS initiatives.
2. **Coherence Among Initiatives**
    - Avoid siloed programs by integrating existing efforts (e.g., SEL curriculum, PBIS practices, technology integration) under the MTSS umbrella (McIntosh & Goodman, 2016).
    - Clearly articulate how each initiative contributes to the collective vision and goals so stakeholders see a unified plan rather than disjointed projects.
3. **Stakeholder Engagement**
    - Communicate the newly crafted MTSS mission and goals to staff, students, families, and community members. Solicit feedback to ensure buy-in and relevance.
    - Present the alignment between MTSS goals and broader strategic priorities at school board meetings, parent-teacher organizations, and community forums.

Reflection & Planning

1. **Assess Your Current Mission Statement**
    - Does it address the whole child—academic, behavior, and SEL?
    - How explicitly does it commit to equity, inclusivity, and culturally responsive practices?
2. **Review and Refine Existing Goals**
    - Are your objectives SMART?
    - Do they align with district-wide improvement plans, or do they need updating to reflect MTSS priorities?
3. **Plan for Ongoing Review**
    - Establish a routine (e.g., every quarter or semester) for reviewing progress on MTSS goals.

- Involve leadership teams, grade-level or department teams, and community stakeholders in assessing goal attainment and identifying adjustments.

By articulating a clear vision and developing SMART goals, school and district leaders lay the groundwork for a cohesive MTSS that fosters high-quality instruction, timely interventions, and equitable outcomes for all students. The next sections will detail how to build and empower leadership teams to put these visions and goals into action, while also ensuring that robust policies and procedures are in place to support MTSS success.

2.2 Building Leadership Teams

At the heart of every successful Multi-Tiered System of Supports (MTSS) is **effective leadership**—a distributed, collaborative effort that brings together administrators, teachers, support staff, and community stakeholders (Spillane, 2006). By establishing leadership teams at both the district and school levels, you create the infrastructure needed to champion MTSS, align resources, and sustain continuous improvement. This section explores key considerations for forming and nurturing these leadership groups, including roles and responsibilities, team composition, and scheduling strategies.

Roles and Responsibilities (District vs. School-Level)

District Leadership Team (DLT)

- **Strategic Direction:** The DLT defines the overarching MTSS vision and ensures alignment with district goals (Fullan, 2014). This includes setting broad policies related to screening, data management, and funding for interventions.
- **Resource Allocation:** DLT members—often including the superintendent or assistant superintendent, special education director, curriculum coordinators, and department heads—collaborate on budgetary decisions and professional development needs across the district.
- **Monitoring and Accountability:** The DLT tracks districtwide progress toward MTSS goals (e.g., reductions in behavior incidents, improved reading proficiency) and provides implementation support to individual schools.

School-Based MTSS Team (SBT)

- **Implementation and Fidelity:** SBTs translate district policies into concrete school-level actions, ensuring that universal screening, data reviews, and tiered interventions are implemented consistently and accurately (McIntosh & Goodman, 2016).
- **Data Analysis:** School teams gather and review academic, behavioral, and social-emotional data to identify students' needs, assign interventions, and monitor progress (Burns & Gibbons, 2012).
- **Problem-Solving:** Through regular meetings, the SBT addresses challenges such as student motivation, staffing limitations, and curriculum adaptations. They also collaborate with grade-level or department teams to refine instructional strategies.

By clarifying responsibilities at both the district and school levels, you establish **shared ownership** and **clear lines of communication** that keep MTSS initiatives moving forward. Effective leadership is at the heart of MTSS implementation, with roles and teams working collaboratively at all levels. Figure 2.2 outlines the structure of MTSS leadership teams, showing their interconnected roles and responsibilities

Figure 2.2 Leadership Team Structure

Role	Responsibilities	Examples of Actions
District MTSS Coordinator	Oversees implementation across schools, allocates resources, and ensures alignment with district goals	Provides training, secures funding
School Administrator	Leads school-wide MTSS efforts, monitors fidelity, and supports staff	Conducts progress meetings, observes practices
Data Analyst	Collects, analyzes, and reports on MTSS data to guide decision-making	Generates progress reports, tracks trends
Intervention Specialist	Designs and delivers interventions aligned with student needs	Provides Tier 2 and 3 supports, coaches staff
Classroom Teacher	Implements Tier 1 interventions and refers students needing additional supports	Differentiates instruction, maintains data logs
Family Liaison	Engages families in the MTSS process and provides support	Organizes family workshops, communicates progress

Creating Cross-Functional and Interdisciplinary Teams

A hallmark of effective MTSS leadership is **inclusivity**—teams that represent the diversity of perspectives and expertise within the school community (McIntosh & Goodman, 2016). Consider the following guidelines:

1. **Include Key Stakeholder Groups**
   - **Administrators:** Principals, vice principals, or district-level leaders to ensure top-down support and policy alignment.
   - **Teachers:** General education, special education, and English learner (EL) teachers who bring front-line experience of student needs and classroom dynamics.
   - **Support Staff:** School psychologists, counselors, social workers, and instructional coaches to inform decisions about behavioral interventions, mental health, and pedagogy.
   - **Families and Community Members:** Representation from parent organizations or local community agencies can offer valuable insights into student experiences and supports beyond school walls (Bryk et al., 2010).
2. **Capitalizing on Individual Strengths**
   - **Instructional Expertise:** Some members may have deep content knowledge or expertise in culturally responsive pedagogy (Gay, 2018).
   - **Data Literacy:** Others might excel at analyzing student performance data or using data-management systems.
   - **Relationship Building:** Members who demonstrate strong interpersonal skills can lead initiatives for family engagement, peer coaching, or community partnerships.
3. **Cultivating a Collaborative Culture**
   - Encourage open dialogue and shared decision-making where each member's voice is valued (DuFour & Fullan, 2013).
   - Rotate meeting facilitators, share meeting minutes, and maintain transparency around decision-making and next steps.

Scheduling Effective Team Meetings

Consistent and well-structured team meetings are crucial for sustaining momentum and addressing issues before they become barriers. Below are suggestions for scheduling and facilitating productive sessions:

1. **Regular Cadence**
   - **District Leadership Team:** Monthly or quarterly, depending on the scope of districtwide initiatives. Meetings often focus on broad policy updates, reviewing aggregated data trends, and planning professional development (Fullan, 2014).

- **School-Based MTSS Team:** Biweekly or monthly meetings allow teams to review updated screening or progress monitoring data, discuss student support plans, and refine intervention processes (McIntosh & Goodman, 2016).

2. **Structured Agendas**
   - Begin each meeting with a review of **action items** from the previous session.
   - Allocate time for **data review**, **problem-solving**, and **action planning**—ensuring discussions remain focused and solution-oriented (Bryk et al., 2010).
   - End with a clear **summary of decisions** and **next steps**, assigning responsibilities and deadlines to specific individuals.
3. **Efficient Use of Data**
   - Share data ahead of time (e.g., via a secure platform) so members can come prepared with insights or questions (Burns & Gibbons, 2012).
   - Use data dashboards or summary reports that highlight key metrics (e.g., academic benchmarks, office referrals, attendance rates) in a user-friendly format.
4. **Flexible Formats**
   - In-person meetings foster team cohesion and relationship-building.
   - Virtual or hybrid formats can be used to accommodate districtwide teams with limited travel time or to include community partners who cannot attend in person.

Reflection & Planning

1. **Assess Current Team Structures**
   - Do you already have a functional MTSS or RTI team, and how frequently do they meet?
   - Which stakeholders are missing from the table, and how can you invite them to participate?
2. **Define Roles and Responsibilities**
   - Clarify tasks and expectations for each team member.
   - Align individual strengths with leadership opportunities (e.g., data analysis, coaching, family outreach).
3. **Review Your Meeting Calendar**
   - Are meetings scheduled frequently enough to keep momentum, but not so often as to become burdensome?
   - Can the current agenda format be improved to ensure purposeful discussion and follow-through?

By intentionally building and supporting leadership teams, schools and districts create **the core organizational structure** that drives MTSS success. When roles are well-defined, members are empowered to contribute their expertise, and consistent meeting routines are in place, these teams can effectively oversee data-based decisions, maintain fidelity of interventions, and foster a culture of continuous improvement. In the next section, we will explore the development of **policies and procedures** essential to sustaining a robust MTSS framework.

2.3 Developing Policies and Procedures

Behind every effective Multi-Tiered System of Supports (MTSS) lies a strong backbone of **well-defined policies and procedures**. These guidelines help ensure consistency, transparency, and fidelity as schools work to provide equitable, evidence-based support for all students (Burns & Gibbons, 2012). Districts and schools that clearly document their procedures for data collection, intervention protocols, and tier transitions are better equipped to implement MTSS with fidelity, evaluate its impact, and make ongoing improvements.

Data Privacy, Access, and Sharing Policies

Protecting Student Information

- **Compliance with Legal Requirements:** Schools must adhere to federal and state regulations that protect student data, such as the Family Educational Rights and Privacy Act (FERPA) in the U.S. (U.S. Department of Education, 2022). Define who has permission to view student records, how data is stored, and how it may be securely shared.
- **Anonymizing and Aggregating Data:** When presenting progress monitoring outcomes or screening data to broader audiences (e.g., board meetings or community partners), ensure student identifiers are removed to maintain confidentiality (Burns & Gibbons, 2012).
- **Staff Training:** Provide regular training for teachers, administrators, and support personnel on ethical data use. Emphasize adherence to established protocols, such as secure digital platforms and password protection.

Clear Data Pathways

- **Data Stewardship:** Assign responsibility for data collection and distribution to specific roles (e.g., data coordinators, school psychologists, instructional coaches). Clarity on who pulls reports, updates dashboards, and oversees data entry prevents confusion and errors.
- **Timely Access:** Ensure teachers and interventionists have **real-time** or **regularly updated** access to student performance data (McIntosh & Goodman, 2016). Quick and accurate data retrieval enables timely adjustments in interventions and instructional strategies.

Data is the backbone of MTSS, driving informed decisions and interventions. Figure 2.3 demonstrates the cyclical flow of data within MTSS, from collection to analysis and action.

Figure 2.3 Data Flow in MTSS

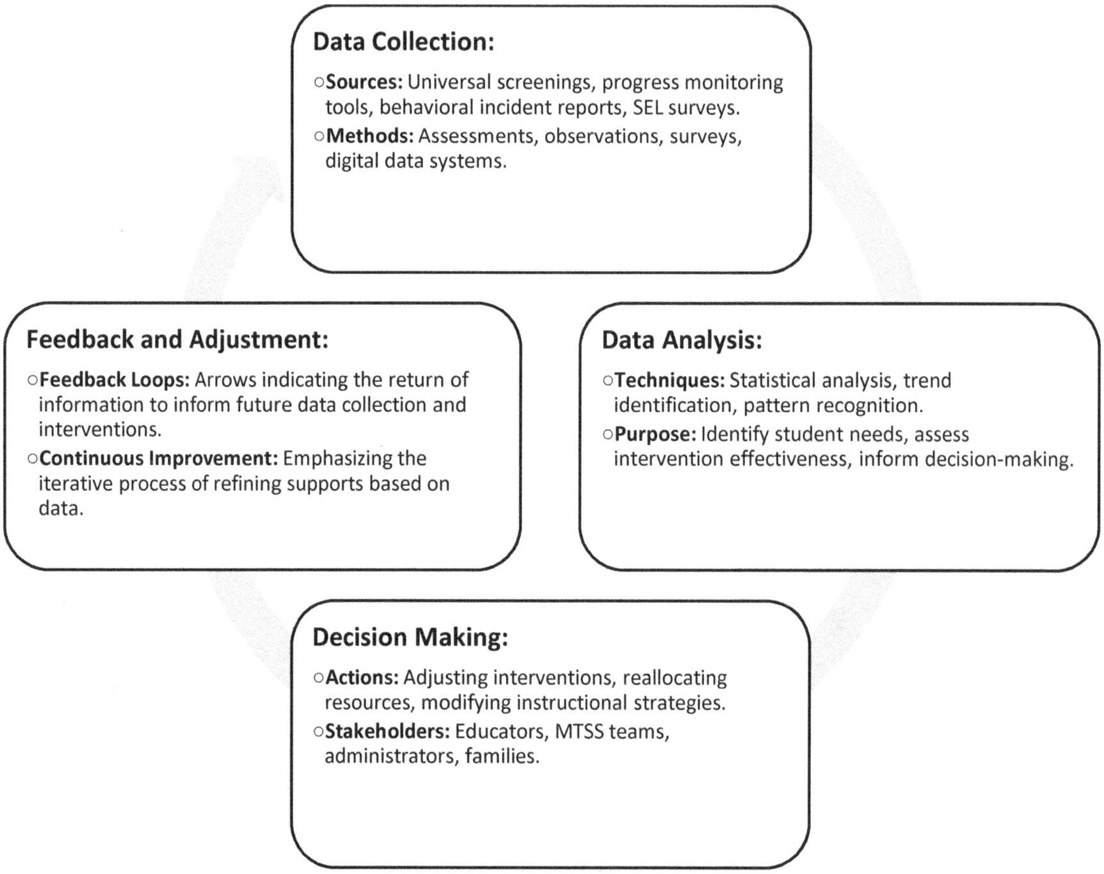

Data Collection:
- **Sources:** Universal screenings, progress monitoring tools, behavioral incident reports, SEL surveys.
- **Methods:** Assessments, observations, surveys, digital data systems.

Feedback and Adjustment:
- **Feedback Loops:** Arrows indicating the return of information to inform future data collection and interventions.
- **Continuous Improvement:** Emphasizing the iterative process of refining supports based on data.

Data Analysis:
- **Techniques:** Statistical analysis, trend identification, pattern recognition.
- **Purpose:** Identify student needs, assess intervention effectiveness, inform decision-making.

Decision Making:
- **Actions:** Adjusting interventions, reallocating resources, modifying instructional strategies.
- **Stakeholders:** Educators, MTSS teams, administrators, families.

Universal Screening and Progress Monitoring Protocols

Selecting Screening Tools

- **Multiple Domains:** Effective MTSS addresses academics, behavior, and social-emotional learning (SEL). Choose or develop screening tools that capture student performance in all three domains to get a complete picture of needs (Greenberg et al., 2017).

- **Evidence-Based and Culturally Responsive:** Pick tools validated by research and sensitive to cultural and linguistic differences, ensuring that all student populations are assessed accurately (Gay, 2018).
- **User-Friendliness:** Opt for assessments that are easy to administer and interpret. Overly complex or time-consuming screenings can overwhelm staff and lead to inconsistent implementation.

Screening Schedules

- **Frequency:** Most schools conduct universal screening at least three times per year (e.g., fall, winter, spring). Some may screen behavior or SEL less frequently but still benefit from periodic checks (McIntosh & Goodman, 2016).
- **Coordinated District Calendars:** Align screening windows across schools to facilitate timely comparisons, identify districtwide trends, and centralize data storage (Buffum, Mattos, & Weber, 2010).

Progress Monitoring Guidelines

- **Tiered Frequency:**
  - **Tier 1:** Occasional benchmark assessments for all students (e.g., every 8–12 weeks).
  - **Tier 2:** Bi-weekly or monthly checks to track response to targeted interventions.
  - **Tier 3:** Weekly or bi-weekly progress monitoring to inform rapid adjustments in high-intensity supports (Fuchs, Fuchs, & Vaughn, 2014).
- **Clear Documentation Protocols:** Specify how often teachers must record data, in what format (e.g., digital platforms, spreadsheets), and who is responsible for analyzing results. Consistency ensures no student slips through the cracks (Burns & Gibbons, 2012).

Screening Tools

Tool Name	Purpose	Target Areas	Frequency	Example Providers
STAR Assessments	Benchmark and monitor progress	Reading, Math	3 times per year	Renaissance Learning
DIBELS	Early literacy skills assessment	Phonemic awareness, fluency	3-4 times per year	University of Oregon
Behavior Assessment System for Children (BASC)	Assess emotional and behavioral strengths and needs	Behavior, Social-Emotional	As needed	Pearson
NWEA MAP Growth	Measure academic growth over time	Reading, Math, Science	3 times per year	NWEA
Panorama Surveys	Gather SEL-related insights	SEL competencies	Twice per year	Panorama Education

Referral and Exit Criteria for Each Tier

A core strength of MTSS is its **fluid movement** between tiers based on student performance. To support this, schools need transparent, data-informed criteria that guide decisions about entering or exiting each tier (McIntosh & Goodman, 2016).

1. **Tier 1 to Tier 2 Referral**
   - **Data Thresholds:** For academics, a certain score on universal screening or frequent mid-tier assessments might trigger further evaluation. For behavior, repeated discipline referrals or teacher nominations could initiate referral (Sugai & Horner, 2009).
   - **Timeframe:** Decide how many screening cycles or how many weeks of consistent data a student must show before referral to Tier 2.
2. **Progression from Tier 2 to Tier 3**
   - **Lack of Adequate Growth:** If a student is not making expected gains despite fidelity of Tier 2 interventions, teams should refer the student for more intensive support. Document the duration of Tier 2 interventions and ensure interventions have been implemented consistently (Fuchs et al., 2014).
   - **Significant Need Emerges:** Severe behavior incidents or sudden changes in academic performance may necessitate direct movement to Tier 3 without prolonged Tier 2 interventions.

3. **Exit Criteria for Tiered Interventions**
    - **Sustained Improvement:** A student demonstrating progress for a set number of consecutive data points (e.g., six to eight weeks) may be able to transition back to a lower tier or Tier 1 alone.
    - **Ongoing Monitoring:** Even after exiting a more intensive tier, continue periodic checks to ensure the student maintains progress.

By making referral and exit criteria explicit, schools reduce subjective judgments and maintain **equitable** practices (McIntosh & Goodman, 2016).

MTSS operates across three tiers, providing varying levels of support tailored to student needs. Figure 2.4 visually represents how these tiers integrate to create a seamless continuum of support.

Figure 2.4 Tiered Support Integration

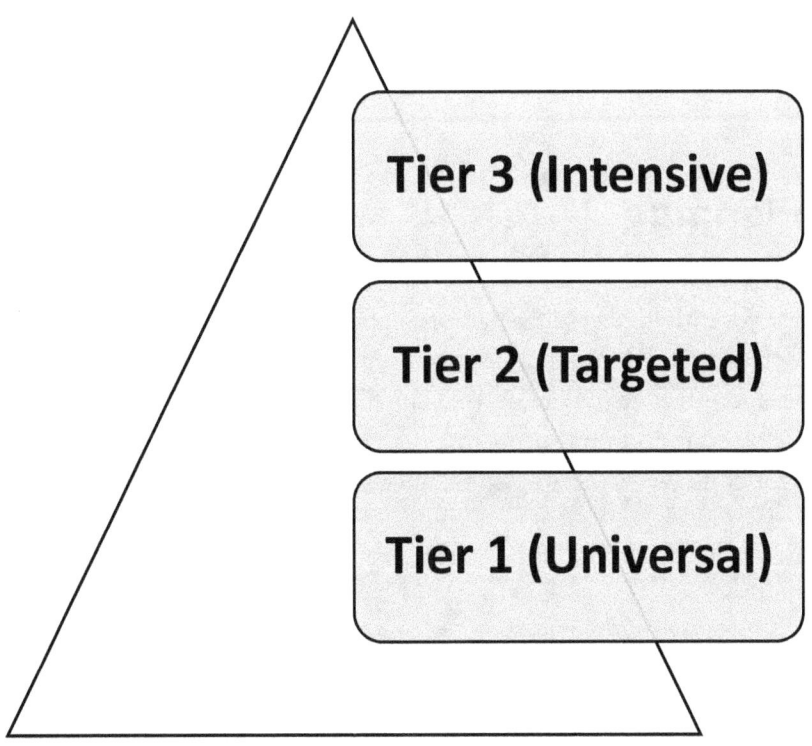

Reflection & Planning

1. **Policy Inventory**
    - Which written policies exist regarding data management, screening, and intervention placement?
    - Are these policies up to date, aligned with MTSS best practices, and understood by staff?

2. **Consistency Across Schools**
    - If you work in a district setting, do building-level procedures vary significantly?
    - Where can you standardize processes (e.g., universal screening schedules) to streamline student support?
3. **Training and Communication**
    - How are new policies introduced to staff and families?
    - Do stakeholders know how to navigate referral processes, interpret screening data, and apply tier movement guidelines?

By developing **clear, consistent, and equitable policies and procedures**, districts and schools create the operational framework for a robust and effective MTSS. When everyone—from central office staff to classroom teachers—knows their roles, understands how data is gathered, and follows established criteria for tier movement, MTSS can function as a **unified system** rather than a collection of isolated efforts. In Section 2.4, we'll revisit reflection questions that further guide you in assessing readiness and next steps, ensuring you have the foundation to implement MTSS with fidelity.

2.4 Reflection & Planning

Building a strong foundation for your Multi-Tiered System of Supports (MTSS) involves much more than developing a vision, assembling teams, and drafting policies—it requires **ongoing self-assessment** to ensure your system remains responsive and effective (Fullan, 2014). This final section of Chapter 2 provides guiding questions and action steps to help you reflect on the information covered in Sections 2.1 through 2.3, identify areas for refinement, and plan for cohesive MTSS implementation.

Reflection on Vision and Goals (Section 2.1)

1. **Alignment with District Priorities**
    - Have you clearly articulated how the MTSS vision and SMART goals support broader district or school improvement efforts?
    - Are stakeholders (teachers, families, community members) aware of and committed to these goals?
2. **Equity and Inclusivity in the Vision**
    - Do the stated goals explicitly address the academic, behavioral, and social-emotional needs of **all** learners?
    - In what ways do your goals ensure culturally responsive teaching and equitable outcomes for diverse student groups (Gay, 2018)?
3. **Measurable Success**
    - How will you track progress toward your goals?

- Do you have a plan for regular goal reviews (e.g., quarterly or semi-annually) to make data-based adjustments (Doran, 1981)?

Reflection on Leadership Structures (Section 2.2)

1. **Team Composition**
   - Do your District Leadership Team (DLT) and School-Based MTSS Team (SBT) include a broad range of expertise (e.g., general educators, special educators, administrators, mental health professionals)?
   - Have you identified potential gaps in representation, such as family or community partners (Bryk et al., 2010)?
2. **Collaboration and Communication**
   - How often do these teams meet, and are the meetings structured with clear agendas, action items, and follow-up procedures?
   - Is there a feedback loop between the district and school levels so that priorities are aligned, and progress is continuously shared (McIntosh & Goodman, 2016)?
3. **Team Efficacy**
   - Does each team member understand their role and responsibilities for MTSS planning and implementation?
   - Have you explored ways to leverage individual strengths (e.g., data analysis, coaching skills) to enhance overall team effectiveness (Spillane, 2006)?

Reflection on Policies and Procedures (Section 2.3)

1. **Data Management and Privacy**
   - Are there clear guidelines ensuring FERPA compliance or other relevant regulations (U.S. Department of Education, 2022)?
   - Do staff members have sufficient training on data handling and interpretation to maintain confidentiality and protect student privacy (Burns & Gibbons, 2012)?
2. **Universal Screening and Progress Monitoring**
   - Have you selected (or created) tools that assess students' academic, behavioral, and SEL needs in a valid, reliable, and culturally responsive manner (Greenberg et al., 2017)?
   - Is there a schedule in place—e.g., three benchmark screenings per year—to catch problems early and address them promptly (McIntosh & Goodman, 2016)?
3. **Referral and Exit Criteria**

- Are your thresholds for Tier 2 or Tier 3 entry and exit based on data-driven benchmarks to ensure objectivity and equity (Sugai & Horner, 2009)?
- How will you document intervention fidelity and student progress to make fair, timely decisions about tier movement (Fuchs, Fuchs, & Vaughn, 2014)?

Building staff capacity through professional development ensures fidelity in MTSS implementation. Figure 2.5 outlines the critical components of professional learning that empower educators to support student success.

Figure 2.5 Professional Development Components

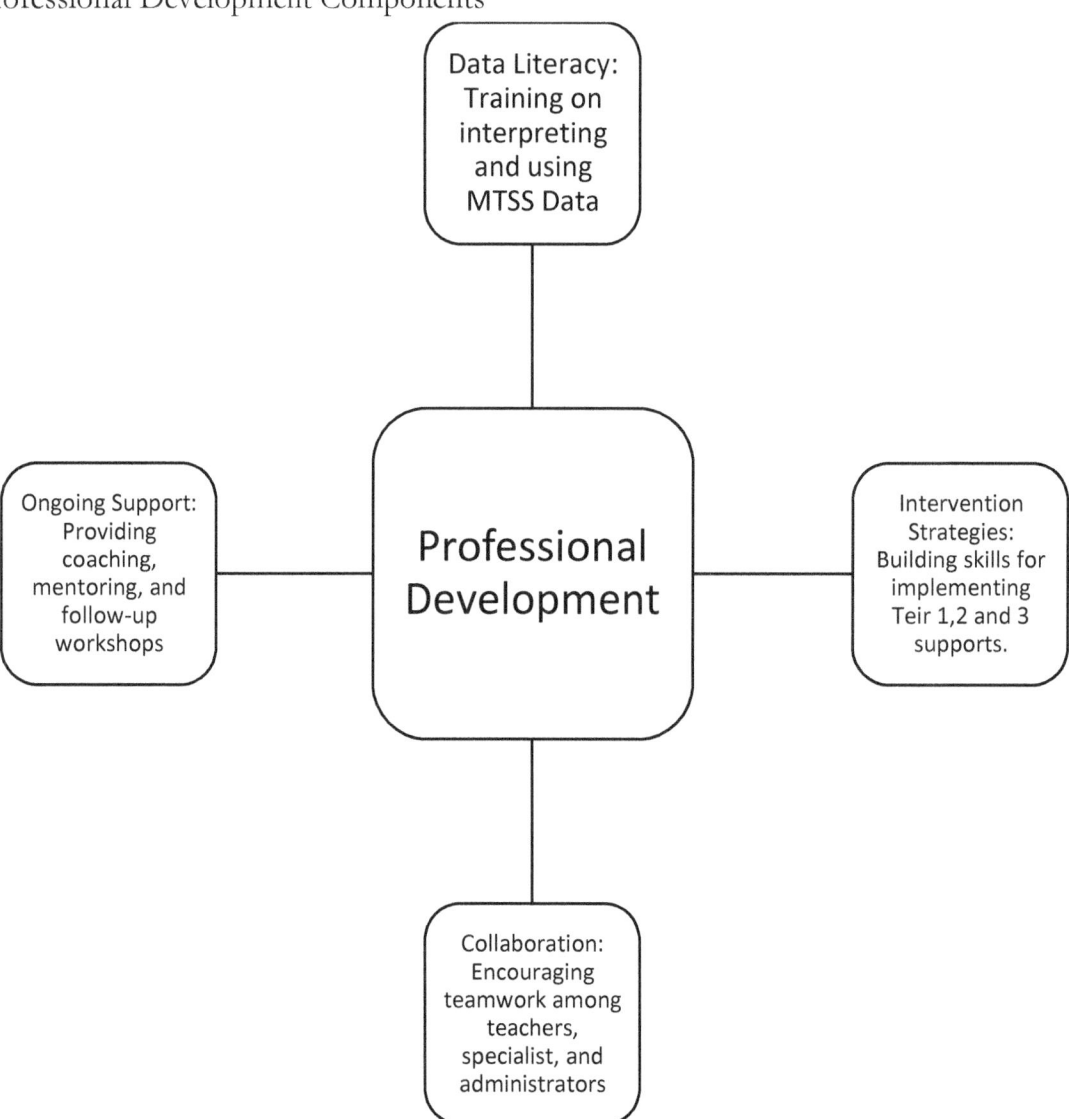

Action Steps for Cohesive MTSS Implementation

1. **Consolidate Documentation**
    - Gather your newly refined mission statement, SMART goals, leadership team rosters, and policy documents into a central handbook or digital resource.

- Ensure that all staff know where to find these documents and how to reference them for day-to-day MTSS operations (Buffum, Mattos, & Weber, 2010).

2. **Plan for Professional Development**
   - Identify gaps in staff knowledge related to data literacy, culturally responsive teaching, or intervention strategies.
   - Schedule regular, ongoing training sessions or coaching cycles to build capacity and maintain momentum (DuFour & Fullan, 2013).

3. **Establish Review and Accountability Processes**
   - Set up a recurring schedule (e.g., monthly or quarterly) for both district and school teams to review progress on MTSS initiatives.
   - Use a structured data protocol to evaluate interventions, discuss fidelity, and determine any necessary course corrections (Burns & Gibbons, 2012).

4. **Strengthen Stakeholder Engagement**
   - Communicate current MTSS efforts and achievements to staff, families, and the broader community through newsletters, open houses, and workshops.
   - Invite feedback and collaboration from parents, especially those representing diverse cultural or linguistic backgrounds (Gay, 2018).

Successful MTSS implementation requires a structured, step-by-step process. Figure 2.6 illustrates the workflow for implementing MTSS, highlighting key stages from planning to continuous improvement.

Figure 2.6 MTSS Workflow

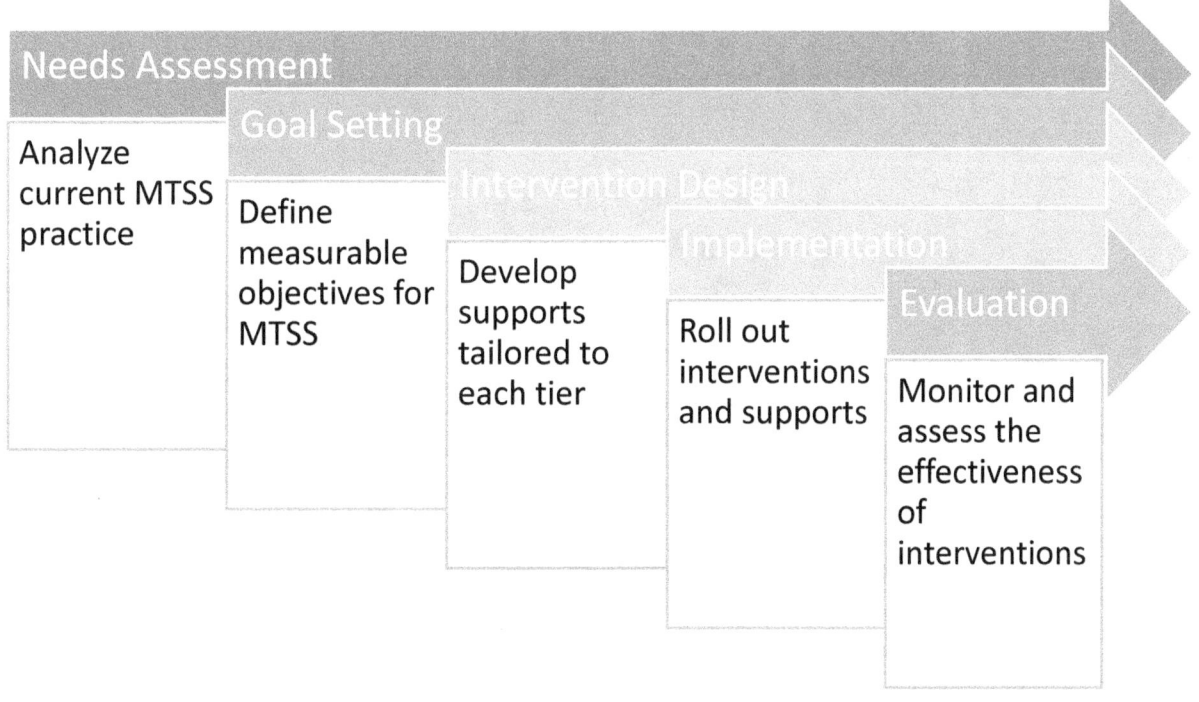

Moving Forward

By reflecting on the foundational elements covered in Chapter 2—your mission and goals, leadership teams, and operational procedures—you set the stage for **sustainable MTSS success**. These steps ensure that everyone involved understands the system's purpose, knows their role, and follows clear guidelines for data-driven decision-making. In **Chapter 3**, we will delve deeper into **data-driven decision-making**, exploring how to select appropriate screening and assessment tools, interpret results, and use data cycles to refine interventions.

Implementing MTSS with intentionality is an ongoing journey. By revisiting and refining your approach regularly, you cultivate a dynamic learning environment where every student's needs are met in a proactive, equitable, and evidence-based manner.

Chapter 3: Data-Driven Decision-Making

3.1 The Role of Data in MTSS

Data is the **lifeblood** of a Multi-Tiered System of Supports (MTSS). From identifying students who need extra help to evaluating whether interventions are effective, data serves as both a compass and a catalyst for continuous improvement (Burns & Gibbons, 2012). When used thoughtfully and consistently, data provides educators with a clear picture of student progress across academic, behavioral, and social-emotional domains—ensuring that decisions are grounded in evidence rather than guesswork.

Data serves as the backbone of MTSS, guiding decisions from early identification to program evaluation. Figure 3.1 illustrates the key roles data plays in driving effective, equitable practices.

Figure 3.1 The Role of Data in MTSS

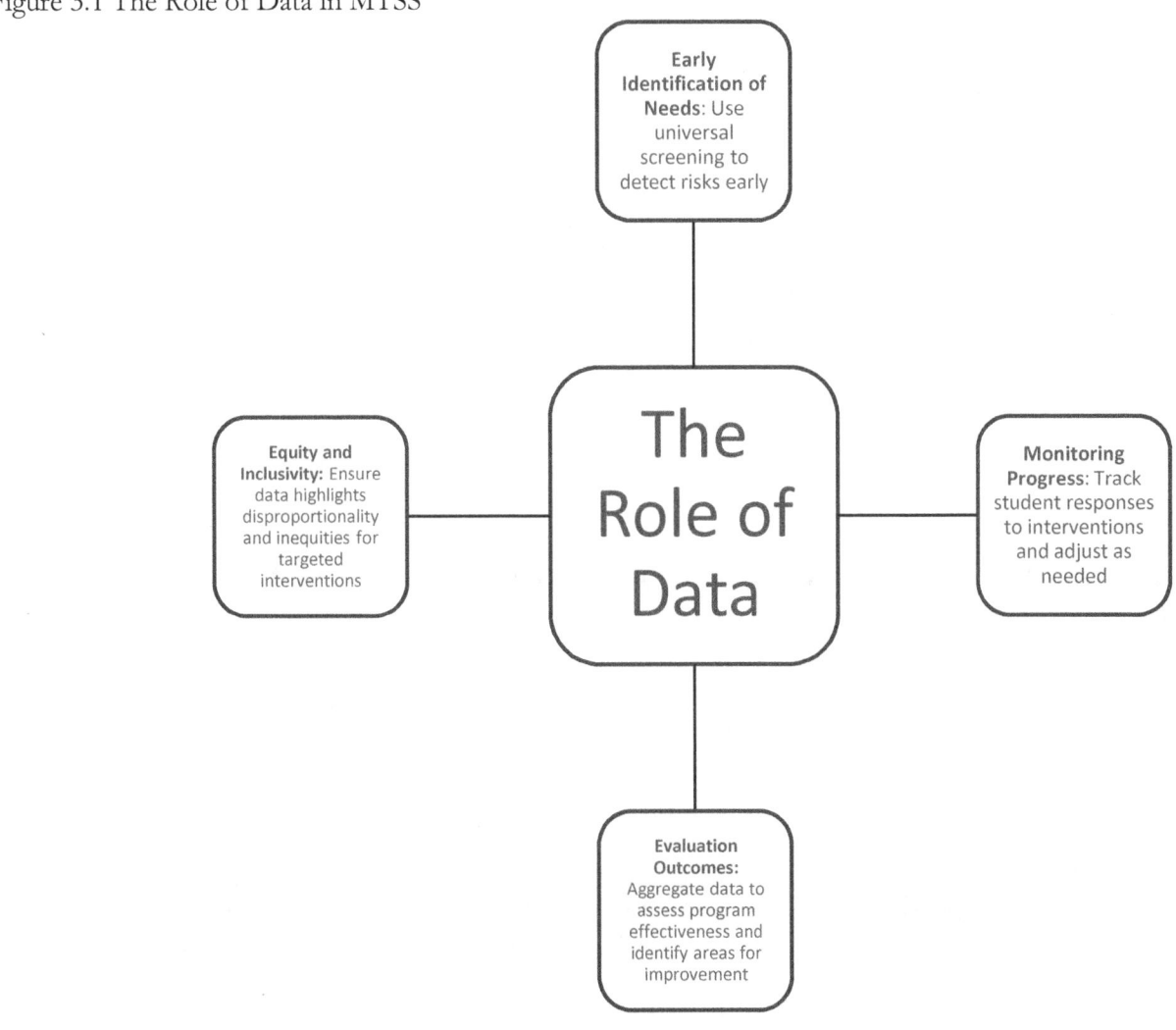

Why Data Matters in MTSS

1. **Early Identification of Student Needs**
   - **Universal Screening**: By administering brief, validated assessments at regular intervals, educators can quickly identify students who may be at risk academically, behaviorally, or socially-emotionally (McIntosh & Goodman, 2016). This proactive approach helps prevent small problems from becoming big ones.
   - **Equity and Inclusivity**: Data makes it easier to spot patterns of underachievement or disproportionate discipline rates among specific student groups, prompting more equitable interventions (Fergus, 2017).
2. **Monitoring Progress and Measuring Growth**
   - **Frequent Check-Ins**: Progress monitoring tools—ranging from curriculum-based measures in reading and math to daily behavior tracking—provide snapshots of how students are responding to interventions (Fuchs, Fuchs, & Vaughn, 2014).
   - **Adjusting Interventions**: Timely data enables teams to tweak or intensify supports at Tiers 2 and 3 if students aren't making expected gains. This ensures that resources are used efficiently and students receive interventions that match their evolving needs.
3. **Evaluating Outcomes and Program Effectiveness**
   - **School- and District-Wide Insights**: Aggregate data (e.g., attendance trends, discipline incidents, SEL survey results) highlights areas of strength and areas needing improvement across the entire organization (McIntosh & Goodman, 2016).
   - **Continuous Improvement Cycles**: By consistently examining results, leadership teams can refine or replace strategies that aren't having the desired impact (Bryk et al., 2010).

Using Data to Identify Needs, Monitor Progress, and Evaluate Outcomes

While the overarching purpose of data is to drive decisions, data-informed practices can be broken down into three interconnected phases:

1. **Identify Needs**
   - **Screening and Diagnostic Assessments**: Tools such as universal screeners, formative classroom assessments, and behavior checklists reveal gaps in knowledge or skills. These tools also indicate whether students may need targeted or intensive support.

- **Root Cause Analysis**: After identifying a problem area (e.g., low reading fluency), teams conduct further assessments to pinpoint contributing factors—like decoding struggles, limited vocabulary, or lack of practice (Burns & Gibbons, 2012).

2. **Monitor Progress**
   - **Frequent, Focused Measures**: Progress monitoring instruments are brief assessments that directly align with the targeted skill or behavior. For instance, a weekly fluency passage or daily self-regulation checklist (Fuchs et al., 2014).
   - **Goal-Setting**: Establish clear, measurable targets for each student. Regular check-ins determine whether growth is on pace or if adjustments are needed (Deno, 2016).

3. **Evaluate Outcomes**
   - **Mid- and End-of-Year Data Reviews**: Leadership teams compare progress against goals. If an intervention consistently yields positive results, it can be scaled up or sustained; if not, new strategies or resources may be needed (Bryk et al., 2010).
   - **Actionable Feedback**: Sharing outcomes with teachers, families, and even students fosters transparency and collective ownership of results.

The use of data in MTSS follows a continuous improvement cycle. Figure 3.2 highlights the interconnected phases of identifying needs, monitoring progress, and evaluating outcomes.

Figure 3.2 Phases of Data-Informed Practices

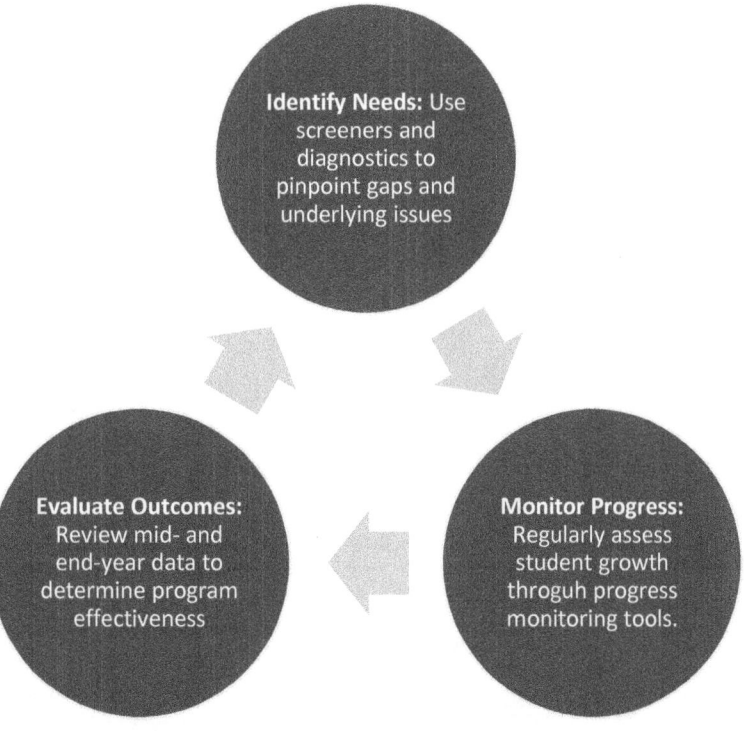

Connecting MTSS Data to Broader School/District Systems

Rather than existing in a silo, MTSS data should integrate seamlessly with **overall district and school data systems** (McIntosh & Goodman, 2016). This integration ensures that:

1. **Leaders Make Informed Policy Decisions**
   - By examining comprehensive data sets—encompassing academics, discipline, attendance, and SEL—district and school leaders can align MTSS strategies with other priorities such as strategic planning, resource allocation, and professional development.
2. **Schools Maintain a Unified Student Record**
   - A centralized platform or student information system (SIS) allows relevant staff to view performance trends, intervention histories, and notes in **one** location. This shared record prevents duplication of services and missed opportunities for collaboration.
3. **Families and Community Partners Stay Informed**
   - Regularly sharing data updates through newsletters, parent portals, or community forums builds trust and engagement.
   - Community agencies (e.g., mental health providers) can tailor their supports when they understand how a student is progressing academically, behaviorally, and socially.

MTSS data must integrate seamlessly into school and district systems to inform decisions and foster collaboration. Figure 3.3 outlines the connections between MTSS data and broader organizational priorities.

Figure 3.3 Connecting MTSS Data to Broader Systems

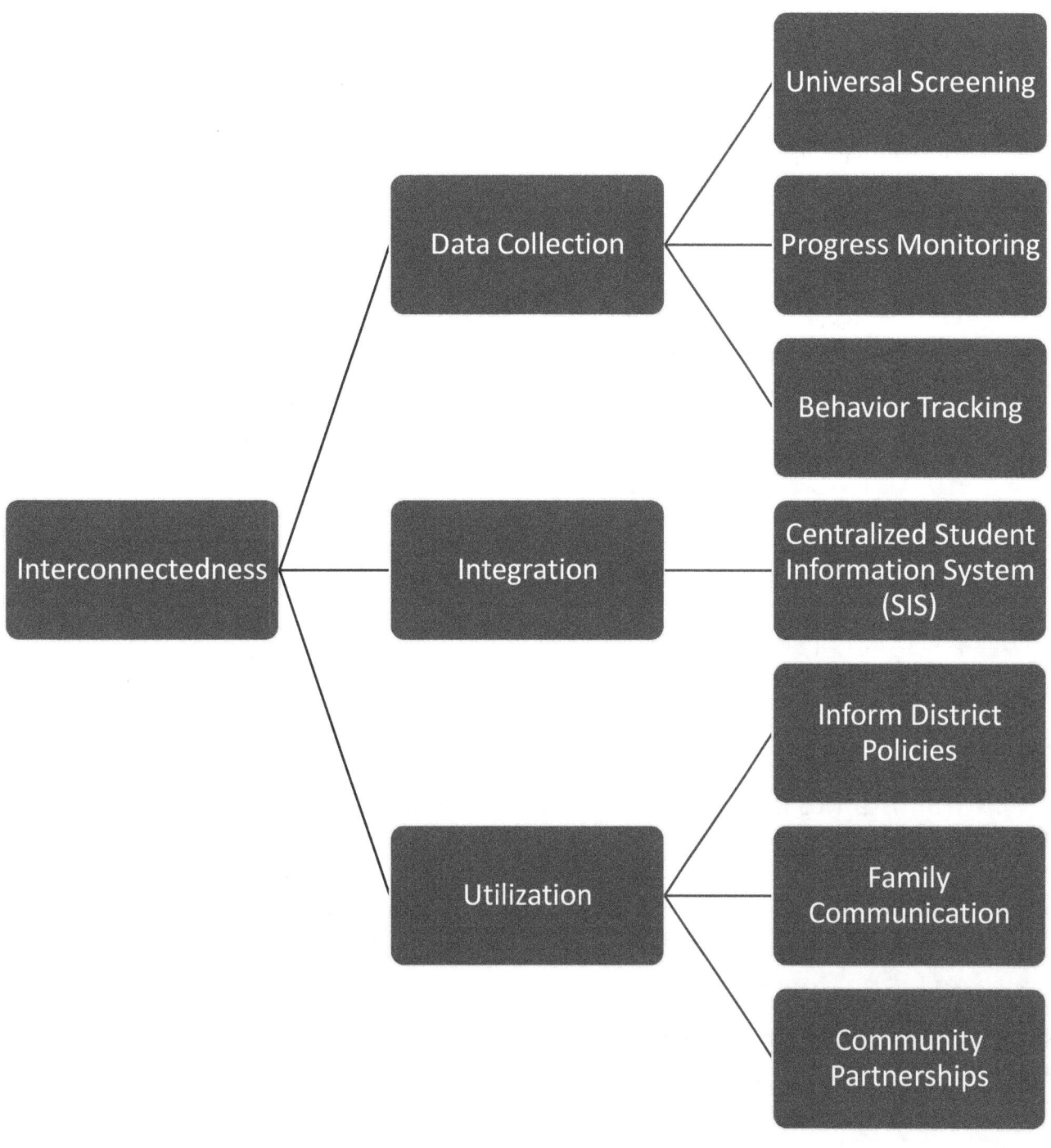

Practical Tips for Data-Driven Success

1. **Build Data Literacy**
   - Provide ongoing professional development to ensure that teachers, administrators, and support staff feel confident interpreting assessments and using data to inform instruction (DuFour & Fullan, 2013).
2. **Use Visualizations**
   - Charts, graphs, and color-coded reports make data more accessible, helping teams quickly spot trends and decide on next steps (Burns & Gibbons, 2012).
3. **Keep Data Cycles Manageable**
   - While frequent progress monitoring is essential for some students, not all data needs to be collected or reviewed at the same rate. Balance the desire for detail with realistic time constraints (McIntosh & Goodman, 2016).
4. **Celebrate Small Wins**
   - Highlight positive trends—such as improved attendance or fewer office referrals—to motivate staff and students. Recognizing growth fosters a positive school culture that values continual improvement (Bryk et al., 2010).

To maximize the impact of data-driven practices, schools can adopt actionable strategies to streamline processes and foster a culture of continuous improvement. Figure 3.4 provides practical tips for success.

Figure 3.4 Practical Tips for Data-Driven Success

Build Data Literacy
- Train staff to interpret and use data effectively

Use Visualizations
- Leverage graphs and dashboards for accessibility

Keep Data Cycles Manageable
- Avoid data overload by setting realistic timelines

Celebrate Small Wins
- Highlight success to build morale and encourage progress

Looking Ahead

Section 3.1 underscores how data underpins every facet of MTSS, serving as a roadmap for identifying needs, monitoring growth, and evaluating impact. In the upcoming sections, we will delve deeper into **universal screening and assessment strategies** (3.2), **progress monitoring protocols** (3.3), and practical tools and exercises for creating or refining your data cycle (3.4). Armed with the right data and a systematic approach to using it, your school or district can make smarter decisions that lead to better outcomes for all students.

3.2 Universal Screening and Assessment

Universal screening is a cornerstone of a Multi-Tiered System of Supports (MTSS). By administering **brief, systematic assessments** to all students—often multiple times per year—schools can quickly identify individuals who may need additional academic, behavioral, or social-emotional support (Burns & Gibbons, 2012). This proactive approach ensures that no student's needs go unnoticed and provides a consistent method for monitoring school- and district-wide trends.

Selecting Screening Tools for Academic, Behavior, and SEL Needs

1. **Academic Screening**
   - **Curriculum-Based Measures (CBMs):** Short, fluency-based probes in reading (e.g., oral reading fluency), math (e.g., computation), and writing (e.g., spelling or sentence construction) have a strong research base (Fuchs, Fuchs, & Vaughn, 2014).
   - **Standards-Aligned Assessments:** Some districts use computer-based tests aligned to local or state standards (e.g., IRLA, NWEA MAP, STAR Assessments) to gauge proficiency and growth.
2. **Behavioral Screening**
   - **Teacher Rating Scales:** Tools like the Student Risk Screening Scale (SRSS) or the Strengths and Difficulties Questionnaire (SDQ) offer quick insights into externalizing and internalizing behaviors (McIntosh & Goodman, 2016).
   - **Office Discipline Referrals (ODRs):** While these data can help detect patterns, they should not be the **only** source of information, as they may reflect staff referral practices rather than actual student need (Sugai & Horner, 2009).

3. **Social-Emotional Learning (SEL) Screening**
   - **Self-Report Surveys:** Age-appropriate questionnaires (e.g., Devereux Student Strengths Assessment, Panorama SEL Surveys) can highlight strengths and challenges in self-management, social awareness, and relationship skills (Greenberg et al., 2017).
   - **Teacher or Parent Ratings:** Observational tools can capture SEL competencies if students are too young or have difficulty self-reporting.
4. **Criteria for Selecting Tools**
   - **Validity and Reliability:** Ensure chosen screeners have robust evidence supporting their accuracy and consistency across diverse student populations (Burns & Gibbons, 2012).
   - **Cultural and Linguistic Responsiveness:** Assess whether a screener is culturally fair and accounts for linguistic differences (Gay, 2018).
   - **Practicality:** Tools should be cost-effective, time-efficient, and straightforward to administer and score.

Implementing Efficient Screening Practices

1. **Scheduling and Logistics**
   - **Frequency:** Most schools screen 3–4 times per year (e.g., fall, winter, spring). Behavior or SEL screeners may be administered less frequently, though at least one or two times per year is recommended (McIntosh & Goodman, 2016).
   - **Testing Environment:** Strive for consistency across classrooms or computer labs to reduce testing anxiety and ensure data integrity.
   - **Staff Training:** Teachers and support personnel need clear guidelines on administration procedures to maintain **fidelity** (Buffum, Mattos, & Weber, 2010).
2. **Data Management**
   - **Centralized Platforms:** Digital assessment tools often provide dashboards that quickly aggregate results, making it easier for educators to spot trends and flag at-risk students (DuFour & Fullan, 2013).
   - **Roles and Responsibilities:** Assign a data coordinator or team to oversee the collection, organization, and distribution of screening data to relevant stakeholders (Burns & Gibbons, 2012).
3. **Equity Considerations**
   - **Language Accessibility:** Provide screeners in students' home languages where possible, or use adapted versions with proven validity (Gay, 2018).
   - **Bias Awareness:** Regularly review data disaggregated by race, gender, socioeconomic status, and other demographics to identify potential biases and ensure fair identification of students needing support (Fergus, 2017).

Interpreting Screening Results

1. **Cut Scores and Benchmarks**
   - **Defined Thresholds:** Collaborate with district and school leadership to set clear benchmarks that determine risk levels (e.g., "At Risk," "Some Risk," or "On Track") (McIntosh & Goodman, 2016).
   - **Local Norms vs. National Norms:** Some schools may rely on national norms, while others create local norms specific to their student population. A blend of both can provide a more complete picture.
2. **Data Triangulation**
   - **Multiple Measures:** Pair screening data with other sources—classroom grades, teacher input, and attendance records—to verify whether a student truly needs additional support (Fuchs et al., 2014).
   - **Contextual Information:** Explore potential root causes (e.g., English language proficiency, recent family changes) that could influence a student's performance (Burns & Gibbons, 2012).
3. **Next Steps and Action Plans**
   - **Identify Interventions:** Students flagged by universal screening may need targeted Tier 2 support (e.g., small-group reading intervention) or individualized Tier 3 support if the skill gap or concern is severe.
   - **Set Goals:** Establish specific, measurable goals for each student, and schedule progress monitoring to track responsiveness to interventions (Deno, 2016).
   - **Referral to School-Based MTSS Team:** For students whose screening results indicate urgent or complex needs, refer them to the building-level team for a thorough review and comprehensive intervention plan.

Reflection & Planning

1. **Current Screening Tools**
   - Are your existing academic, behavior, and SEL screeners evidence-based and culturally responsive?
   - Do the tools produce actionable data that leads to **timely** intervention decisions?
2. **Administration and Fidelity**
   - How consistently are screeners administered across classrooms or schools in your district?
   - Do staff have the training and resources needed to implement screening protocols with fidelity?
3. **Interpretation and Follow-Through**
   - Is there a clear, documented process for assigning interventions based on screening results (e.g., Tier 2, Tier 3)?
   - How frequently and in what format do you share screening data with teachers, families, and community partners?

Universal screening is the gateway to effective, equitable MTSS implementation. By choosing robust, culturally aligned tools and establishing consistent protocols for administration and interpretation, you ensure that every student's needs are identified early and addressed systematically. In the next section, **3.3: Progress Monitoring**, we'll explore how to follow up these initial screenings with ongoing data checks that guide intervention adjustments and measure student growth in real time.

3.3 Progress Monitoring

Progress monitoring is the **ongoing, systematic collection and analysis of data** to gauge student growth and the effectiveness of interventions within a Multi-Tiered System of Supports (MTSS). Unlike universal screening, which casts a wide net to identify students who may need help, progress monitoring hones in on students receiving targeted or intensive supports—ensuring that educators can adjust instructional or behavioral strategies as soon as data indicates a need (Burns & Gibbons, 2012). This proactive, iterative process is vital for addressing academic, social-emotional, and behavioral gaps before they become more entrenched.

Setting Benchmarks and Tracking Growth

1. **Defining Clear Goals**
   - **Specific and Measurable:** Establish concise targets for each intervention. For instance, a Tier 2 reading goal might specify "improve oral reading fluency by 10 words per minute over six weeks."
   - **Appropriate Ambition:** Goals should be attainable yet challenging to ensure both rigor and motivation (Deno, 2016).
2. **Baseline Data**
   - **Accurate Starting Point:** Before launching an intervention, assess the student's current level of performance—academically (e.g., math computation rate), behaviorally (e.g., frequency of out-of-seat behavior), or socially-emotionally (e.g., rating-scale scores on self-regulation).
   - **Comparison to Norms or Past Performance:** Use universal screening results, local norms, or previous intervention data as a point of reference (Fuchs, Fuchs, & Vaughn, 2014).
3. **Incremental Checkpoints**
   - **Regular Intervals:** Progress monitoring often occurs weekly or bi-weekly for students in Tier 3, and every two to four weeks for those in Tier 2 (Burns & Gibbons, 2012).
   - **Frequent Feedback:** These check-ins provide a continuous stream of data, helping teachers quickly determine whether the student is on track to meet the set goals—or if adjustments are warranted.

Tools and Techniques for Progress Monitoring

1. **Curriculum-Based Measurements (CBMs)**
   - **Skill-Specific Probes:** Often used in reading, math, and writing to measure foundational skills (e.g., fluency, accuracy) in short intervals (Fuchs et al., 2014).
   - **Easy Administration and Scoring:** Teachers can collect data efficiently and plot a student's progress on a graph for quick visual reference.
2. **Behavioral Checklists and Observations**
   - **Frequency Counts and Duration Measures:** Track how often a specific behavior occurs or how long it lasts during a given period (McIntosh & Goodman, 2016).
   - **Daily Behavior Reports:** Students and/or teachers rate adherence to behavioral goals (e.g., self-control, cooperation), facilitating swift intervention if problems arise (Sugai & Horner, 2009).
3. **Social-Emotional and SEL Metrics**
   - **Rating Scales and Rubrics:** Incorporate short surveys or rubrics that assess SEL competencies (e.g., empathy, self-management) every few weeks (Greenberg, Domitrovich, Weissberg, & Durlak, 2017).
   - **Goal-Setting with Students:** Empower students to track their own social-emotional growth by reflecting on weekly or monthly progress toward SEL targets.
4. **Digital Progress Monitoring Tools**
   - **Online Platforms:** Many modern CBM, behavioral, and SEL assessment tools feature real-time dashboards, simplifying data collection and analysis (DuFour & Fullan, 2013).
   - **Automatic Alerts:** Built-in notifications can flag when a student is not meeting expected growth rates, prompting immediate action by intervention teams.

Analyzing Data to Adjust Interventions

1. **Graphing and Visual Analysis**
   - **Trend Lines:** Plot student data points over time to reveal whether progress is accelerating, remaining flat, or regressing (Deno, 2016).
   - **Goal Lines:** Overlay an expected rate of improvement on the graph to compare actual versus desired performance. If the student consistently falls below the goal line, consider intensifying or altering the intervention (Burns & Gibbons, 2012).
2. **Team Collaboration**
   - **Structured Data Meetings:** Regularly scheduled sessions (e.g., bi-weekly, monthly) where teams examine progress monitoring data for individual students (McIntosh & Goodman, 2016).
   - **Action Plan Adjustments:** If growth is inadequate, teams can modify intervention dosage (e.g., more frequent sessions), methodology (e.g., switching to a different evidence-based program), or environment (e.g., smaller group size).
3. **Decision Rules for Next Steps**

- **Timely Change:** Waiting too long to shift an ineffective intervention delays student progress. Typically, if a student shows insufficient growth for a predetermined number of data points (e.g., three to four consecutive data checks), the team considers altering the support plan (Fuchs et al., 2014).
- **Graduation Back to Core:** When a student consistently meets or exceeds goals, teams decide whether the individual can move back to Tier 1 or Tier 2 supports, while still monitoring to prevent regression.

Reflection & Planning

1. **Current Progress Monitoring Practices**
   - Do you have established guidelines for how frequently to collect data?
   - Are tools aligned with the skills or behaviors you aim to improve?
2. **Staff Training and Fidelity**
   - How confident are teachers, counselors, and support staff in administering and interpreting progress monitoring tools?
   - Do you have a system for periodically reviewing fidelity (i.e., ensuring the intervention is delivered as intended)?
3. **Data-Driven Adjustments**
   - Is there a clear, documented procedure for when and how teams decide to alter or escalate interventions based on progress data?
   - How frequently do you review student growth with families, and what role do they play in the process?

Through consistent and strategic progress monitoring, schools and districts can **fine-tune** the level of support each student receives, ensuring no one slips through the cracks. By regularly measuring progress, educators can celebrate successes, identify persistent challenges, and pivot interventions accordingly—ultimately creating a responsive, data-driven culture that propels every student toward success. In **Section 3.4**, we will explore how to streamline these practices through an organized data cycle (Plan-Do-Study-Act) and offer tools for refining your approach to continuous improvement.

3.4 Reflection & Planning

After establishing universal screening processes, selecting and administering valid assessments, and conducting systematic progress monitoring, the final step in effective data-driven decision-making is **ongoing reflection and strategic planning**. This phase ensures that teams use collected data to inform improvements, celebrate successes, and refine Multi-Tiered System of Supports (MTSS) practices. Central to this effort is a **Plan-Do-**

Study-Act (PDSA) cycle, a continuous improvement model that encourages schools to remain proactive, responsive, and adaptable (Bryk, Gomez, Grunow, & LeMahieu, 2015).

Creating or Refining Your Data Cycle (Plan-Do-Study-Act)

1. **Plan**
   - **Identify a Focus**: Decide which specific aspect of MTSS implementation or student outcome you aim to improve (e.g., increasing reading fluency in Tier 2, reducing disruptive classroom behaviors, or expanding SEL supports).
   - **Set Measurable Goals**: Outline clear objectives, including criteria for success. Goals should be **SMART** (Specific, Measurable, Achievable, Relevant, Time-Bound) to provide direction (Doran, 1981).
   - **Outline Action Steps**: Determine who will collect data, how often, and what tools or methods (e.g., curriculum-based measures, behavior checklists) will be used.
2. **Do**
   - **Implement Interventions**: Execute the agreed-upon strategies or interventions with fidelity. For instance, if you plan to pilot a new behavior tracking system, ensure all teachers receive the necessary training and resources.
   - **Collect Data**: Record results systematically—weekly progress monitoring, teacher observations, or digital logs.
   - **Document Observations**: Note any challenges or unexpected developments, such as schedule disruptions or resource constraints (Burns & Gibbons, 2012).
3. **Study**
   - **Analyze the Data**: Review quantitative measures (e.g., progress monitoring graphs, universal screening scores) and qualitative inputs (e.g., teacher feedback, student surveys).
   - **Compare Against Goals**: Are students making the progress you anticipated within the set timeframe? Look for patterns, trends, and anomalies.
   - **Consider Root Causes**: If growth is lagging, dig into potential reasons. Are interventions implemented consistently? Are goals realistic? Are there external factors (e.g., student attendance, motivation) affecting outcomes (Fergus, 2017)?
4. **Act**
   - **Refine or Scale**: If the intervention shows promise, consider scaling it up to additional classrooms or grade levels. If results are inadequate, revise the strategy—adjust the duration, intensity, or delivery method (Fuchs, Fuchs, & Vaughn, 2014).
   - **Create Next Steps**: Document the lessons learned and share them with stakeholders (e.g., leadership teams, families, community partners). Establish new cycles of data collection to maintain momentum (Bryk et al., 2015).

By cycling through **Plan-Do-Study-Act** regularly, schools foster a culture of continuous improvement—rapidly identifying what works, discarding or modifying what doesn't, and scaling effective practices so that all students benefit.

The PDSA cycle provides a structured framework for continuous improvement in MTSS practices. Figure 3.5 illustrates each phase of this iterative process, guiding schools toward data-informed refinement.

Figure 3.2 Plan-Do-Study-Act (PDSA) Cycle

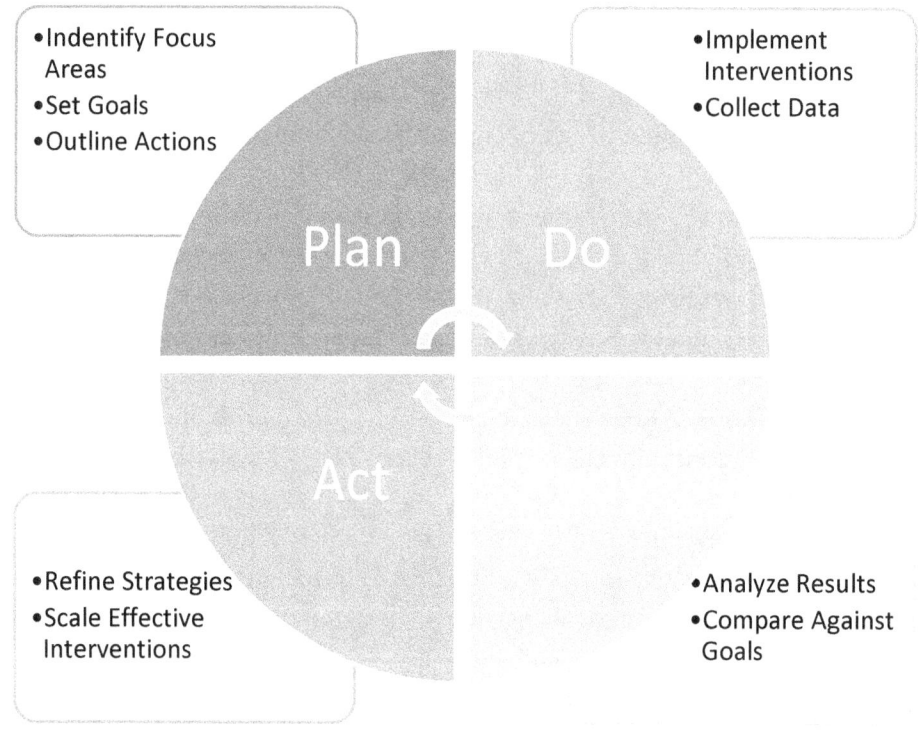

Identifying Trends and Prioritizing Intervention Areas

Even the most robust PDSA cycles can be overwhelming if schools try to tackle too many initiatives at once. Streamlining data review and prioritizing interventions ensures resources are used effectively (DuFour & Fullan, 2013).

1. **Aggregate and Disaggregate Data**
   - **Big-Picture Insights**: Look for trends at the school, grade, or district level (e.g., overall improvements in reading proficiency).
   - **Equity Lens**: Examine disaggregated data by race, ethnicity, language status, gender, or special education identification to identify and address achievement gaps or disproportionality (McIntosh & Goodman, 2016).
2. **Prioritizing High-Impact Areas**
   - **Identify "Critical Need" Domains**: For instance, if a large percentage of students are struggling with behavior in unstructured settings (cafeteria, hallways), focus resources there first.
   - **Leverage Quick Wins**: Addressing manageable concerns early can build confidence and momentum among staff, families, and students (Bryk et al., 2015).
3. **Collaborative Decision-Making**
   - **Data Dialogues**: Hold regular meetings (e.g., monthly) with leadership teams, teacher PLCs, and other stakeholders. Use agendas or protocols to keep discussions focused on actionable solutions (DuFour & Fullan, 2013).
   - **Consensus Building**: Where disagreements arise (e.g., on how to interpret data or which interventions to adopt), use established decision-making processes or voting methods to ensure equitable input.

Reflection & Planning

1. **Assess Your Current PDSA Cycles**
   - Do you already have a structured improvement cycle in place, or are changes needed to make it more consistent and transparent?
   - How often are these cycles revisited? Are they ongoing or intermittent?
2. **Review Roles and Responsibilities**
   - Who on your team is best suited to lead each phase of the PDSA cycle?
   - How do you involve key stakeholders—teachers, families, support staff, and community partners—in reviewing data and planning next steps?
3. **Evaluate Your Intervention Priorities**
   - Are you trying to tackle too many areas at once, or are your priorities clear?
   - Are you systematically monitoring both academic and non-academic domains (behavior, SEL) to capture a holistic view of student needs?

Progress in MTSS hinges on educators' willingness to reflect, adapt, and refine practices based on **accurate, timely data** (Burns & Gibbons, 2012). By embedding the Plan-Do-Study-Act cycle into your school or district's culture—and systematically identifying trends and prioritizing interventions—you create an environment where continuous improvement is the norm. In **Chapter 4**, we will transition from the system-wide lens of data-driven decision-making to exploring **Tier 1 universal supports**, examining how high-quality instruction, effective classroom management, and universal social-emotional practices set the stage for success.

Chapter 4: Tier 1 – Universal Supports

4.1 Core Instructional Practices

Tier 1 is the **foundation** of a Multi-Tiered System of Supports (MTSS). At this level, every student benefits from high-quality, evidence-based instruction that is culturally responsive, engaging, and differentiated to meet diverse learning needs (Fisher, Frey, & Hattie, 2021). Strong Tier 1 practices reduce the number of students who require additional interventions in Tier 2 or Tier 3, ensuring that your school or district's time and resources are used most effectively. This section explores the essential components of **core instructional practices** and how they align with an MTSS framework.

Tier 1 instruction hinges on the implementation of core practices that ensure every student receives high-quality, engaging, and differentiated learning experiences. Figure 4.1 highlights these foundational elements.

Figure 4.1 Core Instructional Practices in Tier 1

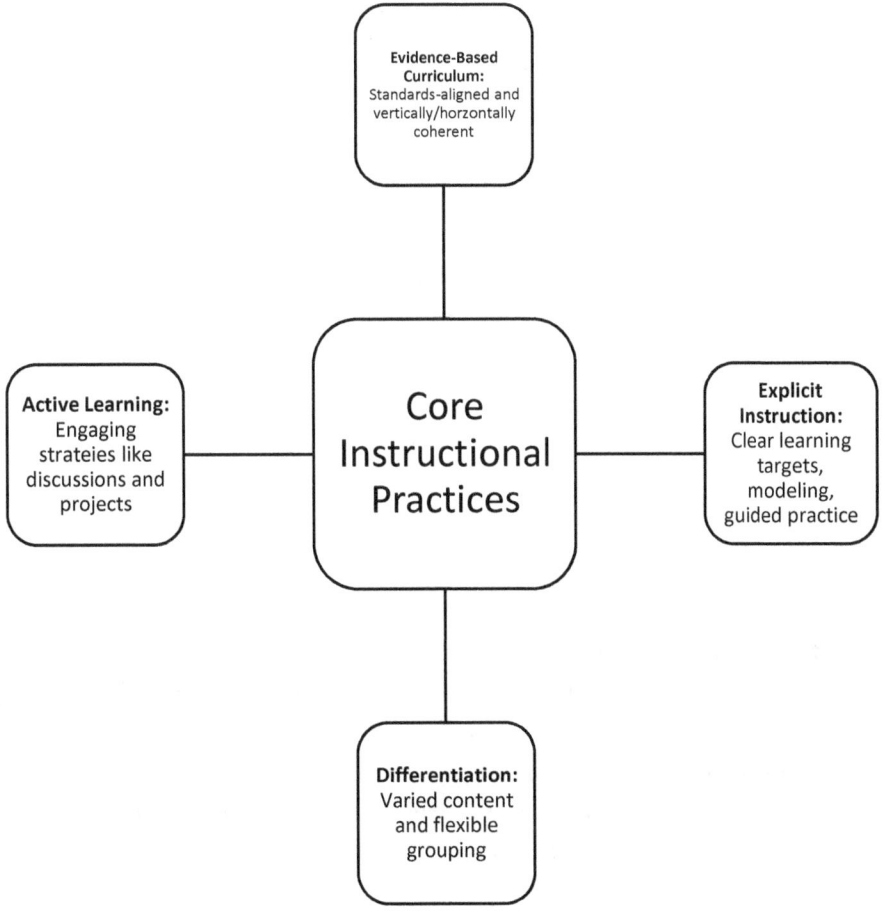

Evidence-Based Curriculum and Instructional Strategies

1. **Standards-Based Curriculum**
   - **Alignment with State or National Standards:** Instructional materials should directly connect to grade-level expectations, ensuring clarity and consistency across classrooms (Marzano, 2007).
   - **Vertical and Horizontal Alignment:** Collaboration among grade-level teams and subject-area departments helps maintain coherence and prevents instructional gaps or redundancies.
2. **Explicit and Systematic Instruction**
   - **Clarity of Learning Targets:** Begin each lesson by clearly stating what students will learn and why it's relevant. This anchors attention and allows students to gauge their own progress (Fisher et al., 2021).
   - **Modeling and Practice:** Demonstrate new skills or content using "think-alouds," followed by guided practice with prompt feedback. Gradually release responsibility to students for independent work (Duke & Pearson, 2002).
3. **Differentiated Instruction**
   - **Varied Content, Process, and Product:** Adapt materials, groupings, and tasks to meet students' readiness levels, interests, and learning profiles (Tomlinson, 2017).
   - **Flexible Grouping:** Rotate between whole-group, small-group, and independent activities based on skill level, allowing all students to engage with content at an appropriate challenge level (Fuchs, Fuchs, & Vaughn, 2014).
4. **Active Learning and Student Engagement**
   - **Interactive Strategies:** Incorporate discussions, hands-on projects, technology integration, and peer collaboration to maintain student motivation and deepen understanding (DuFour & Fullan, 2013).
   - **Frequent Checks for Understanding:** Use quick formative assessments (e.g., exit tickets, mini-quizzes, polls) to gauge comprehension and adjust instruction in real time (Black & Wiliam, 2018).

Culturally Responsive Teaching and Learning

1. **Cultural Awareness and Respect**
   - **Inclusive Curriculum:** Reflect diverse cultures, languages, and experiences in examples, literature, and historical perspectives (Gay, 2018).
   - **Classroom Climate:** Foster an environment of mutual respect, ensuring all voices are heard and valued. Encourage students to bring their cultural backgrounds into discussions and projects.
2. **Validating and Affirming Student Identities**

- **Relating Content to Real-Life Contexts:** Make connections between the curriculum and students' cultural or community experiences. This helps learners see the relevance of what they are studying (Ladson-Billings, 1995).
- **Positive Teacher-Student Relationships:** Show genuine interest in each student's background and aspirations. Personalized feedback and rapport-building can boost engagement and academic achievement (Hattie, 2009).

3. **Equitable Access to Rigorous Instruction**
    - **High Expectations for All Learners:** Provide challenging tasks paired with appropriate scaffolds, ensuring every student has opportunities to experience both struggle and success (Fisher et al., 2021).
    - **Culturally and Linguistically Responsive Supports:** Offer language accommodations (e.g., visuals, sentence frames) for English learners, and adapt materials for students with diverse needs.

Culturally responsive teaching strengthens Tier 1 by validating student identities and fostering equity. Figure 4.2 illustrates the interconnected components of this approach.

Figure 4.2 Components of Culturally Responsive Teaching

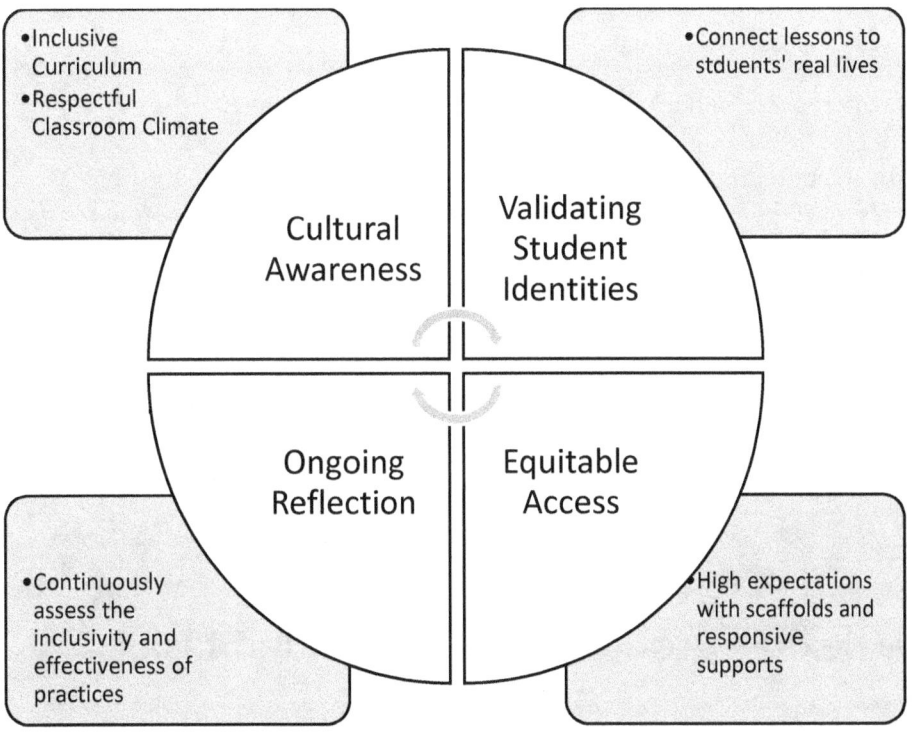

Instructional Differentiation to Meet Diverse Needs

1. **Ongoing Assessment for Grouping**
   - **Data-Driven Flexibility:** Use screening, formative assessments, and quick checks to adjust groups, ensuring students receive just-right instruction (Burns & Gibbons, 2012).
   - **Targeted Skill Building:** In reading, for example, students requiring support in phonemic awareness might work together, while advanced readers explore higher-level comprehension tasks.
2. **Scaffolding Techniques**
   - **Gradual Release Model:** Provide explicit teaching and modeling, then guide practice with feedback, followed by independent or collaborative tasks (Duke & Pearson, 2002).
   - **Layered Supports:** Use graphic organizers, sentence starters, or peer modeling to help students bridge gaps in understanding or skill.
3. **Flexible Use of Technology**
   - **Digital Tools:** Differentiation apps, instructional software, and online tutorials can reinforce lessons, offer extra practice, or extend learning (McIntosh & Goodman, 2016).
   - **Blended Learning Models:** Rotate students between online learning stations and teacher-led small groups, enabling more personalized instruction.

Differentiation in Tier 1 enables educators to address diverse needs effectively. Figure 4.3 categorizes key strategies for tailoring content, process, and products to optimize learning outcomes.

Figure 4.3 Differentiated Instruction Strategies

Content
- Use varied texts, videos, and resources to cater to different readiness levels

Process
- Incorporate flexible grouping and scaffolded tasks

Product
- Allow multiple formats for demonstrative mastery (e.g., presentations., essays, and projects)

Reflection & Planning

1. **Reviewing Current Tier 1 Practices**
   - Are your instructional materials aligned to state or national standards?
   - How consistently do teachers across grade levels or departments implement evidence-based strategies and formative assessments?
2. **Equity and Cultural Responsiveness**
   - Do students see their lived experiences, languages, and cultures represented in classroom materials and discussions?
   - How do teachers build relationships and maintain high expectations for learners from all backgrounds?
3. **Differentiation and Engagement**
   - Are there adequate structures (e.g., instructional planning time, coaching support) to help teachers differentiate effectively?
   - What technology tools or blended learning approaches could further personalize learning for your students?

Core instructional practices are the engine that drives Tier 1 success in an MTSS framework. When teachers provide explicit, systematic, and culturally responsive instruction—tailored to the diverse strengths and needs of their classrooms—most students can achieve academic standards without additional supports. In **Section 4.2**, we will explore **schoolwide positive behavior supports** that align with and complement these academic practices, ensuring that all students thrive in a safe, structured, and supportive environment.

4.2 Schoolwide Positive Behavior Supports

A positive and proactive school climate sets the stage for effective Tier 1 instruction. **Schoolwide Positive Behavior Supports (SWPBS)**—often implemented through frameworks like Positive Behavioral Interventions and Supports (PBIS)—aim to **prevent** problematic behaviors before they escalate, while simultaneously promoting a safe, respectful, and engaging environment for all students (Sugai & Horner, 2009). By clearly defining, teaching, and reinforcing consistent behavioral expectations, schools create a culture where students are more receptive to academic learning and social-emotional growth.

Establishing Clear Expectations and Consistent Routines

1. **Schoolwide Behavior Matrix**
    - **Common Language and Rules:** Develop 3–5 core values or behavioral expectations (e.g., "Be Safe, Be Responsible, Be Respectful") that apply in every setting—classrooms, hallways, cafeterias, and buses (McIntosh & Goodman, 2016).
    - **Behavior Matrix:** Clearly outline what each expectation looks like in different contexts (e.g., "Be Responsible" in the cafeteria means cleaning up your tray and table area). Consistency across all school areas reduces ambiguity for students.
2. **Direct Teaching of Behaviors**
    - **Lesson Plans for Expectations:** Just as you would teach math or reading strategies, dedicate time to modeling, role-playing, and practicing the desired behaviors. Reinforce these lessons throughout the year, not just at the start (Simonson, Fairbanks, Briesch, Myers, & Sugai, 2008).
    - **Visual Reminders:** Post charts, signs, or infographics around the school to keep expectations at the forefront of students' minds (Colvin, 2007).
3. **Predictable Routines**
    - **Structured Transitions and Procedures:** Predictability in daily schedules and classroom routines fosters a sense of security and helps students anticipate what comes next (Sprick, 2009).
    - **Consistent Implementation:** Align routines among all teachers and staff, so students experience the same expectations and procedures across classrooms, grade levels, and common areas (DuFour & Fullan, 2013).

A schoolwide behavior framework provides consistency across settings, helping students internalize expectations. Figure 4.4 illustrates a sample behavior matrix for various contexts.

Figure 4.4 Schoolwide Positive Behavior Supports Framework

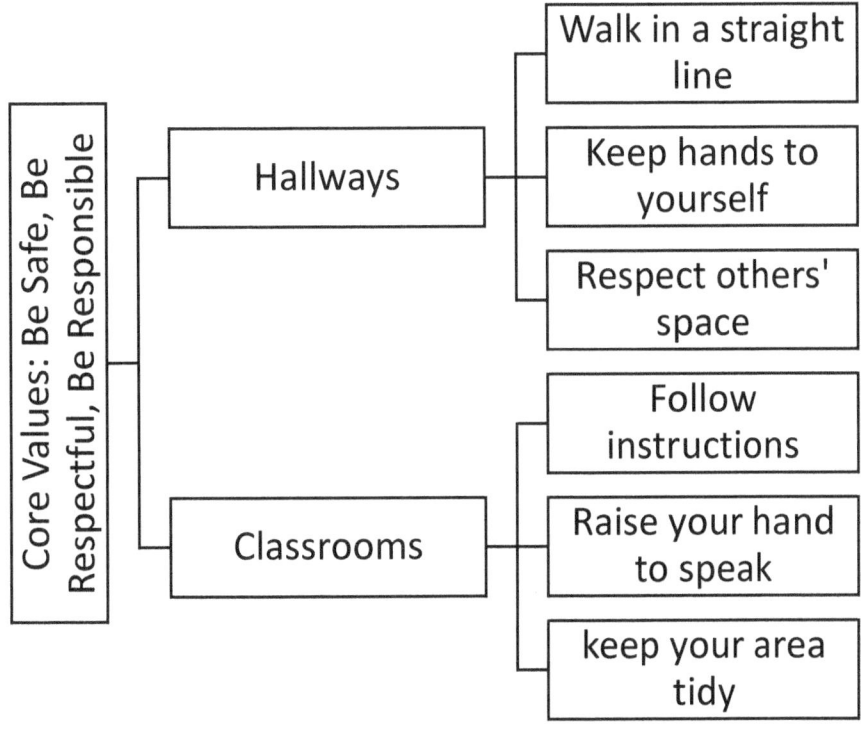

Positive Reinforcement Systems (PBIS Alignment)

1. **Acknowledging and Celebrating Positive Behavior**
    - **Immediate, Specific Feedback:** Recognize desired behaviors by telling students exactly what they did well (e.g., "Thank you for following directions quickly!"). Specific praise is more impactful than general remarks (Hattie & Yates, 2014).
    - **Schoolwide Recognition Programs:** Implement token economies, point systems, or "gotcha" tickets that can be redeemed for privileges or small rewards. Make sure these systems are **fair** and **equitable** so all students can succeed (McIntosh & Goodman, 2016).
2. **Building a Positive School Climate**
    - **Staff Modeling:** When adults consistently model respectful, caring interactions, students are more likely to mirror those behaviors (Sugai & Horner, 2009).
    - **Group Celebrations and Assemblies:** Periodically highlight collective achievements, such as zero referrals in a week or improved hallway conduct. Public celebrations foster a sense of community pride (Colvin, 2007).
3. **Data-Driven Behavior Management**

- **Tracking Office Discipline Referrals (ODRs):** Analyze patterns in ODRs to determine problem locations or times. Use this information to proactively address common triggers (McIntosh, Filter, Bennett, Ryan, & Sugai, 2010).
- **Continuous Improvement:** Review behavioral data in the same spirit as academic data—using results to refine routines, reteach expectations, or adjust reinforcement strategies (Sugai & Horner, 2009).

Positive reinforcement is a cornerstone of behavior management in Tier 1. Figure 4.5 showcases strategies that encourage and sustain desired behaviors.

Figure 4.5 Positive Reinforcement and Behavior Management

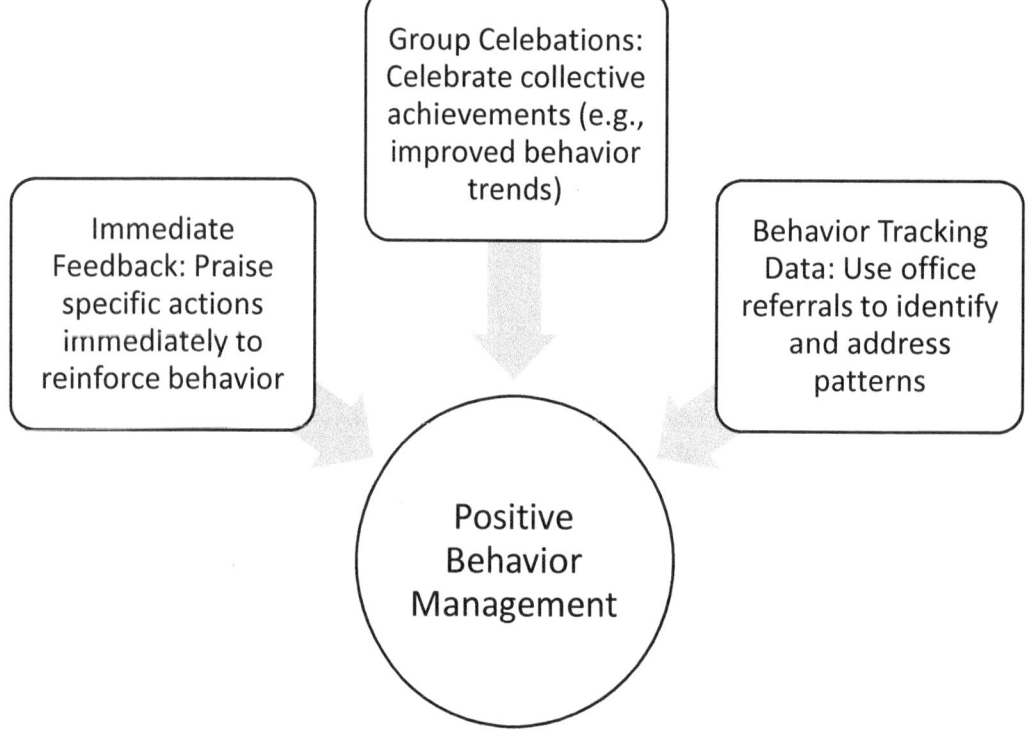

Classroom Management Strategies

1. **Active Supervision and Proximity**
    - **Strategic Positioning:** Move around the room to prevent off-task behavior and provide timely feedback (Sprick, 2009).
    - **Early Intervention:** Address minor issues immediately and privately, preventing small disruptions from becoming major discipline problems.
2. **Positive Teacher-Student Relationships**
    - **Rapport and Respect:** Greet students at the door, learn about their interests, and involve them in setting class norms. Such relationship-building has a powerful impact on engagement and behavior (Hattie & Yates, 2014).

- **Empathy and Understanding:** When students misbehave, explore underlying causes (e.g., frustration, social-emotional skill deficits) rather than solely applying punitive measures (Greenberg, Domitrovich, Weissberg, & Durlak, 2017).

3. **Differentiated Behavior Supports**
   - **Flexible Seating and Task Variety:** Just as academic tasks are differentiated, tailor behavioral supports to meet diverse student needs (Tomlinson, 2017).
   - **Clear, Predictable Consequences:** Ensure that students understand the logical outcomes of misbehavior (e.g., loss of a privilege tied directly to the misused behavior). Consistency, fairness, and transparency reduce power struggles (Sprick, 2009).

Reflection & Planning

1. **Reviewing Your Behavior Framework**
   - Do you have a schoolwide system for defining, teaching, and reinforcing behavioral expectations?
   - Are these expectations clearly communicated and consistently upheld by all staff?
2. **Gathering and Using Behavioral Data**
   - How do you collect and analyze data on office referrals, attendance, or classroom incidents?
   - Are staff trained to interpret behavioral patterns and respond proactively?
3. **Ongoing Staff Development**
   - Have teachers and support staff received recent training on PBIS or other positive behavior models?
   - What coaching or follow-up opportunities exist to ensure fidelity of implementation?

By focusing on **schoolwide positive behavior supports**, schools create an environment where respectful, engaged interactions are the norm, allowing students to feel safe, valued, and ready to learn. Effective Tier 1 behavior strategies not only reduce the need for more intensive interventions down the road but also enhance the overall school climate. In **Section 4.3**, we will delve into how Tier 1 can further support students' social-emotional and mental health needs, broadening our commitment to the holistic well-being of every learner.

4.3 Social-Emotional and Mental Health Promotion

Strong academic and behavioral supports thrive in an environment where students' **social-emotional** needs are also prioritized. In Tier 1, schools and districts embed universal practices that promote self-awareness, self-management, social awareness, relationship skills, and responsible decision-making—collectively known as **social-emotional learning (SEL)** (Greenberg, Domitrovich, Weissberg, & Durlak, 2017). By integrating SEL and mental health supports into core instruction, educators proactively foster a sense of belonging, resilience, and well-being for **all** students, reducing the likelihood that more intensive interventions will be needed later.

Universal SEL Curriculum and Practices

1. **Explicit SEL Instruction**
    - **Dedicated Lessons:** Implement a research-based SEL curriculum (e.g., PATHS, Second Step, RULER) that teaches skills such as emotional regulation, empathy, and conflict resolution (Durlak, Weissberg, Dymnicki, Taylor, & Schellinger, 2011).
    - **Integration with Academics:** Embed SEL strategies into academic lessons—for instance, by using cooperative learning structures that develop communication and teamwork skills during math or reading activities (Fisher, Frey, & Hattie, 2021).
2. **Modeling and Reinforcement**
    - **Teacher Demonstration:** Just as educators model problem-solving in math, they should also model self-reflection and emotional regulation (Jennings & Greenberg, 2009).
    - **Opportunities for Practice:** Encourage students to apply SEL skills throughout the day—during group work, in peer mediation, and while reflecting on personal goals.
3. **Regular Check-Ins and Assessments**
    - **Brief SEL Surveys:** Short, age-appropriate questionnaires can gauge how students feel about their school climate or relationships with peers (Greenberg et al., 2017).
    - **Goal-Setting and Reflection:** Incorporate self-assessment tools, journals, or conferences where students evaluate their social-emotional growth and set new goals (Deno, 2016).

SEL integrates seamlessly into Tier 1 to build resilient, empathetic learners. Figure 4.6 demonstrates how universal practices, explicit instruction, and restorative approaches work together.

Figure 4.6 Social-Emotional Learning Integration

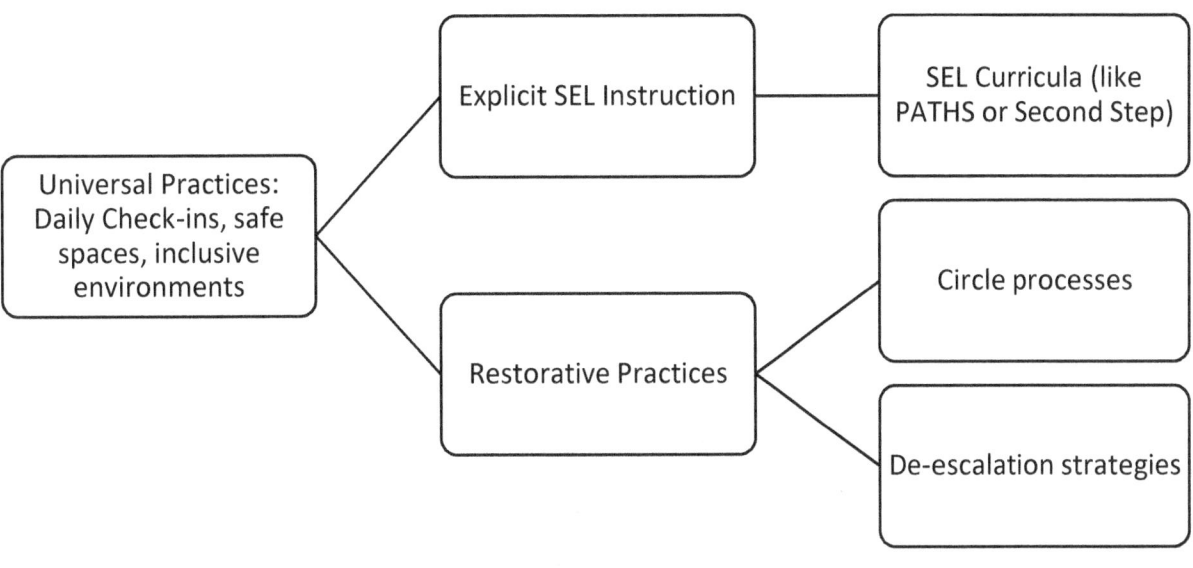

Building Trauma-Informed and Restorative Classroom Environments

1. **Trauma-Informed Practices**
    - **Understanding Trauma's Impact:** Recognize that adverse childhood experiences (ACEs) can affect students' behavior, emotions, and learning. Offer consistent, predictable routines to help students feel safe and supported (Substance Abuse and Mental Health Services Administration [SAMHSA], 2014).
    - **De-Escalation and Calming Strategies:** Teach techniques like mindfulness, breathing exercises, or movement breaks that help students self-regulate when overwhelmed (Jennings & Greenberg, 2009).
2. **Restorative Approaches**
    - **Circle Processes:** Use restorative circles for classroom discussions, conflict resolution, and community building. Circles provide a structured format for respectful, empathetic dialogue (Costello, Wachtel, & Wachtel, 2019).
    - **Repairing Harm, Not Punishing:** When disruptions occur, shift from punitive discipline to restorative conversations that address root causes, promote accountability, and repair relationships (Gregory & Evans, 2020).
3. **Empathy and Belonging**
    - **Responsive Class Environment:** Validate students' feelings and experiences, ensuring that cultural or personal backgrounds are respected (Gay, 2018).

- **Safe Spaces and Flexible Seating:** Create areas in the classroom where students can calm themselves or seek peer or adult support, reducing the stigma around mental or emotional challenges.

Family and Community Engagement for SEL

1. **Collaborative Partnerships**
    - **Parent Workshops and Resources:** Offer sessions that equip families with strategies to reinforce SEL skills at home (e.g., building routines, using positive language) (Greenberg et al., 2017).
    - **Community Connections:** Partner with local mental health agencies or youth organizations to provide wraparound services for students who need additional support (Fergus, 2017).
2. **Consistent Communication**
    - **Regular Updates:** Include SEL progress, upcoming lessons, and useful tips in newsletters or online portals. Communicate how families can reinforce classroom strategies (DuFour & Fullan, 2013).
    - **Cultural Responsiveness:** Translate materials and host events in languages spoken by your school's population. Invite community leaders to co-facilitate discussions about mental health and wellness.
3. **Shared Vision and Responsibility**
    - **Co-Created SEL Goals:** Involve families and community members in defining schoolwide social-emotional goals. Collective buy-in enhances fidelity and sustainability (McIntosh & Goodman, 2016).
    - **Celebrations and Showcases:** Publicly honor milestones or projects that highlight social-emotional growth (e.g., peer mentoring initiatives, service-learning projects). These events build pride and ownership among stakeholders.

Reflection & Planning

1. **Assessing Universal SEL Practices**
    - Which SEL curricula or strategies are already in place at your school or district?
    - Are these integrated consistently across grade levels and content areas, or do they function as isolated lessons?
2. **Trauma-Informed and Restorative Readiness**
    - How prepared is your staff to address the effects of trauma and employ restorative practices?
    - What additional professional development or resources might be needed?
3. **Family and Community Engagement**
    - Are families aware of your schoolwide SEL or mental health initiatives?

- How can you strengthen partnerships with local mental health services or youth organizations?

By weaving social-emotional learning and mental health promotion into **everyday** Tier 1 instruction, schools nurture resilient, empathic students who can navigate academic and life challenges. These universal supports also build a robust foundation for higher-tier interventions, helping educators identify and address emerging concerns earlier and more effectively. In **Section 4.4**, we will reflect on these universal practices, guiding you to evaluate current Tier 1 systems and plan next steps for continuous improvement in academics, behavior, and social-emotional learning.

4.4 Reflection & Planning

A robust Tier 1 ensures that all students receive high-quality instruction, proactive behavior supports, and integrated social-emotional learning. When these universal strategies are consistently implemented and regularly evaluated, schools minimize the need for more intensive interventions in Tier 2 or Tier 3 (McIntosh & Goodman, 2016). This final section of Chapter 4 provides guiding questions and action steps to help you assess your current Tier 1 practices, celebrate successes, and identify areas for improvement.

Reflecting on Academic Core (Sections 4.1 & 4.2)

1. **Instructional Alignment and Quality**
    - **Standards-Based Alignment:** Are your curriculum and instructional materials clearly tied to state or national learning standards (Marzano, 2007)?
    - **Differentiation:** Do teachers regularly use data to group students flexibly, offer scaffolds, and adjust instruction based on readiness, interest, and learning profile (Tomlinson, 2017)?
    - **Student Engagement:** Are there systems (e.g., frequent formative assessments, cooperative learning strategies) in place to keep students actively involved in lessons (Fisher, Frey, & Hattie, 2021)?
2. **Positive Behavior Supports**
    - **Consistency and Clarity:** Are schoolwide expectations explicitly taught and displayed in all areas of the school (Sugai & Horner, 2009)?
    - **Reinforcement and Recognition:** Do staff consistently praise positive student behaviors and use data (e.g., office referrals) to adjust supports (McIntosh et al., 2010)?
    - **Fair and Equitable Discipline:** How do you ensure that behavioral policies and consequences are applied consistently and without bias (Fergus, 2017)?

Reflecting on SEL and Mental Health (Section 4.3)

1. **Universal SEL Integration**
   - **Curriculum Implementation:** Is a research-based SEL curriculum delivered with fidelity across all grade levels (Durlak, Weissberg, Dymnicki, Taylor, & Schellinger, 2011)?
   - **Daily Integration:** Do teachers embed SEL competencies (e.g., self-regulation, conflict resolution) within academic lessons, rather than viewing SEL as an "add-on" (Greenberg, Domitrovich, Weissberg, & Durlak, 2017)?
2. **Trauma-Informed and Restorative Practices**
   - **Staff Training:** Are educators trained to recognize and respond to signs of trauma in students (SAMHSA, 2014)?
   - **Repairing Harm:** Do restorative conversations or circle processes replace punitive measures when misbehavior occurs (Costello, Wachtel, & Wachtel, 2019)?
3. **Family and Community Engagement**
   - **Outreach and Communication:** Are families kept informed about SEL initiatives and invited to practice strategies at home?
   - **Community Partnerships:** Do you have links with mental health agencies or community organizations for wraparound services when students or families need additional help (Fergus, 2017)?

Assessing Overall Tier 1 Fidelity

1. **Consistency Across Classrooms**
   - **Observational Data:** Conduct walkthroughs or peer observations to verify that Tier 1 strategies (e.g., clear learning targets, posted behavioral expectations) are used schoolwide.
   - **Staff Collaboration:** Do teams (PLCs, grade-level groups) meet frequently to discuss instructional approaches, share materials, and review data (DuFour & Fullan, 2013)?
2. **Student Outcomes and Equity**
   - **Achievement and Behavior Data:** Compare screening results, progress monitoring data, and discipline trends among different subgroups (e.g., race/ethnicity, English learners, special education) to identify possible inequities (Fergus, 2017).
   - **Stakeholder Feedback:** Solicit input from students, families, and community members about what's working and what can be improved, ensuring multiple voices shape Tier 1 improvements (Gay, 2018).
3. **Resource Allocation**
   - **Professional Development Needs:** Do teachers and support staff have the training, coaching, and materials needed to provide high-quality Tier 1 supports (Sprick, 2009)?
   - **Time and Scheduling:** Are there enough collaboration periods, planning sessions, or staff meetings allocated to sustain and refine universal practices?

Action Steps for Strengthening Tier 1

1. **Conduct a Tier 1 "Audit"**
   - Use a self-assessment or fidelity checklist (e.g., PBIS Tiered Fidelity Inventory, SEL Implementation Rubric) to get a baseline measure of current strengths and challenges (Sugai & Horner, 2009).
   - Share findings with leadership teams, grade-level or department PLCs, and the broader school community to encourage transparent dialogue and collective problem-solving (DuFour & Fullan, 2013).
2. **Set Improvement Goals**
   - **SMART Goals:** Identify a manageable set of objectives (e.g., "Reduce the number of office referrals by 20% over the next semester") tied to specific Tier 1 strategies (Doran, 1981).
   - **Align Resources:** Ensure budgets, schedules, and professional development align with these goals. If the aim is to strengthen SEL practices, prioritize training on trauma-informed approaches or restorative discipline.
3. **Create a Continuous Improvement Cycle**
   - **Plan-Do-Study-Act (PDSA):** Adopt a structured routine to implement, monitor, and refine Tier 1 improvements. Gather ongoing data, compare results to your goals, and adjust as needed (Bryk, Gomez, Grunow, & LeMahieu, 2015).
   - **Celebrate and Scale Successes:** Recognize teachers or teams that demonstrate excellence in Tier 1 practices. Share their strategies with the entire school to encourage replication of effective methods (Fisher et al., 2021).

Reflecting on Tier 1 practices ensures continuous improvement and better outcomes for all students. Figure 4.7 outlines a systematic approach to evaluating and enhancing universal supports.

Figure 4.7 Reflecting and Planning for Tier 1

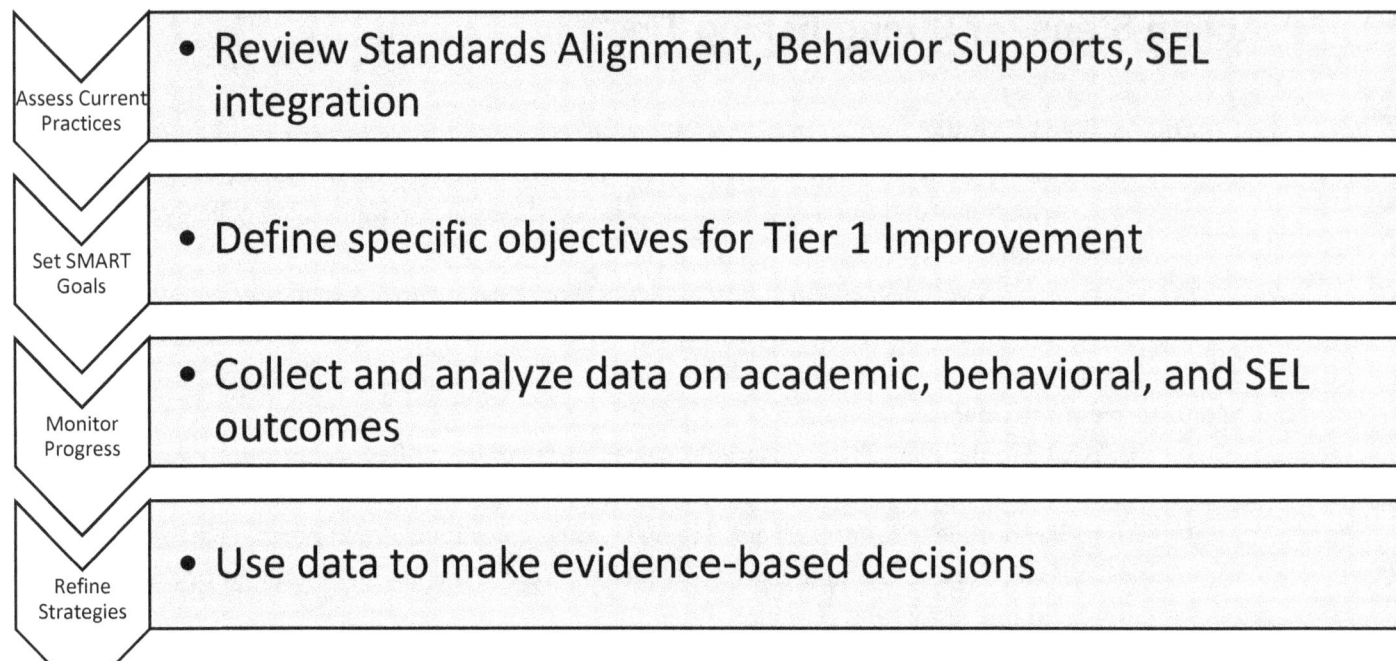

Looking Ahead

Reflecting on your Tier 1 foundation is vital for ensuring that universal supports meet the needs of the majority of students, academically, behaviorally, and socially-emotionally. By examining current practices, analyzing data, and involving the entire school community in continuous improvement, you pave the way for a more efficient and equitable Multi-Tiered System of Supports.

In **Chapter 5**, we will shift our focus to **Tier 2**—exploring targeted interventions and small-group supports for students who need more than Tier 1 can provide. However, remember that **the strength of your Tier 1** directly influences how many students ultimately require Tier 2 or Tier 3 interventions. Maintain your momentum in refining universal instruction and supports to foster a thriving learning environment for **all** students.

Chapter 5: Tier 2 – Targeted/Small Group Interventions

5.1 Identifying Students for Tier 2 Supports

Not all students will respond to Tier 1 instruction and supports at the same pace or level. **Tier 2** is designed for those who need more focused, small-group interventions to close skill gaps or address emerging behavioral or social-emotional challenges (McIntosh & Goodman, 2016). A successful Tier 2 system begins with **accurate and equitable** identification, ensuring that the right students receive additional support as soon as they show signs of risk. This section explores data-driven criteria, the role of collaboration among educators, and methods for preventing bias in identifying students for Tier 2.

Tier 2 identification relies on data-driven, equitable practices. Figure 5.1 summarizes key criteria used to determine eligibility for additional support.

Figure 5.1 Identifying Students for Tier 2 Supports

Performance Below Benchmark
- Universal screeners, formative assessments, SEL survey results

Rate of Progress in Tier 1
- Progress monitoring trends and multiple data points

Equity Considerations
- Disaggregated data and team consensus for decision-making

Data-Driven Criteria for Entry

1. **Performance Below Established Benchmarks**
   - **Academic Indicators:** Students who consistently score below the proficiency threshold on universal screeners, classroom formative assessments, or district benchmarks may need extra support in reading, math, or other content areas (Burns & Gibbons, 2012).
   - **Behavioral or Social-Emotional Indicators:** Frequent minor discipline referrals, teacher ratings on behavior checklists, or SEL survey results indicating heightened risk can flag students for additional intervention (McIntosh & Goodman, 2016).
2. **Rate of Progress in Tier 1**
   - **Progress Monitoring Trends:** Even if students are somewhat below benchmarks, a steadily upward trajectory may suggest they can succeed with continued high-quality Tier 1 instruction. Conversely, those with flat or declining progress lines might require Tier 2 interventions (Fuchs, Fuchs, & Vaughn, 2014).
   - **Multiple Data Points:** Rely on a **body of evidence** rather than a single score or event—this could include classroom performance, attendance patterns, discipline referrals, and teacher observations (Marzano, 2017).
3. **Equitable Decision-Making**
   - **Disaggregated Data:** Regularly review data by student subgroups (e.g., race/ethnicity, language proficiency, socioeconomic status) to detect patterns of disproportionality or potential bias (Fergus, 2017).
   - **Team Consensus:** Use a collaborative process (e.g., MTSS or RTI teams) to discuss borderline cases. Collective input reduces the risk of individual bias influencing who is placed in Tier 2 (McIntosh & Goodman, 2016).

Collaboration Between Teachers, Counselors, and Support Staff

1. **Regular Student Review Meetings**
   - **Structured Agendas:** Schedule biweekly or monthly meetings specifically to review at-risk students, ensuring data (e.g., screening results, teacher logs) is shared beforehand (DuFour & Fullan, 2013).
   - **Cross-Functional Teams:** Include content-area teachers, school psychologists, counselors, social workers, and administrators. Each brings a unique lens to interpreting data and recommending next steps (Spillane, 2006).
2. **Clarifying Roles and Responsibilities**
   - **Teachers:** Provide ongoing classroom-based assessments, behavioral observations, and anecdotal notes about student engagement.
   - **Counselors & School Psychologists:** Offer insights on social-emotional indicators, mental health concerns, and possible external factors impacting the student (Greenberg, Domitrovich, Weissberg, & Durlak, 2017).

- **Administrators:** Ensure resources (e.g., time, funding, professional development) are allocated to support Tier 2 interventions and coordinate consistency across grade levels or subject areas.
3. **Communication with Families**
    - **Early and Frequent Outreach:** Inform parents or guardians when their child is being considered for Tier 2. Share the data behind the decision, the goals of the intervention, and how progress will be tracked (Buffum, Mattos, & Weber, 2010).
    - **Family Voice:** Families often have valuable context—such as recent life changes, cultural values, or health issues—that can explain or influence a student's performance. Involving them from the outset fosters trust and increases likelihood of student success (Gay, 2018).

Collaboration among educators and families is crucial for Tier 2 success. Figure 5.2 illustrates the cyclical process of decision-making and communication.

Figure 5.2 Collaboration in Tier 2 Decision-Making

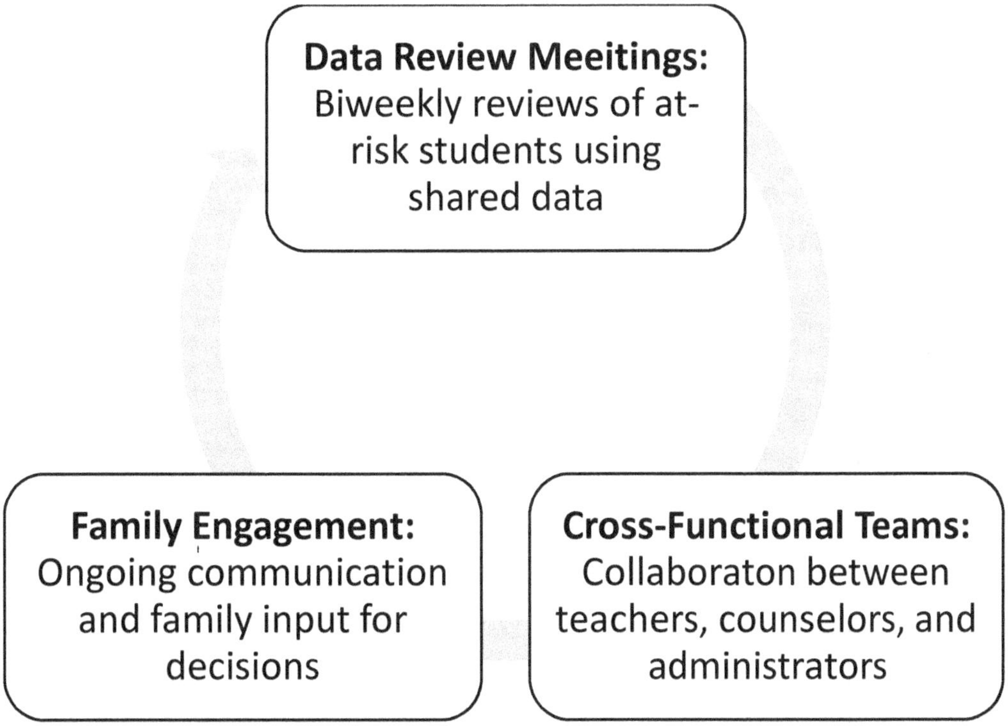

Data Review Meeitings: Biweekly reviews of at-risk students using shared data

Family Engagement: Ongoing communication and family input for decisions

Cross-Functional Teams: Collaboraton between teachers, counselors, and administrators

Preventing Over-Identification and Bias

1. **Multiple Measures and Triangulation**
    - **Beyond Grades and Test Scores:** Incorporate teacher recommendations, attendance and discipline data, and student self-assessments to gain a comprehensive view of a student's need (Burns & Gibbons, 2012).

- **Behavior Observations:** Document frequency, intensity, and context of any behavior concerns. Is the behavior pervasive across multiple settings, or limited to certain classes or times of day (McIntosh & Goodman, 2016)?

2. **Culturally Responsive Approaches**
    - **Review Discipline Practices:** Check whether certain student groups are disproportionately referred for behavior issues. Examine potential implicit biases and provide training on culturally responsive classroom management (Gay, 2018; Fergus, 2017).
    - **Language Considerations:** Students who are still developing English proficiency might need linguistic supports rather than a Tier 2 intervention for a learning disability (Esparza Brown & Sanford, 2011).

3. **Monitoring Misplacement and Exit Criteria**
    - **Periodic Review:** Students placed in Tier 2 should not remain there indefinitely. Regular progress monitoring ensures that if they catch up, they can return to Tier 1 (Fuchs et al., 2014).
    - **Structured Exit Criteria:** Establish data thresholds (e.g., consistent performance above a certain benchmark for multiple weeks) so students exit Tier 2 promptly when they're ready (Burns & Gibbons, 2012).

Reflection & Planning

1. **Current Identification Processes**
    - How do you currently determine which students need Tier 2 interventions?
    - Are these decisions made systematically and consistently across grade levels or subject areas?
2. **Data Sources and Equity**
    - Do you rely on multiple data points (screeners, classwork, behavioral referrals) to inform placement decisions?
    - Are you reviewing disaggregated data to check for potential biases or patterns of over-identification among specific groups?
3. **Collaboration and Communication**
    - How frequently do teachers, counselors, and support staff meet to discuss students who may require Tier 2?
    - Are families involved early in the discussion, and do they feel empowered to share insights or concerns?

By adopting clear, data-informed criteria and engaging a cross-functional team in the process, schools can accurately identify students who need targeted support while minimizing misplacements or unintended bias. In **Section 5.2**, we will outline **practical academic interventions** appropriate for Tier 2, offering guidelines on small-group instruction, resource allocation, and progress monitoring protocols to ensure every student's needs are met swiftly and effectively.

5.2 Academic Interventions

Tier 2 academic interventions provide **targeted, small-group support** to students who are not meeting key benchmarks through Tier 1 instruction alone (McIntosh & Goodman, 2016). By using data to pinpoint specific skill deficits, educators can deliver short-term, evidence-based interventions that accelerate growth in reading, math, or other core areas. This section details how to design and implement effective Tier 2 academic interventions, covering small-group models, the selection of evidence-based programs, and co-teaching or push-in/pull-out services.

Small-Group Instruction Models

1. **Focused Skills Groups**
   - **Needs-Based Grouping:** After analyzing screening and classroom assessment data, place students with similar skill gaps (e.g., phonemic awareness, number sense) in groups of three to five (Fuchs, Fuchs, & Vaughn, 2014).
   - **Flexible Groupings:** Students may move in or out of groups as they master certain skills or demonstrate new needs. Regular progress monitoring ensures that group composition remains responsive and dynamic (Burns & Gibbons, 2012).
   - **Intensive Practice and Feedback:** These sessions often involve systematic review of previously taught content, guided practice with immediate feedback, and opportunities to apply new skills in context (Vaughn & Swanson, 2015).
2. **Structured Intervention Sessions**
   - **Frequent, Consistent Sessions:** Schedule interventions at least three to four times per week for 20–30 minutes per session. Shorter, more frequent sessions tend to be more effective than sporadic, longer blocks (Denton, 2012).
   - **Dedicated Intervention Blocks:** Some schools implement a "What I Need (WIN)" or "Intervention" period within the master schedule, ensuring all students have access to support without missing core instruction (DuFour & Fullan, 2013).
   - **Clear Routines and Expectations:** Students should know the purpose of each intervention session, materials needed, and how their progress will be measured (Buffum, Mattos, & Weber, 2010).

Small-group instruction models form the backbone of Tier 2 academic interventions. Figure 5.3 illustrates the key steps in designing effective small-group supports.

Figure 5.3 Small-Group Academic Intervention Models

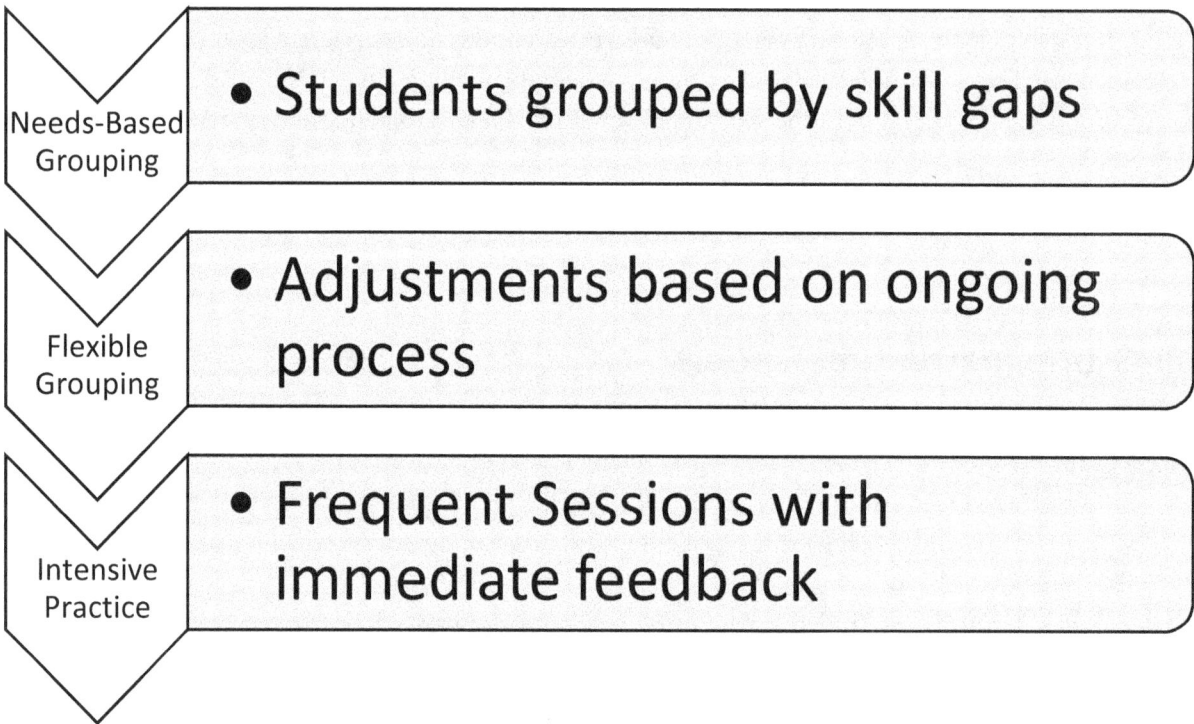

Use of Evidence-Based Intervention Programs

1. **Selecting Research-Validated Materials**
    - **Alignment with Tier 1 Curriculum:** Choose programs that complement your core materials and instructional approach, minimizing instructional conflicts for students (Burns & Gibbons, 2012).
    - **Reviewed and Rated Resources:** Tools such as the National Center on Intensive Intervention or Evidence for ESSA databases can guide educators in selecting interventions with a strong evidence base (Gersten et al., 2009).
2. **Targeting Specific Skill Deficits**
    - **Academic Domains:** In reading, interventions might focus on phonics, fluency, or comprehension; in math, they might emphasize numeracy, computation, or problem-solving (Fuchs et al., 2014).
    - **Diagnostic Assessments:** Administer short, skill-based diagnostics to refine intervention focus (e.g., a decoding inventory to pinpoint phonics gaps, a math fact fluency probe) (Vaughn & Swanson, 2015).

3. **Fidelity of Implementation**
   - **Program Training:** Ensure staff receive adequate training on the program's content, pacing, and instructional routines (Burns & Gibbons, 2012).
   - **Observation and Feedback:** Use fidelity checklists or peer observations to confirm that key program components are delivered consistently and with quality (DuFour & Fullan, 2013).
   - **Regular Data Checks:** Monitor student progress weekly or bi-weekly; if growth is insufficient, adjust the intervention's frequency, intensity, or grouping structure (McIntosh & Goodman, 2016).

Co-Teaching and Push-In/Pull-Out Services

1. **Co-Teaching Models**
   - **General and Special Educator Collaboration:** A general educator and an intervention specialist (e.g., reading specialist, special education teacher) plan and deliver lessons together, offering targeted support within the classroom (Friend & Cook, 2016).
   - **Station Teaching:** Divide the class into small groups rotating through stations—one led by the general educator, another by the intervention specialist—providing intensive practice or re-teaching for those who need it (Murawski & Lochner, 2017).
2. **Push-In Supports**
   - **Within Core Instruction:** An interventionist "pushes in" to the general education classroom to work with a small group on targeted skills. This model avoids removing students from Tier 1 instruction and fosters consistent alignment with core content (Marzano, 2017).
   - **Coordination with Classroom Teacher:** Regular planning time ensures that the push-in support complements the day's lesson objectives, maximizing relevancy and continuity (Murawski & Lochner, 2017).
3. **Pull-Out Services**
   - **Separate, Focused Environment:** In some cases—especially when a student needs highly specialized or intensive work—pull-out sessions may be beneficial (Fuchs et al., 2014).
   - **Minimal Disruption to Core Learning:** Schedule pull-out sessions during non-core instructional times (e.g., homeroom, elective blocks) so students do not miss essential Tier 1 content (Denton, 2012).

Figure 5.4 outlines key delivery models for Tier 2 academic interventions, ensuring tailored support for diverse student needs.

Figure 5.4 Co-Teaching and Push-In/Pull-Out Models

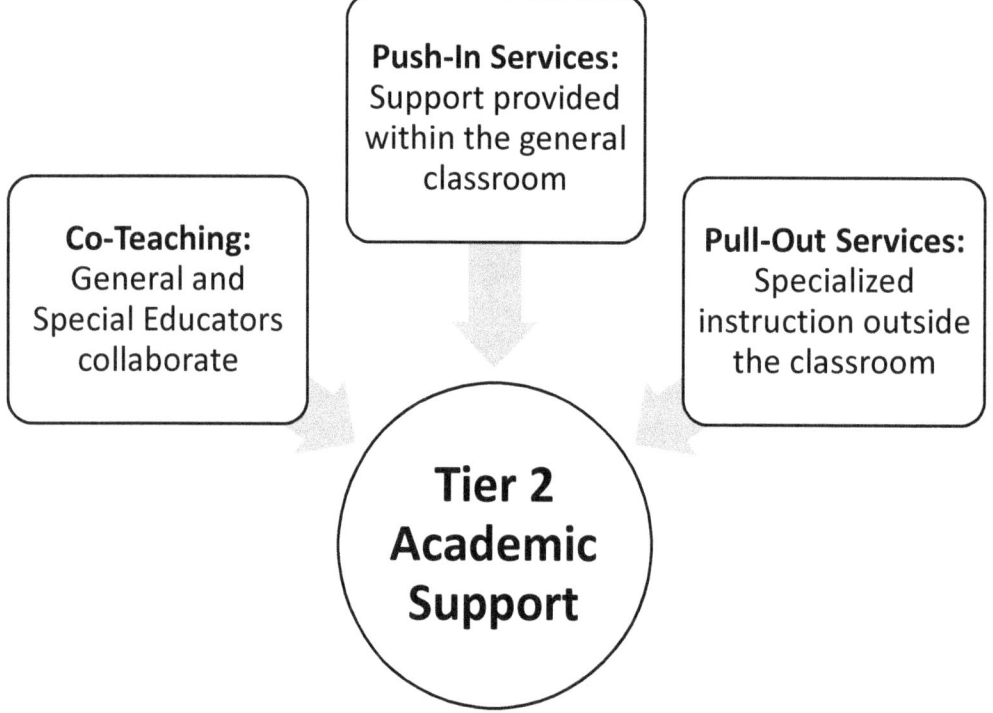

Reflection & Planning

1. **Current Tier 2 Interventions**
   - Which academic areas (e.g., reading fluency, basic math facts) are most in need of small-group support based on recent data?
   - Are there existing intervention programs and materials, and do staff feel confident in their effectiveness?
2. **Scheduling and Logistics**
   - Do you have a dedicated intervention block or a flexible schedule that allows small-group sessions without impacting core instruction?
   - Are there enough trained interventionists, co-teachers, or paraprofessionals to deliver targeted support at the necessary frequency?
3. **Fidelity and Accountability**

- How do you monitor whether interventions are delivered consistently and according to program guidelines?
- What data do you collect (e.g., weekly progress monitoring) to determine if students are responding to the intervention, and how do you share this information with families?

Effective Tier 2 academic interventions bridge the gap for students who need more than strong Tier 1 instruction can provide. By offering systematic, evidence-based, and closely monitored support in small-group settings—whether within or outside the general education classroom—educators can quickly address skill deficits, prevent future academic struggles, and empower students to succeed. In **Section 5.3**, we will discuss **behavioral and SEL interventions** specifically designed for students requiring additional help beyond universal (Tier 1) practices, ensuring a comprehensive approach to student success.

5.3 Behavioral and SEL Interventions

Not all student needs are strictly academic. For some learners, a lack of engagement, self-regulation, or appropriate social skills can significantly hinder success. **Tier 2 behavioral and social-emotional learning (SEL) interventions** provide small-group supports for students who need more than universal (Tier 1) strategies but do not necessarily require the intensive, individualized services of Tier 3 (Sugai & Horner, 2009). By proactively addressing emerging concerns, schools can help students develop the skills and resilience they need to thrive in and out of the classroom.

Small-Group Counseling and Skill-Building Sessions

1. **Focus on Targeted Skill Deficits**
   - **Identifying Specific Needs:** Use teacher observations, behavior checklists, discipline data, or SEL screening tools to pinpoint areas such as conflict resolution, anxiety management, or social communication (Greenberg, Domitrovich, Weissberg, & Durlak, 2017).
   - **Structured Curriculum:** Programs like "Skillstreaming," "WhyTry," or "Second Step" often include small-group modules for students who benefit from explicit instruction in social or emotional competencies (Durlak, Weissberg, Dymnicki, Taylor, & Schellinger, 2011).
2. **Group Size and Frequency**
   - **Small, Consistent Groups:** Aim for 3–6 students with similar skill gaps or behavioral concerns. Consistency allows the group to build trust and practice strategies collectively (McIntosh & Goodman, 2016).
   - **Regular Sessions:** Schedule 20–30 minute meetings two to three times per week for a defined period (e.g., 6–10 weeks). This provides enough practice and repetition for new skills to take root (Han & Weiss, 2005).

3. **Interactive and Experiential Activities**
   - **Role-Playing and Scenarios:** Have students practice conflict resolution, communication, or stress-management skills with real-life scenarios relevant to their experiences (Jennings & Greenberg, 2009).
   - **Reflection and Goal-Setting:** Encourage journaling, self-assessment, or partner check-ins to help students internalize and apply newly learned strategies (Deno, 2016).

Check-In/Check-Out (CICO) Systems

1. **Daily Positive Contact**
   - **Mentoring Relationship:** Each student is paired with a staff member (teacher, counselor, or paraprofessional) who greets them each morning and briefly reviews goals or behavioral expectations (McIntosh & Goodman, 2016).
   - **Individualized Feedback:** At day's end, students "check out" with the same mentor, reviewing progress toward their goals and celebrating achievements or setting targets for the next day (Crone, Hawken, & Horner, 2010).
2. **Progress Tracking and Rewards**
   - **Point Sheets or Digital Tracking:** Students earn points or ratings for meeting daily expectations, creating a tangible record of improvement over time (Hawken, Bundock, Kladis, & Johnson, 2014).
   - **Small but Meaningful Incentives:** Rewards might include verbal praise, extra computer time, or a note home highlighting positive behavior. Link incentives to the student's interests for maximum motivation (Sugai & Horner, 2009).
3. **Collaboration with Teachers and Families**
   - **Teacher Input:** Classroom teachers provide quick feedback on a student's participation, behavior, and goal adherence throughout the day, ensuring consistency of support (McIntosh et al., 2009).
   - **Home-School Connection:** Send point sheets or digital logs home so families can reinforce progress and discuss challenges with their child (Greenberg et al., 2017).

Mentoring and Peer Support Programs

1. **Adult-Student Mentoring**
   - **Regular Check-Ins:** Mentors—school staff or community volunteers—meet weekly with students to build rapport, discuss goals, and provide academic or emotional encouragement (DuBois & Karcher, 2014).
   - **Resource Connection:** Mentors can help students access tutoring, extracurriculars, or community resources that build their confidence and sense of belonging.

2. **Peer Mentoring or Buddy Systems**
   - **Structured Peer Support:** Pair students who exhibit strong leadership or social skills with peers who need extra help navigating school routines or social interactions (Thompson & Kelly-Vance, 2001).
   - **Ongoing Coaching:** Train peer mentors to model appropriate behaviors, offer constructive feedback, and encourage positive habits (McIntosh & Goodman, 2016).
3. **SEL-Focused Clubs or Groups**
   - **Interest-Based Engagement:** After-school clubs around common interests (e.g., gaming, arts, sports) can provide a less formal setting for students to practice prosocial skills, form relationships, and gain leadership experience (Greenberg et al., 2017).
   - **Adult Facilitation:** An adult advisor ensures group norms and activities reinforce core SEL competencies (e.g., empathy, responsible decision-making).

Targeted behavioral and SEL interventions are critical for Tier 2 success. Figure 5.5 categorizes the most effective strategies used in small-group settings.

Figure 5.5 Behavioral and SEL Intervention Strategies

Small-Group Sessions

Conflict Resolution, Stress Management, Social Communication

Check-In/Check-Out (CICO)

Daily Mentoring, Progress Tracking, Small Incentives

Mentoring and Peer Support

Adult Mentoring, Buddy Systems, SEL Clubs

Monitoring and Communication

1. **Ongoing Data Collection**
   - **Behavior Logs and Observations:** Track frequency, duration, or intensity of target behaviors in a systematic way (Burns & Gibbons, 2012).
   - **Short SEL Surveys or Rating Scales:** Allow students and teachers to periodically evaluate progress on goals like self-regulation or social interactions (Greenberg et al., 2017).
2. **Regular Team Debriefs**
   - **Review Student Progress:** School counselors, social workers, teachers, and administrators should meet biweekly or monthly to examine data on students in Tier 2 (McIntosh & Goodman, 2016).
   - **Adjust Interventions as Needed:** If a student isn't making progress, modify the approach—switch from small-group to individualized counseling, increase session frequency, or explore new SEL strategies.
3. **Family Engagement**
   - **Frequent Updates:** Provide brief reports or phone calls after each cycle (e.g., every 4–6 weeks) to inform families about gains, challenges, and next steps (Sugai & Horner, 2009).
   - **Collaborative Planning:** If concerns persist, invite families to problem-solving meetings, ensuring that all stakeholders have a voice in refining the Tier 2 intervention plan (Gay, 2018).

Effective monitoring ensures timely decisions about Tier 2 interventions. Figure 5.6 outlines the structured process for tracking progress and making adjustments.

Figure 5.6 Monitoring and Decision-Making in Tier 2

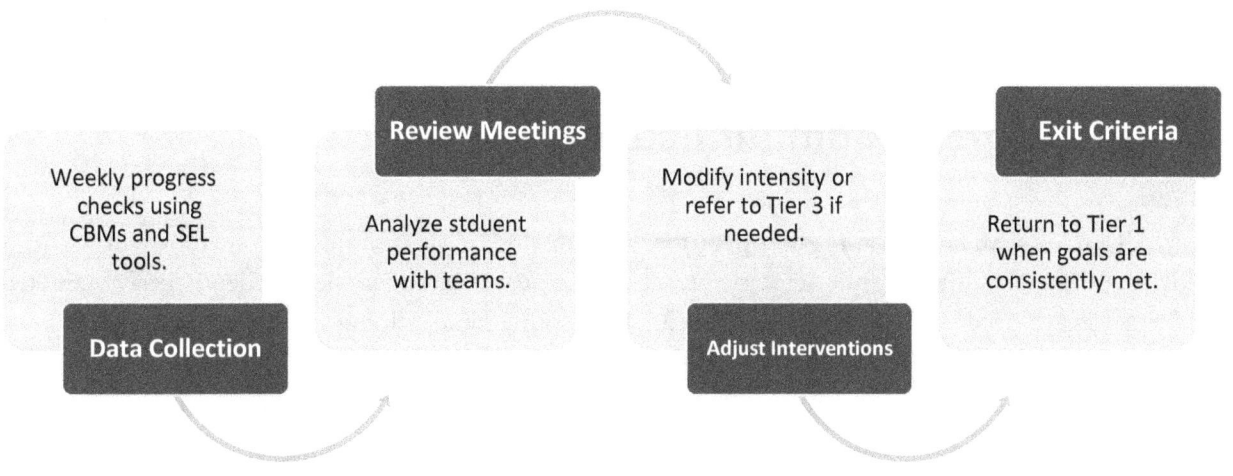

Reflection & Planning

1. **Assess Your Current Supports**
   - Are there existing small-group SEL or behavioral programs you can expand?
   - How effectively are Check-In/Check-Out or mentoring systems implemented in your school?
2. **Identify Staff and Resource Needs**
   - Do school counselors, social workers, or behavior specialists have enough time and capacity to run small-group sessions?
   - What professional development or program materials might you need to improve fidelity?
3. **Fidelity and Accountability**

- How will you monitor whether Tier 2 behavioral or SEL interventions are delivered as intended?
- Do you have clear data protocols for deciding when a student should move back to Tier 1 or advance to Tier 3 supports?

By providing **targeted behavioral and SEL interventions** in small-group settings, schools help students navigate challenges that could otherwise undermine their academic performance and overall well-being. These Tier 2 supports align closely with Tier 1 practices—reinforcing positive behaviors, building self-regulation skills, and deepening students' sense of connection to the school community. In **Section 5.4**, we will examine how to **track progress, engage families, and make data-driven decisions** about whether students in Tier 2 need to intensify their interventions or return to universal supports.

5.4 Monitoring and Communication

A successful Tier 2 system hinges on **regular progress monitoring**, clear communication among all stakeholders, and **timely adjustments** to interventions. These processes ensure that students receive targeted support for as long as needed—but no longer—freeing up resources and helping students return to Tier 1 successfully. This section details how to track academic, behavioral, and social-emotional progress, involve families and caregivers, and make data-informed decisions about when to shift students to either less or more intensive supports.

Tracking Progress in Tier 2 and Adjusting Strategies

1. **Frequent Data Collection**
   - **Short, Skill-Focused Measures:** For academic interventions, use quick curriculum-based measures (CBMs) or targeted assessments (e.g., fluency probes, math fact checks) weekly or biweekly (Fuchs, Fuchs, & Vaughn, 2014). For behavioral or SEL interventions, employ brief rating scales or behavior logs (Greenberg, Domitrovich, Weissberg, & Durlak, 2017).
   - **Consistent Documentation:** Maintain up-to-date records in a shared data system or spreadsheet. This ensures team members can quickly access and analyze student progress over time (Burns & Gibbons, 2012).
2. **Goal Setting and Progress Graphing**
   - **Visual Data Displays:** Plot student performance on graphs or charts that show the "goal line" compared to actual performance. This makes it easier to spot whether a student is on track or lagging behind (Deno, 2016).
   - **Actionable Benchmarks:** Establish concrete, time-bound goals (e.g., "increase reading fluency from 50 wpm to 70 wpm within six weeks") to guide instructional adjustments (Marzano, 2017).
3. **Regular Review Cycles**

- **Structured Team Meetings:** School teams (e.g., MTSS, PLCs) should meet every 2–4 weeks to examine data for students in Tier 2. Use a problem-solving protocol to identify barriers and brainstorm solutions (McIntosh & Goodman, 2016).
- **Mid-Intervention Checks:** If data shows flat or declining trends after several data points, intensify or modify the intervention—change group size, adjust the content focus, or increase session frequency (Fuchs et al., 2014).

Engaging Families and Caregivers in Tier 2 Support

1. **Early and Ongoing Communication**
   - **Initial Notification:** Once a student is placed in Tier 2, promptly inform families about the specific skill or behavior targeted, the rationale for intervention, and the intended duration (Buffum, Mattos, & Weber, 2010).
   - **Frequent Updates:** Provide short, regular progress reports or phone calls summarizing student gains, challenges, and next steps. When families see improvement and understand how to help at home, they become valuable partners in the intervention process (Gay, 2018).
2. **Sharing Strategies and Resources**
   - **Home Practice Ideas:** Offer simple skill-building exercises or conversation prompts for families to reinforce. For behavioral or SEL needs, share calming techniques or reflection questions (Greenberg et al., 2017).
   - **Workshops or Tutorials:** Host brief sessions—either in person or via video conferencing—on topics like reading fluency practice, homework strategies, or using praise and positive reinforcement effectively (DuFour & Fullan, 2013).
3. **Two-Way Dialogue and Cultural Responsiveness**
   - **Listening to Family Insights:** Families can shed light on external factors influencing the student, such as health issues, shifting schedules, or trauma (SAMHSA, 2014).
   - **Language Accessibility and Respectful Communication:** Provide translated materials and interpreters as needed. Recognize cultural norms around parent-teacher interactions and adjust communication styles accordingly (Gay, 2018).

Decision Points: When to Transition Students or Escalate to Tier 3

1. **Meeting Exit Criteria**
   - **Evidence of Growth:** If a student consistently meets weekly or biweekly targets for a defined period (e.g., 4–6 consecutive data points above the goal line), teams may decide to gradually reduce the intervention's frequency or intensity (Burns & Gibbons, 2012).

- **Monitoring After Exit:** Even after returning to Tier 1, continue periodic checks to ensure the student maintains progress without additional supports (Fuchs et al., 2014).
2. **Insufficient Progress or Worsening Trends**
    - **Intensify the Intervention:** Before moving a student to Tier 3, consider increasing session frequency, reducing group size, or trying a different evidence-based program (McIntosh & Goodman, 2016).
    - **Comprehensive Review:** If performance remains static or declines despite fidelity checks and adjustments, the team may recommend a deeper evaluation in Tier 3, which could include diagnostic testing or referral for specialized services (Fergus, 2017).
3. **Behavioral or SEL Escalation**
    - **Increased Severity:** For students exhibiting serious or recurrent behaviors (e.g., aggression, extreme withdrawal), a functional behavioral assessment (FBA) may be warranted, leading to Tier 3 supports (Sugai & Horner, 2009).
    - **Collaboration with Mental Health Professionals:** If Tier 2 SEL interventions are not enough, consult with school counselors, psychologists, or external clinicians for more individualized strategies (Greenberg et al., 2017).

Reflection & Planning

1. **Current Progress Monitoring**
    - Are Tier 2 interventions tracked consistently, with clear procedures for collecting and reviewing data?
    - How do you ensure that staff have the time and training to conduct regular progress monitoring?
2. **Communication Protocols**
    - Do families receive timely, understandable updates about their child's progress?
    - Are cultural and linguistic differences accounted for, so all families can engage in meaningful dialogue?
3. **Data-Driven Transitions**
    - What criteria do you use to decide if a student is ready to exit Tier 2 or needs more intensive Tier 3 support?
    - Are these criteria consistently applied and well-documented, so decisions are transparent and equitable?

By **closely monitoring** student progress and **maintaining open lines of communication** with families, Tier 2 teams can refine supports, celebrate gains, and make confident, data-informed decisions about the path forward. In **Section 5.5**, we will synthesize the key takeaways from Chapter 5, providing a final reflection on targeted interventions and offering guidelines to ensure fidelity, sustainability, and seamless coordination with Tier 1 and Tier 3 systems.

5.5 Reflection & Planning

Throughout Chapter 5, we've examined the **core components** of Tier 2, covering how to **identify** students who need additional academic or behavioral/SEL supports, design **targeted small-group interventions**, and **monitor** progress to ensure timely adjustments. The next step is to reflect on your current Tier 2 practices and plan strategically for **sustainability** and **continuous improvement**. This section provides guiding questions, best practices for fidelity checks, and a look ahead to how Tier 2 seamlessly connects with Tiers 1 and 3.

Reflecting on Tier 2 Implementation

1. **Consistency and Fidelity**
   - **Alignment with Tier 1:** Are Tier 2 strategies clearly building on your school's core curriculum and universal behavior/SEL practices? Gaps between Tier 1 and Tier 2 can create confusion and reduce student buy-in (McIntosh & Goodman, 2016).
   - **Evidence-Based Interventions:** Have you verified that the academic and behavioral/SEL programs you're using have a strong research base? If so, are staff trained to deliver them with fidelity (Fuchs, Fuchs, & Vaughn, 2014)?
2. **Equity and Access**
   - **Data Disaggregation:** Do you regularly check whether certain student groups are overrepresented in Tier 2, and investigate possible reasons (Fergus, 2017)?
   - **Culturally Responsive Support:** How are you adapting interventions—particularly SEL or behavioral supports—to acknowledge students' cultural contexts, languages, and lived experiences (Gay, 2018)?
3. **Staff Capacity and Collaboration**
   - **Scheduling and Resources:** Is there enough flexibility in the daily or weekly schedule for small-group sessions? Are interventionists or co-teachers available as needed (Burns & Gibbons, 2012)?
   - **Team Communication:** Do you have regular Tier 2 meetings where teachers, counselors, and specialists share updates on student progress, discuss barriers, and make decisions collaboratively (DuFour & Fullan, 2013)?

Ensuring Sustainability and Fidelity

1. **Ongoing Professional Development**
   - **Targeted Training:** Provide ongoing PD on the specific interventions or curricula used in Tier 2—especially when staff turnover occurs (Buffum, Mattos, & Weber, 2010).

- **Peer Observations and Coaching:** Encourage teachers and interventionists to learn from one another through classroom visits and feedback sessions, reinforcing consistent delivery of supports (Tomlinson, 2017).
2. **Fidelity Checklists and Observations**
    - **Structured Tools:** Develop or adopt simple checklists that outline the critical components of each intervention (e.g., session frequency, instructional protocols). Observers can use these to gauge adherence (DuFour & Fullan, 2013).
    - **Self-Reflection:** Encourage interventionists to video record a session or self-assess using a fidelity rubric, promoting continuous improvement and confidence (Marzano, 2017).
3. **Resource Management**
    - **Budgeting for Materials:** Ensure sufficient funding for workbooks, technology licenses, or other materials required for small-group sessions (Burns & Gibbons, 2012).
    - **Time Allocation:** Protect dedicated Tier 2 periods from disruptions such as assemblies or testing, underscoring the importance of consistent intervention delivery (McIntosh & Goodman, 2016).

Connecting Tier 2 with Tier 1 and Tier 3

1. **Seamless Transitions**
    - **Exit Back to Tier 1:** When students meet their goals, create a clear plan for monitoring them post-intervention to ensure they continue to thrive without Tier 2 supports (Fuchs et al., 2014).
    - **Escalation to Tier 3:** If a student's needs persist or intensify, move swiftly to a Tier 3 evaluation. Have clear data and documentation ready to guide the process (McIntosh & Goodman, 2016).
2. **Collaboration with Tier 1 Educators**
    - **Shared Data and Practices:** Keep Tier 1 teachers informed of the strategies and progress made in Tier 2 so they can reinforce skills or behaviors in the general classroom (Marzano, 2017).
    - **Professional Learning Communities:** Maintain regular PLC meetings where Tier 1 and Tier 2 staff exchange insights on student needs, curriculum alignment, and potential universal enhancements (DuFour & Fullan, 2013).
3. **Preventing Tier 2 "Drift"**
    - **Periodic System Reviews:** Evaluate whether students remain in Tier 2 too long without re-evaluation, or if interventions have unintentionally replaced robust Tier 1 instruction (Burns & Gibbons, 2012).
    - **Feedback Loops:** Collect input from students and families about their experiences with Tier 2, using it to refine or modify interventions to be more relevant and engaging (Gay, 2018).

Action Steps and Future Directions

1. **Self-Audit of Tier 2**
   - Use an existing rubric or create a schoolwide self-check tool to measure your Tier 2 practices against best practices outlined in this chapter (Sugai & Horner, 2009).
   - Present findings to leadership teams, grade-level groups, and families for transparency and collective problem-solving.
2. **Plan for Improvements**
   - Set **SMART** goals (Doran, 1981) for strengthening Tier 2—like improving fidelity rates, boosting family engagement, or reducing the average time students spend in interventions by a specific margin.
   - Align resources (budget, staffing, PD) with these goals, ensuring Tier 2 remains a top priority for continuous schoolwide improvement (Fergus, 2017).
3. **Maintain a Culture of Reflection**
   - Celebrate student successes, teacher innovations, and family engagement wins.
   - Use data as a guide for iterative refinements, maintaining the focus on **proactive** and **equitable** supports for all students (Buffum et al., 2010).

Moving Forward

A well-executed Tier 2 ensures that students receive **targeted, data-driven** interventions at the moment they need them, bridging gaps before they widen. By reflecting on your identification criteria, fidelity of interventions, and communication strategies, you strengthen the likelihood of successful outcomes and smooth transitions—whether back to Tier 1 or forward to Tier 3.

In **Chapter 6**, we will explore **Tier 3**—the most intensive level of support—for those students who continue to struggle despite robust Tier 1 and Tier 2 interventions. A cohesive, well-managed Tier 2 makes Tier 3 more precise and effective, ensuring students receive the **right** help at the **right** time in their educational journey.

Chapter 6: Tier 3 – Intensive/Individualized Interventions

6.1 Criteria for Tier 3 Support

When students do not make sufficient progress despite robust Tier 1 (universal) and Tier 2 (targeted) interventions, it may be time to consider **Tier 3**—the most intensive level of support within a Multi-Tiered System of Supports (MTSS). Tier 3 interventions are typically **highly individualized**, addressing significant academic, behavioral, or social-emotional needs that require specialized expertise. This section examines data-based criteria for determining whether a student requires Tier 3 support, as well as how these decisions align with special education evaluations and schoolwide equity goals.

Figure 6.1 highlights the key criteria schools use to determine whether a student requires Tier 3 interventions.

Figure 6.1 Criteria for Tier 3 Support

Using Data to Determine the Need for High-Intensity Interventions

1. **Insufficient Response to Tier 2**
   - **Lack of Adequate Growth:** If a student's performance remains static or declines after **multiple** progress monitoring data points—even when Tier 2 interventions have been delivered with fidelity—Tier 3 may be warranted (Fuchs, Fuchs, & Vaughn, 2014).
   - **Extended Intervention Trials:** Ensure that Tier 2 interventions have been given enough time (e.g., 8–12 weeks) to yield results, unless the student's data clearly indicates an urgent need for more individualized support (McIntosh & Goodman, 2016).
2. **Frequent or Significant Risk Indicators**
   - **Academic Red Flags:** Students significantly below benchmark or grade-level expectations (e.g., multiple levels below in reading) may need diagnostic testing to identify the root cause of their struggles (Burns & Gibbons, 2012).
   - **Severe Behavioral/SEL Issues:** Repeated office referrals for aggression, high levels of anxiety or depression, or chronic disengagement could signal that Tier 2 supports are insufficient (Greenberg, Domitrovich, Weissberg, & Durlak, 2017).
   - **Chronic Attendance Problems:** Students with extensive absenteeism or tardiness might require Tier 3 strategies—such as wraparound services—to address factors outside the classroom contributing to inconsistent attendance (Chang & Romero, 2008).
3. **Equity Considerations**
   - **Data Disaggregation:** Before assigning Tier 3 services, review data by subgroups (e.g., race/ethnicity, language proficiency) to avoid automatically attributing achievement gaps or behavioral patterns to a "deficit" within the student (Fergus, 2017).
   - **Ensuring Culturally Responsive Practices:** Verify that Tier 2 interventions have been culturally and linguistically appropriate. If not, a culturally tailored approach at Tier 2 might still be a better starting point than Tier 3 (Gay, 2018).

Aligning with Special Education Evaluations (When Appropriate)

1. **Overlap Between Tier 3 and Special Education**
   - **Not All Tier 3 Students Have an IEP:** Some students benefit from intensive supports without qualifying for special education services under IDEA. Decisions about IEP eligibility must follow a formal evaluation process (Fuchs & Fuchs, 2006).

- **Documentation and Data Collection:** MTSS data—including Tier 2 progress monitoring, intervention fidelity checks, and performance trends—can support or prompt a special education referral if a suspected disability is indicated (McIntosh & Goodman, 2016).

2. **Collaboration with Special Education Teams**
   - **Shared Data Reviews:** General educators, intervention specialists, and special education professionals should collaborate to interpret a student's growth curves and diagnostic results (National Center on Intensive Intervention, 2013).
   - **Comprehensive Evaluation:** If Tier 3 supports suggest the possibility of a learning disability or other qualifying condition, schools must follow legal guidelines—securing parent/guardian consent for a formal evaluation and ensuring a thorough review of all relevant data (U.S. Department of Education, 2006).

3. **Clear Pathways to Services**
   - **When a Student Qualifies:** If evaluations confirm a student's disability, the individualized education program (IEP) team integrates Tier 3 strategies into a formal plan, potentially including additional accommodations and modifications (Fuchs & Fuchs, 2006).
   - **Continued MTSS Support:** For students who do not qualify for special education, Tier 3 services can still provide intensive instruction or behavior/SEL interventions, revisited or revised based on ongoing progress monitoring (Burns & Gibbons, 2012).

Figure 6.2 illustrates the relationship between Tier 3 interventions and special education, emphasizing areas of overlap and distinction.

Figure 6.2 The Relationship Between Tier 3 Interventions and Special Education

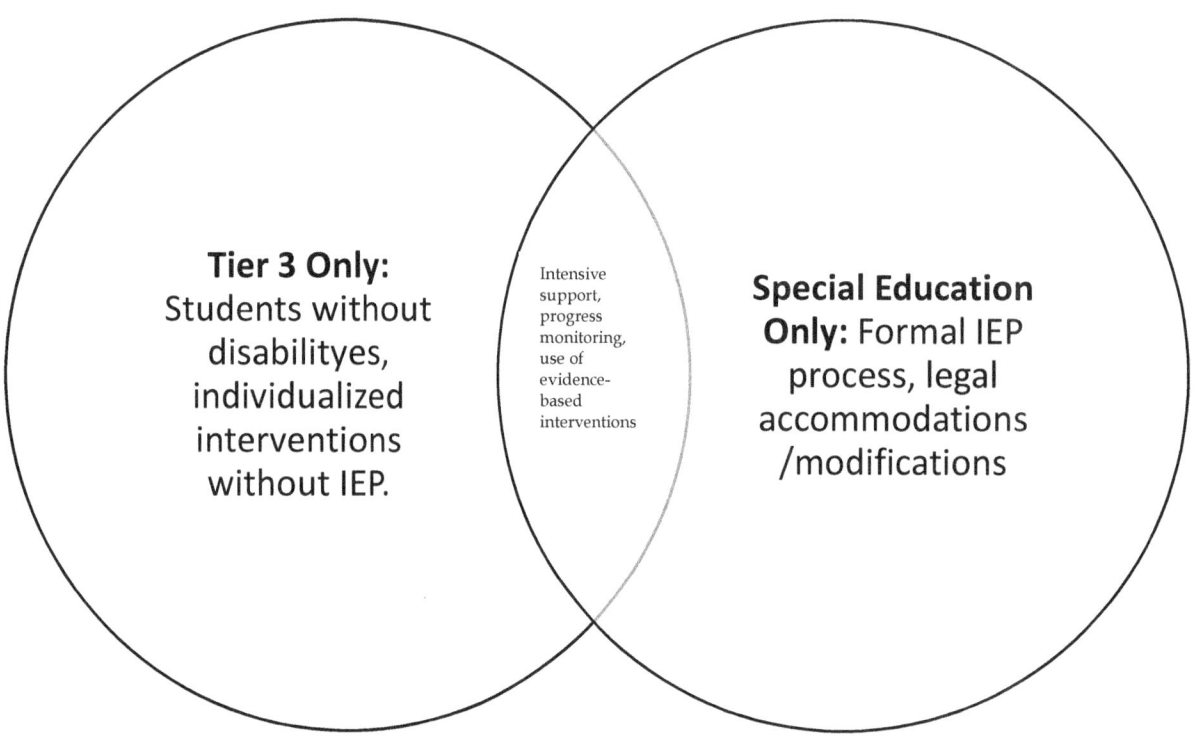

Key Considerations for Determining Tier 3 Eligibility

1. **Fidelity of Lower-Tier Interventions**
   - **Verify Implementation Quality:** Confirm that Tier 1 and Tier 2 supports were consistently delivered and matched to the student's needs (Fuchs et al., 2014).
   - **Professional Development and Coaching:** Provide teachers and interventionists with necessary training or coaching to ensure that lack of progress is not due to inadequate implementation (DuFour & Fullan, 2013).
2. **Diagnostic Assessments**
   - **Pinpoint Specific Skill Gaps:** Administer targeted assessments (e.g., phonological awareness tests, functional behavioral assessments) to clarify which areas require the most intensive focus (Sugai & Horner, 2009).
   - **Collaborative Analysis:** Convene MTSS or problem-solving teams to evaluate assessment data collectively, ensuring multiple perspectives on the student's strengths and needs (McIntosh & Goodman, 2016).
3. **Documentation and Transparency**
   - **Record Keeping:** Maintain organized files of screening data, intervention logs, progress monitoring charts, and fidelity checklists. This evidence base guides Tier 3 decisions and supports special education referrals if needed (Buffum, Mattos, & Weber, 2010).
   - **Family and Student Voice:** Keep parents or guardians informed of all data and decisions, inviting their insights into the student's history, home environment, and cultural context (Gay, 2018). Provide clear explanations of the Tier 3 process and potential next steps.

Reflection & Planning

1. **Current Criteria for Tier 3 Entry**
   - Are your thresholds clear, data-based, and consistently applied across grade levels and subject areas?
   - How do you ensure cultural and linguistic responsiveness when determining whether Tier 3 is appropriate?
2. **Team Coordination**
   - Are general educators, special educators, counselors, and administrators collaborating to interpret data and make Tier 3 decisions?
   - Do you have a structured problem-solving protocol or flowchart to guide these discussions (e.g., standardized forms, checklists)?
3. **Alignment with Special Education**

- How seamlessly does your Tier 3 process connect with formal special education evaluations, if needed?
- Do you have clear communication protocols for engaging families—particularly when the possibility of a learning disability or other eligibility concerns arise?

When students show a **significant** need for more intensive support, a clear, data-driven Tier 3 process prevents unnecessary delays and ensures the **right** interventions at the **right** time. In **Section 6.2**, we'll delve into **designing individualized interventions**, focusing on academic, behavioral, and social-emotional domains, and the critical role of collaboration with specialists in delivering high-intensity services.

6.2 Designing Individualized Interventions

When a student enters **Tier 3**, it signals that they need **highly specialized, personalized support** above and beyond the targeted small-group interventions offered in Tier 2. These interventions are often delivered one-on-one or in very small groups, and they involve **frequent monitoring**, **deep diagnostic assessments**, and **close collaboration with specialists** to determine the best course of action (Fuchs, Fuchs, & Vaughn, 2014). This section outlines how to develop individualized support plans for academic, behavioral, or social-emotional challenges, as well as how to involve key professionals and stakeholders in the process.

Developing Personalized Support Plans (IEPs, 504 Plans, or Other Plans)

1. **Assessing the Root Causes of Struggles**
   - **Diagnostic Assessments:** Go beyond typical screening or progress monitoring. Use in-depth tools (e.g., phonological awareness tests, functional behavioral assessments) to pinpoint specific skill or behavioral deficits (Burns & Gibbons, 2012).
   - **Multiple Data Sources:** Consider factors like attendance, health, language proficiency, and previous interventions. Engage the student's family or caregivers for additional context (Gay, 2018).
2. **Goal-Setting with Precision**
   - **Specific, Measurable Objectives:** For academic deficits (e.g., decoding, math problem-solving), define clear, time-bound targets (e.g., "increase correct words per minute from 30 to 50 in eight weeks").
   - **Behavioral or SEL Targets:** For significant social-emotional needs or challenging behaviors, specify measurable outcomes (e.g., reduce physical aggression incidents from five per week to no more than one per week within six weeks) (Sugai & Horner, 2009).
   - **Student Involvement:** Whenever possible, incorporate student voice to foster ownership and motivation (Greenberg, Domitrovich, Weissberg, & Durlak, 2017).

3. **Choosing the Right Intervention Approach**
    - **Evidence-Based Programs and Strategies:** Select interventions supported by research for the specific skill or behavior (e.g., intensive phonics programs, structured literacy modules, cognitive-behavioral therapy techniques for managing anxiety) (Fuchs et al., 2014).
    - **Structure and Frequency:** Tier 3 often requires daily or near-daily sessions of 30–60 minutes each, depending on the severity of need (McIntosh & Goodman, 2016).
    - **Alignment with Individualized Plans (IEPs, 504 Plans):** If the student has an identified disability or a 504 Plan, ensure the Tier 3 intervention complements the accommodations and goals already in place (U.S. Department of Education, 2006).

Figure 6.3 presents the key steps in designing personalized Tier 3 support plans to address individual student needs.

Figure 6.3 Developing Personalized Support Plans

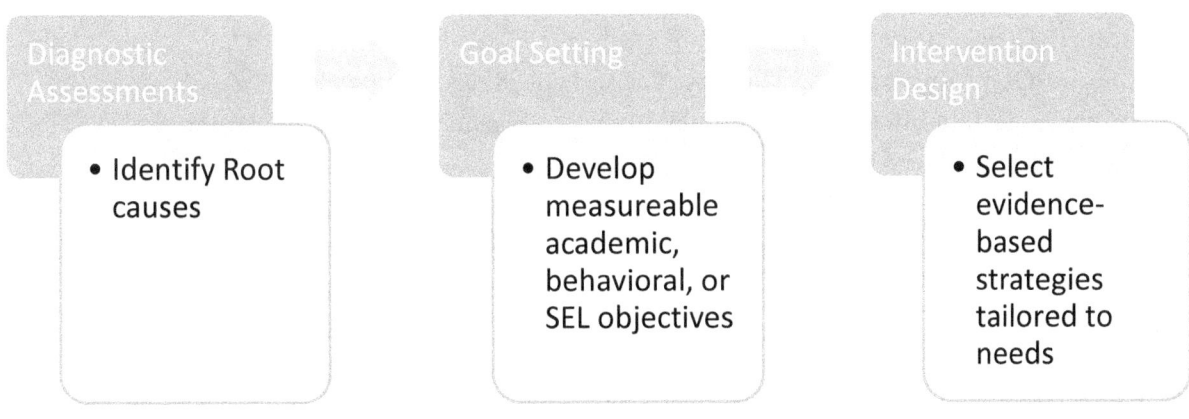

Intervention Techniques for Severe Academic, Behavioral, or SEL Needs

1. **Academic Interventions**
   - **One-on-One Tutoring:** Provide intensive instruction, often using a structured sequence of lessons tailored to the student's gaps (Denton & Vaughn, 2010).
   - **Mastery-Based Progression:** Continually assess mastery of each skill before moving on, revisiting problem areas as needed. Use frequent, detailed feedback to reinforce learning (Burns & Gibbons, 2012).
   - **Assistive Technology:** For some learners, tools such as text-to-speech software, specialized apps, or alternative keyboards can significantly enhance access to academic content (Marzano, 2017).
2. **Behavioral Interventions**
   - **Functional Behavioral Assessment (FBA):** Identify the underlying causes (e.g., avoidance, seeking attention) of severe or chronic behaviors. Develop a Behavior Intervention Plan (BIP) that includes proactive strategies, replacements skills, and de-escalation methods (Sugai & Horner, 2009).
   - **One-on-One Counseling or Therapy:** Collaborate with school psychologists, counselors, or external mental health professionals to address deep-rooted issues (e.g., trauma, anxiety, anger management) (Greenberg et al., 2017).
   - **Wraparound Services:** When home or community factors play a significant role, connect families with external social services, health providers, or community organizations (Fergus, 2017).
3. **Social-Emotional Interventions**
   - **Individualized SEL Coaching:** Work directly with the student on self-awareness, stress management, and relationship skills. Use role-playing, journaling, or guided reflection to practice and internalize skills (Durlak, Weissberg, Dymnicki, Taylor, & Schellinger, 2011).
   - **Trauma-Informed Supports:** For students who have experienced significant adversity, incorporate trauma-sensitive practices—e.g., predictable routines, safe spaces to calm down, and counseling tailored to trauma (SAMHSA, 2014).
   - **Alternative Programs or Placements (if needed):** In rare cases where the standard school environment cannot meet a student's high-level SEL or mental health needs, short-term placement in a specialized program may be considered, with the aim of reintegration once progress is shown (McIntosh & Goodman, 2016).

Figure 6.4 categorizes intervention techniques for addressing intensive academic, behavioral, and SEL needs in Tier 3.

Figure 6.4 Intervention Techniques for Tier 3

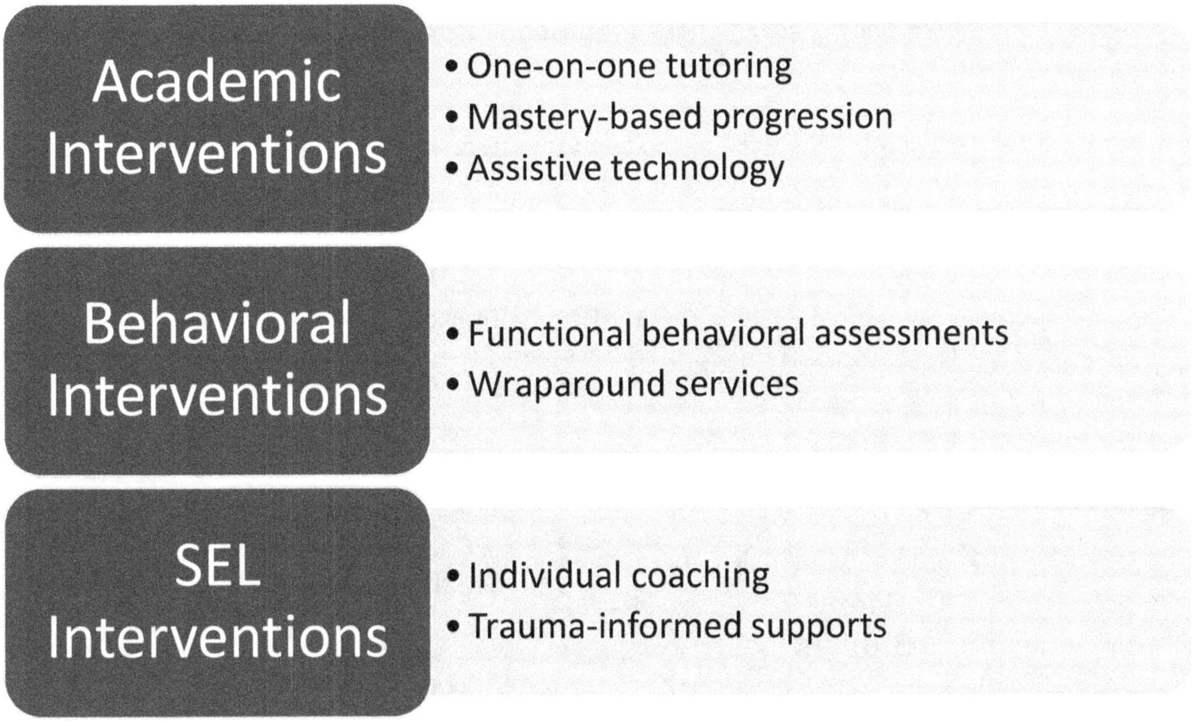

Academic Interventions
- One-on-one tutoring
- Mastery-based progression
- Assistive technology

Behavioral Interventions
- Functional behavioral assessments
- Wraparound services

SEL Interventions
- Individual coaching
- Trauma-informed supports

Collaboration with Specialists (School Psychologists, Social Workers, etc.)

1. **Interdisciplinary Teams**
    - **Multiple Perspectives:** Bring together special educators, school psychologists, social workers, behavior analysts, and other relevant professionals to design and refine Tier 3 plans (Spillane, 2006).
    - **Shared Responsibility:** Define clear roles for each specialist—who conducts assessments, who provides therapy, who tracks progress—to avoid duplication of efforts (Buffum, Mattos, & Weber, 2010).
2. **Ongoing Consultation and Coaching**
    - **Regular Check-Ins:** Schedule biweekly or monthly meetings where the specialist(s) and classroom teacher(s) review data, discuss successes, and troubleshoot challenges (DuFour & Fullan, 2013).
    - **Professional Development:** Provide training to staff in evidence-based, intensive intervention methods or behavior de-escalation techniques, ensuring that Tier 3 strategies remain consistent (Burns & Gibbons, 2012).

3. **Community Partnerships**
   - **External Referrals:** If a student requires outside counseling, medical services, or additional therapies, coordinate efforts with community health agencies. Secure parental consent and maintain confidentiality protocols (U.S. Department of Education, 2006).
   - **Wraparound Support:** Involve local organizations that can address non-academic barriers—such as housing instability or family stressors—that may affect the student's school performance (Fergus, 2017).

Figure 6.5 illustrates the collaborative roles of specialists in supporting students receiving Tier 3 interventions.

Figure 6.5 Collaboration with Specialists

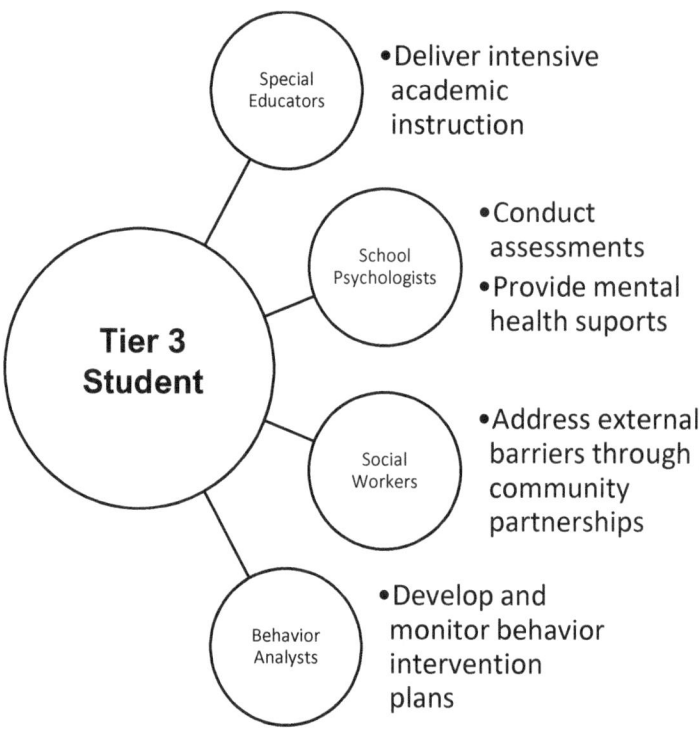

Reflection & Planning

1. **Assessing Your Current Tier 3 Interventions**
   - Do you have a structured process for diagnosing specific skill deficits or behavioral triggers?
   - Are Tier 3 interventions research-based and individualized, rather than a "one-size-fits-all" approach?
2. **Collaboration and Role Clarity**
   - How frequently do specialists and general education staff meet to discuss Tier 3 cases?
   - Are responsibilities (e.g., data collection, progress monitoring, communication with families) clearly assigned and consistently fulfilled?
3. **Family Engagement and Student Voice**

- Are parents/guardians fully aware of the purpose, nature, and anticipated duration of Tier 3 services?
- Do students have an opportunity to set their own goals, provide feedback on interventions, or participate in self-monitoring?

By **designing individualized interventions** that are informed by deep diagnostic data and delivered in close partnership with specialists, schools can effectively support students who face significant academic or behavioral challenges. These personalized plans often mean the difference between ongoing struggle and meaningful progress. In **Section 6.3**, we'll address **ongoing evaluation and adjustment** within Tier 3—examining how frequent data collection, transparent communication, and structured decision-making processes ensure that students receive exactly the level of support they need.

6.3 Ongoing Evaluation and Adjustment

Designing individualized, high-intensity supports for students is only the first step in **Tier 3**. To truly address a student's unique needs, schools must remain flexible and **data-driven**, continually assessing whether interventions are effective and making timely adjustments as necessary (Fuchs, Fuchs, & Vaughn, 2014). This section focuses on how to collect and analyze progress data, maintain transparent communication with families and staff, and adapt interventions or transition students to a different tier of support when appropriate.

Frequent Data Collection and Review

1. **Weekly or Bi-Weekly Progress Checks**
   - **Short, Targeted Assessments:** For academic goals, tools like curriculum-based measures (CBMs) in reading, math, or writing can provide quick snapshots of progress. For behavior or social-emotional goals, use frequent rating scales or logs that track specific actions or skill usage (Greenberg, Domitrovich, Weissberg, & Durlak, 2017).
   - **Visual Monitoring:** Graph student data over time, comparing actual progress to the goal line. This clear visual can help teams spot trends—whether improvement is accelerating, plateauing, or declining (Deno, 2016).
2. **Collaborative Team Meetings**
   - **Structured Conversations:** Assemble specialists, the classroom teacher, and relevant support staff (e.g., counselors, psychologists) every two to four weeks to evaluate the latest data. Follow a problem-solving protocol that frames discussions around observed outcomes, barriers, and potential solutions (DuFour & Fullan, 2013).

- **Action-Oriented Decision-Making:** When data indicates insufficient progress, teams should determine how to intensify or modify the intervention—more frequent sessions, smaller group size, alternative strategies, or additional professional development (Burns & Gibbons, 2012).

3. **Fidelity Checks**
    - **Observation and Feedback:** Ensure the intervention is being implemented as designed. Peer observations, coaching sessions, or fidelity checklists help verify that each session's key components are addressed (McIntosh & Goodman, 2016).
    - **Ongoing Training:** Staff responsible for Tier 3 interventions may need extra support to master evidence-based methods, especially if the intervention is new to the school or district (Fuchs et al., 2014).

Communicating Progress with Stakeholders

1. **Frequent Family Updates**
    - **Progress Reports:** Send short weekly or bi-weekly summaries (via email, notes home, or secure digital platforms) showing the student's performance trajectory and any immediate next steps (Gay, 2018).
    - **Two-Way Communication:** Invite families to share observations from home, ask questions, or offer insights about the student's behavior or motivation. This approach fosters trust and collaborative problem-solving (Fergus, 2017).
2. **Student Involvement**
    - **Goal-Setting and Self-Monitoring:** Encourage older students, in particular, to review their data, reflect on their efforts, and set incremental goals (Greenberg et al., 2017). This practice can increase ownership and motivation.
    - **Celebrating Milestones:** Even small gains in Tier 3 should be recognized. Positive feedback boosts a student's sense of competence and can help sustain effort (Marzano, 2017).
3. **Staff Collaboration and Consistency**
    - **Cross-Department Communication:** General education teachers, special educators, and paraprofessionals need shared access to progress data so they can reinforce Tier 3 strategies throughout the day (Spillane, 2006).
    - **Data Dashboards or Shared Documents:** Utilize secure, user-friendly platforms for real-time updates on attendance, performance, and behavioral indicators. Consistency in communication prevents gaps and duplication of efforts (Burns & Gibbons, 2012).

Making Decisions About Next Steps

1. **Significant Growth and Return to a Lower Tier**

- **Meeting Goals Consistently:** If a student demonstrates sustained growth over multiple data points (e.g., 6–8 consecutive assessments), consider reducing intervention intensity or transitioning the student back to Tier 2, with periodic check-ins (Fuchs et al., 2014).
    - **Post-Exit Monitoring:** After scaling down, regularly monitor the student's progress to ensure regression does not occur. If issues reemerge, reintroduce or adapt supports promptly (McIntosh & Goodman, 2016).
2. **Persistent Struggles Despite Intensive Support**
    - **Reassessing Needs:** If data remains stagnant, intensify the plan—alter the frequency, duration, or content of sessions. Conduct additional diagnostic assessments to rule out overlooked skill deficits or contextual factors (Burns & Gibbons, 2012).
    - **Consideration for Special Education Evaluation:** If a student has not already been evaluated for special education services, the consistent lack of progress may indicate a potential disability. Follow the legal guidelines for obtaining consent and conducting a comprehensive assessment (U.S. Department of Education, 2006).
3. **Revisiting the Intervention Environment**
    - **Classroom Observations:** Ensure the student's entire school day is supportive. Sometimes Tier 3 is undermined by mismatches in Tier 1 or Tier 2 instruction or by environmental factors such as bullying or trauma (SAMHSA, 2014).
    - **Home and Community Factors:** If outside factors (e.g., health, nutrition, family circumstances) significantly impact the student's performance, link families to external supports or community resources as part of the intervention plan (Fergus, 2017).

Reflection & Planning

1. **Current Monitoring Protocols**
    - Are your Tier 3 data collection methods consistent and frequent enough to detect small but meaningful changes?
    - Do teams have structured meeting times to review progress, and does this process lead to concrete action steps?
2. **Communication Strategies**
    - How are you ensuring families and students stay informed and engaged in Tier 3 processes?
    - Do staff members have a clear system (e.g., data dashboards, shared drives) to track and update interventions in real time?
3. **Exit and Transition Criteria**
    - Are there defined benchmarks for reducing the intensity of support once a student shows consistent growth?
    - Is there a plan for how to respond if a student fails to progress, including possible referral for a formal special education evaluation?

Figure 6.6 outlines the key steps for progress monitoring and decision-making in Tier 3 interventions.

Figure 6.6 Monitoring Progress in Tier 3

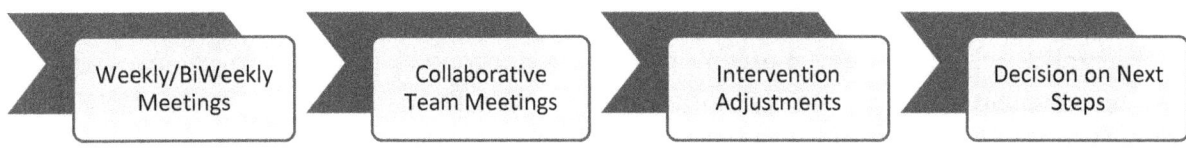

By consistently **evaluating data**, maintaining **transparent communication**, and **adapting interventions** as needed, Tier 3 teams can deliver high-impact, individualized support to students facing the greatest academic or behavioral challenges. In **Section 6.4**, we will conclude our exploration of Tier 3 with a look at long-term planning—ensuring that schools have the resources and capacity to meet intensive needs while remaining agile in their approach to every learner.

6.4 Reflection & Planning

Tier 3 represents the most **intensive level** of support within an MTSS framework. By this stage, students have been unresponsive to Tier 1 and Tier 2 interventions and demonstrate significant academic, behavioral, or social-emotional needs requiring **highly specialized and individualized** assistance (Fuchs, Fuchs, & Vaughn, 2014). Establishing systematic processes for resource allocation, capacity building, and continuous improvement ensures

Tier 3 services remain **effective, sustainable, and equitable**. This final section of Chapter 6 focuses on reflecting on your Tier 3 system, planning for long-term success, and aligning these efforts with the broader goals of your MTSS.

Ensuring Capacity for Intensive Services

1. **Staffing and Expertise**
   - **Specialists on Hand:** School psychologists, instructional specialists, behavior interventionists, counselors, and social workers are often needed to deliver or consult on Tier 3 interventions (Burns & Gibbons, 2012).
   - **Professional Development:** Tier 3 staff may require additional training in areas such as trauma-informed practices, advanced behavior management, or specialized academic interventions (SAMHSA, 2014).
   - **Role Clarity:** Create clear job descriptions that outline who provides which services (e.g., reading specialist vs. special education teacher) and how they collaborate with general education staff (Spillane, 2006).
2. **Time and Scheduling**
   - **Dedicated Intervention Blocks:** Consider setting aside specific times in the master schedule for Tier 3 sessions so students do not consistently miss core instruction (McIntosh & Goodman, 2016).
   - **Flexibility and Responsiveness:** Some students may require daily or even multiple sessions per day. Build in contingencies for adjusting schedules as needs shift (Deno, 2016).
3. **Resource Allocation**
   - **Budget Priorities:** Ensure that district and school budgets account for specialized materials, assistive technology, or additional staffing costs associated with Tier 3 (DuFour & Fullan, 2013).
   - **Community Partnerships:** Collaborate with local agencies and non-profits for wraparound services, such as mental health counseling or academic tutoring programs (Fergus, 2017).

Resource Allocation for Students with Significant Needs

1. **Collaborative Funding Strategies**
   - **Blended Funding Streams:** Explore grants, Title I funds, or state/local initiatives that can support targeted Tier 3 efforts—especially for students from underserved populations (Gay, 2018).

- **Strategic Use of Data:** Demonstrate the **impact** of Tier 3 interventions through documented progress and success stories, which can help secure ongoing funding (Buffum, Mattos, & Weber, 2010).
2. **Prioritizing Equity**
    - **Data Disaggregation:** Monitor which student groups (e.g., by race, gender, socioeconomic status) are most often placed in Tier 3 and evaluate whether there are systemic barriers preventing earlier success (Fergus, 2017).
    - **Culturally Responsive Approaches:** Invest in interventions that affirm students' cultural backgrounds, language needs, and lived experiences to boost engagement and outcomes (Gay, 2018).
3. **Sustainability and Scale**
    - **Building Internal Expertise:** Train a cadre of staff capable of coaching colleagues on Tier 3 practices—this approach extends the school's capacity without relying heavily on external consultants (Burns & Gibbons, 2012).
    - **District-Level Support:** Advocate for policies and procedural guidelines that make Tier 3 interventions a recognized, budgeted priority across all schools within the district (McIntosh & Goodman, 2016).

Next Steps for Your Tier 3 Journey

1. **Continuous Improvement Mindset**
    - **Review and Revise:** Consistently use progress monitoring data to refine interventions, ensuring that every Tier 3 plan remains aligned with the student's evolving needs (Fuchs et al., 2014).
    - **Multi-Stakeholder Feedback:** Involve families, community partners, and especially students to gauge the relevance and effectiveness of Tier 3 services—making adjustments accordingly (Greenberg, Domitrovich, Weissberg, & Durlak, 2017).
2. **Transition Plans**
    - **Stepping Down to Tier 2:** When students reach their goals, design a follow-up plan that includes periodic check-ins to prevent regression (McIntosh & Goodman, 2016).
    - **Coordination with Special Education:** For students with IEPs, ensure Tier 3 interventions complement (rather than duplicate) special education services, and communicate regularly with the IEP team (U.S. Department of Education, 2006).
3. **Celebrating Wins and Modeling Success**
    - **Student Stories:** Share case examples—while maintaining confidentiality—that highlight Tier 3 successes, affirming the impact of intensive interventions and encouraging staff buy-in (Marzano, 2017).
    - **Public Recognition:** Acknowledge staff who effectively deliver Tier 3 supports, fostering a culture of excellence and shared responsibility for all learners (DuFour & Fullan, 2013).

Reflection & Planning

1. **Assess Your Current Tier 3 Capacity**
   - Are there enough specialists available to meet the intensity and frequency demands of students needing Tier 3 supports?
   - How consistent is your master schedule in protecting dedicated intervention time?
2. **Equity and Accountability**
   - Does your MTSS team monitor if certain student groups are overrepresented or underrepresented at the Tier 3 level?
   - How is your school ensuring that every Tier 3 intervention is culturally responsive, well-funded, and implemented with fidelity?
3. **Cultivating Sustainable Practices**
   - Are staff receiving ongoing training that helps them refine Tier 3 strategies?
   - How do you embed Tier 3 best practices into districtwide policy so these services remain a long-term priority?

By addressing these questions and planning strategically for **effective resource allocation, staff capacity building**, and **continuous improvement**, schools create a sustainable, high-impact Tier 3 system. The result is a comprehensive MTSS approach that meets the needs of **all** students—especially those with the most complex academic or social-emotional challenges. In the next chapter, we will explore how schools can integrate **social-emotional learning and equity** principles across **all tiers** to further strengthen MTSS and ensure success for every learner.

Chapter 7: Integrating SEL and Equity Across All Tiers

7.1 Why SEL and Equity Must Be Embedded

As educators refine academic and behavioral frameworks through a Multi-Tiered System of Supports (MTSS), the **social-emotional** and **equity** components are not optional add-ons—they are central to ensuring that all students have access to meaningful learning experiences (McIntosh & Goodman, 2016). Addressing social-emotional learning (SEL) and equity within every tier of MTSS expands the scope of traditional intervention models, shifting the focus to the **whole child** and acknowledging the influence of students' cultural backgrounds, linguistic identities, and societal contexts on their academic and personal success (Gay, 2018). This section examines why SEL and equity are crucial to MTSS, highlighting their shared goals and exploring the research-supported benefits of embedding these principles across Tiers 1, 2, and 3.

Figure 7.1 highlights how SEL impacts foundational skills, school climate, and long-term student outcomes.

Figure 7.1 Impact of SEL on Academic and Behavioral Outcomes

Strengthening Skills
- Self-awareness
- Relationship building
- Decision-making

Positive Climate
- Reduced discipline
- Increased engagement

Long-term Benefits
- Academic resilience
- College readiness

Impact of SEL on Academic and Behavioral Outcomes

1. **Strengthening Foundational Skills**
   - **Self-Awareness and Self-Management:** Skills like recognizing emotions, setting goals, and managing stress directly influence a student's ability to focus, persevere, and engage in learning (Durlak, Weissberg, Dymnicki, Taylor, & Schellinger, 2011).
   - **Relationship Skills and Responsible Decision-Making:** Collaborative projects, peer tutoring, and cooperative discussions depend on students' capacity to communicate effectively, resolve conflicts, and practice empathy (Greenberg, Domitrovich, Weissberg, & Durlak, 2017).
2. **Positive School Climate**
   - **Reduced Discipline Issues:** Schools that intentionally teach and reinforce SEL observe fewer behavior incidents and improved classroom management (Sugai & Horner, 2009).
   - **Increased Engagement and Attendance:** Students who feel emotionally safe and supported by adults and peers are more likely to attend regularly and participate actively in lessons (Chang & Romero, 2008).
3. **Long-Term Benefits**
   - **Academic Resilience:** Students with strong SEL skills can adapt to challenges, such as transitioning to more complex coursework or coping with family stressors, thus improving overall achievement (Durlak et al., 2011).
   - **College and Career Readiness:** Collaboration, problem-solving, and social awareness are competencies that employers and postsecondary institutions increasingly value (Fergus, 2017).

Addressing Disproportionality and Opportunity Gaps

1. **Uncovering Systemic Barriers**
   - **Data Disaggregation:** Analyzing academic and behavioral data by race, gender, language status, and socioeconomic factors can reveal patterns of inequality—such as higher discipline referral rates for certain groups (Fergus, 2017).
   - **Bias and Stereotypes:** Implicit biases may lead teachers and administrators to overlook the potential of some students or to interpret behaviors differently based on cultural assumptions (Gay, 2018). Recognizing and addressing these biases is critical to establishing equity.
2. **Culturally Responsive Practices**
   - **Inclusive Curriculum and Instruction:** Embedding diverse perspectives and real-life contexts in lesson plans allows students from all backgrounds to connect with the material and feel seen in their academic environment (Ladson-Billings, 1995).

- **Equitable Discipline Policies:** Adopting restorative approaches rather than relying on exclusionary measures (e.g., suspensions) helps to break cycles of discrimination and promote positive outcomes for historically marginalized students (Gregory & Evans, 2020).

3. **Elevating Student and Family Voice**
    - **Shared Decision-Making:** Inviting input from students and families—particularly those from underrepresented communities—can inform policy changes, intervention selection, and the allocation of resources (McIntosh & Goodman, 2016).
    - **Trust-Building and Engagement:** Culturally responsive family outreach, such as multilingual communication and community-based events, fosters partnerships that lead to improved attendance, behavior, and academic success (Gay, 2018).

Shared Goals of SEL and Equity within MTSS

1. **Proactive and Preventive**
    - **Early Identification:** Just as universal screening helps identify academic needs, SEL screeners and behavior checklists can pinpoint social-emotional skills or equity challenges before they manifest as severe issues (Greenberg et al., 2017).
    - **Holistic Supports:** Blending SEL and equity considerations into Tier 1 ensures that every student encounters respectful, high-quality instruction—reducing the need for more intensive interventions down the road (Marzano, 2017).
2. **Data-Driven Continuous Improvement**
    - **Ongoing Reflection and Adaptation:** Collecting data on student engagement, discipline disparities, and SEL outcomes allows teams to refine instructional strategies, professional development, and resource allocation (Fergus, 2017).
    - **Consistent Alignment Across Tiers:** Whether a student needs Tier 2 small-group sessions or Tier 3 individualized support, SEL and equity remain central—ensuring interventions address root causes, not just symptoms (Durlak et al., 2011).
3. **Empowering the Whole Child**
    - **Academic, Behavioral, and Emotional Growth:** By integrating SEL and equity into MTSS, schools address the cognitive, emotional, and cultural dimensions of learning simultaneously.
    - **Fostering Belonging and Self-Efficacy:** When students see their identities and experiences validated and respected, their motivation, agency, and confidence grow exponentially (Gay, 2018).

Concluding Thoughts for Section 7.1

Incorporating SEL and equity principles into MTSS is a **transformative shift**—one that moves beyond mere compliance or superficial interventions and instead prioritizes meaningful, inclusive learning for all students. By viewing academic outcomes, social-emotional competence, and cultural responsiveness as interconnected, schools create a powerful, **holistic system** that tackles both individual skill gaps and structural inequities. The following sections will explore how to weave these commitments into every tier—from universal practices (Tier 1) that celebrate diversity and cultivate emotional well-being, to targeted (Tier 2) and intensive (Tier 3) interventions designed to uplift students who face significant challenges.

7.2 Building a Culturally Responsive MTSS

A **culturally responsive** Multi-Tiered System of Supports (MTSS) is not simply about adding a few references to diverse cultures in a lesson plan. Rather, it requires a **systemic shift** in how schools view, value, and engage with students from all backgrounds—racially, linguistically, socioeconomically, and otherwise (Gay, 2018). By deliberately weaving cultural competence into academics, behavior, and social-emotional learning (SEL), educators can ensure that **all** students feel recognized, respected, and empowered. This section explores key strategies for creating a culturally responsive MTSS, emphasizing family engagement and a strengths-based approach that honors every student's unique experiences.

Cultural Competence in Curriculum, Instruction, and Assessment

1. **Asset-Based Mindsets**
   - **Rejecting Deficit Views:** Rather than focusing on "gaps," shift the perspective to see each student's cultural and linguistic assets as invaluable resources for learning and growth (Ladson-Billings, 1995).
   - **Validating Lived Experiences:** When classroom discussions and activities reflect real-life experiences relevant to students' cultures and communities, engagement and motivation increase dramatically (Gay, 2018).
2. **Inclusive and Representative Content**
   - **Diverse Texts and Materials:** Incorporate literature, media, and historical perspectives that feature authors and protagonists from varied backgrounds (Marzano, 2017). This practice fosters identification, empathy, and a deeper connection to learning.
   - **Cross-Curricular Integration:** Embed culturally rich examples across subject areas—such as math word problems involving real-world community contexts or science lessons highlighting contributions from diverse cultures (Gay, 2018).
3. **Culturally Sensitive Assessment and Intervention**
   - **Linguistic Considerations:** For English learners, ensure assessments differentiate between language proficiency issues and actual content mastery (Esparza Brown & Sanford, 2011). Provide translated materials or alternative formats as needed.

- **Classroom Observations and Feedback:** Train staff to recognize how behaviors might manifest differently based on cultural norms, avoiding misinterpretations that could lead to disproportionate referrals to Tier 2 or Tier 3 (Fergus, 2017).

Family and Community Engagement from a Strengths-Based Perspective

1. **Authentic Partnerships**
    - **Inviting Family Expertise:** Recognize that parents and guardians bring deep insights into their children's interests, experiences, and cultural traditions. Engage families as co-educators, co-decision-makers, and co-planners (Ishimaru, 2019).
    - **Welcoming Environment:** Greet families in their home languages when possible, offer flexible meeting times, and host events at accessible community locations to reduce barriers and build trust (Gay, 2018).
2. **Transparent Two-Way Communication**
    - **Sharing Data and Strategies:** Keep parents apprised of screening results, intervention goals, and student progress. Explain these findings in clear, jargon-free language, ensuring families understand how to support learning at home (McIntosh & Goodman, 2016).
    - **Listening and Learning:** Proactively ask families about their aspirations for their child, any challenges they perceive, and suggestions for culturally aligned interventions (Fergus, 2017).
3. **Community Partnerships**
    - **Local Organizations and Cultural Centers:** Collaborate with faith-based institutions, non-profits, and community centers that serve students' cultural or linguistic groups. These partners can offer mentorship programs, after-school support, or resources that enhance Tier 1–3 interventions (Greenberg, Domitrovich, Weissberg, & Durlak, 2017).
    - **Reciprocal Benefits:** When schools partner with community groups—sharing space, funding, or expertise—everyone benefits. Students access expanded services, while community organizations gain an avenue to reach local families (Fergus, 2017).

From Universal to Intensive SEL Supports

1. **Schoolwide Culturally Responsive SEL**
    - **Universal SEL Lessons:** Embed discussions of cultural humility, empathy, and bias recognition into Tier 1 lessons so that students build strong interpersonal skills grounded in respect for diversity (Durlak, Weissberg, Dymnicki, Taylor, & Schellinger, 2011).
    - **Celebrating Cultural Identities:** Encourage student-led cultural showcases, clubs, and classroom projects that affirm students' heritage and build cross-cultural understanding (Gay, 2018).

2. **Targeted SEL Interventions for At-Risk Populations**
   - **Small-Group Counseling:** For students experiencing cultural or language barriers, small-group sessions can address specific social-emotional needs—such as navigating school norms, dealing with discrimination, or coping with identity conflicts (Sugai & Horner, 2009).
   - **Mentoring and Peer Support:** Pairing newcomer students or those facing cultural isolation with peer mentors who share similar backgrounds can offer emotional support and a sense of belonging (DuFour & Fullan, 2013).
3. **Individualized Trauma-Informed Supports**
   - **Recognizing Cultural Trauma:** Students from historically marginalized groups may carry generational or community-based trauma. Tier 3 interventions should integrate trauma-informed strategies that honor the student's cultural context (SAMHSA, 2014).
   - **Healing-Focused Approaches:** Partner with culturally competent therapists, social workers, or community elders who can provide one-on-one or family counseling aligned with the student's background and belief systems (Fergus, 2017).

Figure 7.2 depicts how SEL supports are tailored across Tiers 1, 2, and 3 in MTSS.

Figure 7.2 SEL Supports Across Tiers

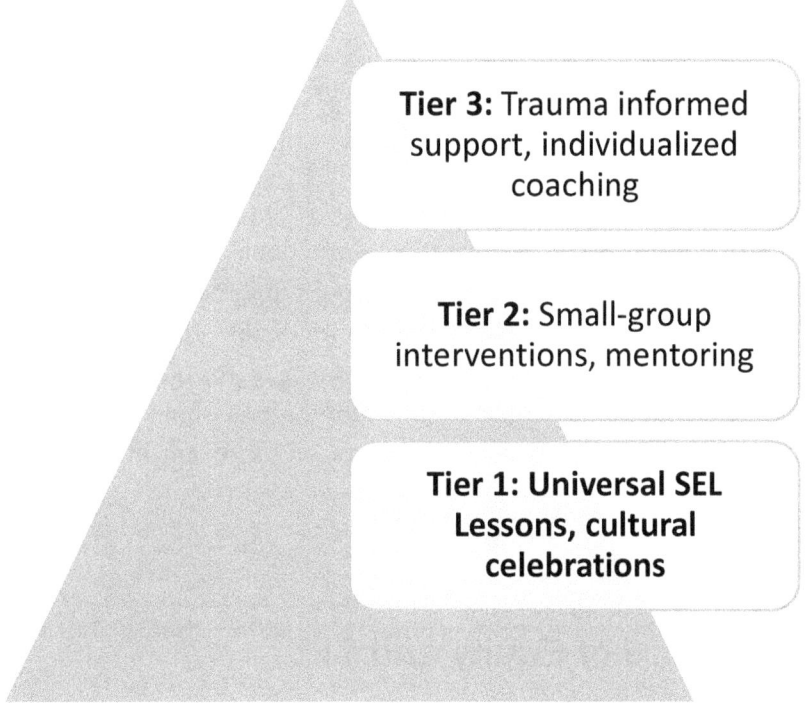

Reflection & Planning

1. **Equity Audit: Identifying and Addressing Gaps in Practice**

- Do Tier 1 materials and teaching strategies consistently reflect the diversity of your student population?
- Are there disparities in who is referred to Tier 2 or Tier 3, and what implicit biases might contribute to these referral patterns?

2. **Action Plan for Embedding Equity and SEL in MTSS**
   - **Professional Development:** Train staff on culturally responsive teaching, SEL facilitation, and bias recognition.
   - **Policy Review:** Examine discipline procedures, homework expectations, and family engagement protocols for hidden inequities (Fergus, 2017).
   - **Ongoing Monitoring:** Set up a schedule for revisiting data (e.g., every quarter) to track improvements in inclusion, engagement, and academic success among all student groups.

By nurturing a **culturally responsive MTSS**, schools expand their capacity to engage students holistically—academically, behaviorally, socially, and emotionally. Families and communities emerge as vital partners, while instruction and intervention practices become firmly rooted in an appreciation for students' diverse assets. In **Section 7.3**, we'll outline how to sustain this focus on **equity and SEL** at every tier, ensuring that practices evolve to meet changing student needs and that no learner is left behind.

7.3 Sustaining SEL and Equity Across Every Tier

Building a **culturally responsive** Multi-Tiered System of Supports (MTSS) requires more than a few stand-alone initiatives—it demands a **long-term commitment** to embed social-emotional learning (SEL) and equitable practices at **every** level. As schools and districts refine Tier 1 (universal supports), Tier 2 (targeted interventions), and Tier 3 (intensive/individualized supports), a consistent focus on **inclusion**, **cultural relevance**, and **student well-being** ensures that no learner is overlooked (McIntosh & Goodman, 2016). This section outlines how schools can align SEL and equity across all tiers, maintain momentum through professional development and data-informed practices, and cultivate a sustainable culture of continuous improvement.

Tier 1: Universal Culture of Equity and SEL

1. **Inclusive Schoolwide Practices**
   - **Proactive Instruction:** Teach SEL skills (e.g., self-management, social awareness) in daily lessons, ensuring that content reflects diverse perspectives, languages, and experiences (Durlak, Weissberg, Dymnicki, Taylor, & Schellinger, 2011).
   - **Positive Environment:** Promote respectful dialogue, restorative discipline, and culturally responsive routines that celebrate student identities (Gay, 2018).
2. **Equity-Focused Data Collection**

- **Universal Screenings:** Track academic, behavioral, and SEL data for **all** students, disaggregating by race, language status, and other demographic factors to spot trends and potential biases (Fergus, 2017).
- **Ongoing Reflection:** Prompt teachers and staff to consider how implicit biases or classroom practices might influence student engagement, participation, or referrals to higher tiers (Ladson-Billings, 1995).

3. **Schoolwide Celebrations and Milestones**
   - **Cultural Showcases:** Encourage student-led events that spotlight different heritages, languages, and traditions, building pride and cross-cultural understanding (Gay, 2018).
   - **SEL Milestones:** Recognize achievements in empathy, conflict resolution, and responsible decision-making with schoolwide acknowledgments or "SEL spotlights."

Tier 2: Targeted, Culturally Responsive SEL Supports

1. **Small-Group Interventions**
   - **Skill-Focused Sessions:** Offer short-term groups for students who need additional SEL practice (e.g., emotion regulation, peer relationship building). Use culturally relevant examples and language supports (Esparza Brown & Sanford, 2011).
   - **Check-In/Check-Out Programs:** Pair students with mentors who understand their cultural context. Frequent feedback can boost motivation and self-efficacy (McIntosh & Goodman, 2016).
2. **Behavioral and Social-Emotional Coaching**
   - **Restorative Circles and Peer Mediation:** Provide opportunities for students to resolve conflicts in a way that respects their cultural norms and family backgrounds (Gregory & Evans, 2020).
   - **Bridge Between Home and School:** Regularly involve families in designing targeted interventions, ensuring strategies align with students' home languages, traditions, and values (Gay, 2018).
3. **Monitoring Equity in Targeted Interventions**
   - **Disaggregated Progress Data:** Examine which student groups are most frequently referred for Tier 2 SEL interventions, ensuring that systemic biases are not driving disproportionate placement (Fergus, 2017).
   - **Timely Adjustments:** Use progress monitoring to gauge each student's SEL and behavioral growth. If improvement stalls, explore whether cultural or linguistic barriers are impeding the intervention's effectiveness.

Tier 3: Intensive, Individualized Support with Cultural Competence

1. **Deep Cultural Understanding**
   - **Family and Community Expertise:** Conduct in-depth interviews or home visits to understand the student's cultural context and any external factors (e.g., family obligations, cultural trauma) that may affect learning or behavior (SAMHSA, 2014).
   - **Specialized Staff Training:** Ensure that counselors, social workers, and interventionists at Tier 3 have advanced skills in trauma-informed care and culturally sensitive counseling techniques (Greenberg, Domitrovich, Weissberg, & Durlak, 2017).
2. **Integrated Wraparound Services**
   - **Community Partnerships:** Collaborate with local health agencies, mental health providers, and cultural organizations to offer holistic support. For instance, a student dealing with family displacement might need both academic tutoring and housing assistance (Fergus, 2017).
   - **Individualized Plans:** Align Tier 3 SEL strategies with the student's cultural values and language needs. If a student also has an Individualized Education Program (IEP) or 504 Plan, ensure that SEL goals are embedded in those plans (U.S. Department of Education, 2006).
3. **Frequent, Data-Driven Adjustments**
   - **Collaborative Case Reviews:** Schedule regular check-ins among teachers, interventionists, specialists, and families to review data on social-emotional milestones, cultural fit, and student engagement (Burns & Gibbons, 2012).
   - **Transition Planning:** If a student shows sustained gains, gradually step down intensity while maintaining cultural responsiveness in ongoing supports at Tier 2 or Tier 1 (McIntosh & Goodman, 2016).

Maintaining Momentum Through Professional Development and Data

1. **Ongoing Staff Training**
   - **Equity and SEL Modules:** Provide repeated, in-depth sessions on bias awareness, culturally responsive pedagogy, trauma-informed practices, and advanced SEL strategies (Gay, 2018).
   - **Peer Observations and Coaching:** Encourage teachers to observe colleagues who excel at embedding SEL and equity, sharing insights on engagement, curriculum adaptations, and relationship-building (DuFour & Fullan, 2013).
2. **Collaborative Data Analysis**
   - **Regular PLC Meetings:** Integrate equity and SEL metrics into professional learning community discussions. Teachers and administrators can brainstorm interventions for students who need additional support (Fergus, 2017).
   - **Transparent Reporting:** Share aggregated, disaggregated, and SEL-focused data with the wider school community—families, students, and community partners—to build collective ownership of equitable outcomes (Marzano, 2017).
3. **Cycle of Continuous Improvement**

- **Plan-Do-Study-Act (PDSA):** Treat SEL and equity goals as dynamic, adjusting strategies based on emerging data or changing student demographics (Bryk, Gomez, Grunow, & LeMahieu, 2015).
- **Celebrating Successes:** Publicly recognize incremental gains—such as improved attendance among a specific subgroup or decreases in discipline referrals—and highlight the SEL and equity practices that contributed to those improvements (Greenberg et al., 2017).

Reflection & Planning

1. **Current Integration of SEL and Equity**
   - How well do Tier 1, Tier 2, and Tier 3 services currently reflect students' cultures, languages, and experiences?
   - Are there specific student groups who are overrepresented in higher tiers, indicating potential systemic or instructional gaps?
2. **Professional Development Needs**
   - What training do teachers, counselors, and administrators need to strengthen their cultural competence and SEL facilitation?
   - Are staff members equipped with strategies for differentiating SEL interventions for English learners or students from diverse backgrounds?
3. **Sustaining the Vision**
   - How does your school or district celebrate and replicate successes in embedding equity and SEL?
   - Do existing policies, schedules, and budgets support the ongoing evolution of culturally responsive, social-emotional practices?

By **systematically weaving SEL and equity** into the fabric of MTSS—across universal, targeted, and intensive supports—schools lay the groundwork for **truly inclusive** learning environments. Through ongoing professional development, strategic data analysis, and partnerships with families and communities, educators can maintain a strong focus on the **whole child**, ensuring that every student, regardless of background, has the skills, confidence, and support to thrive.

Figure 7.3 highlights the core focus areas for professional development in SEL and equity.

Figure 7.3 Professional Development for SEL and Equity

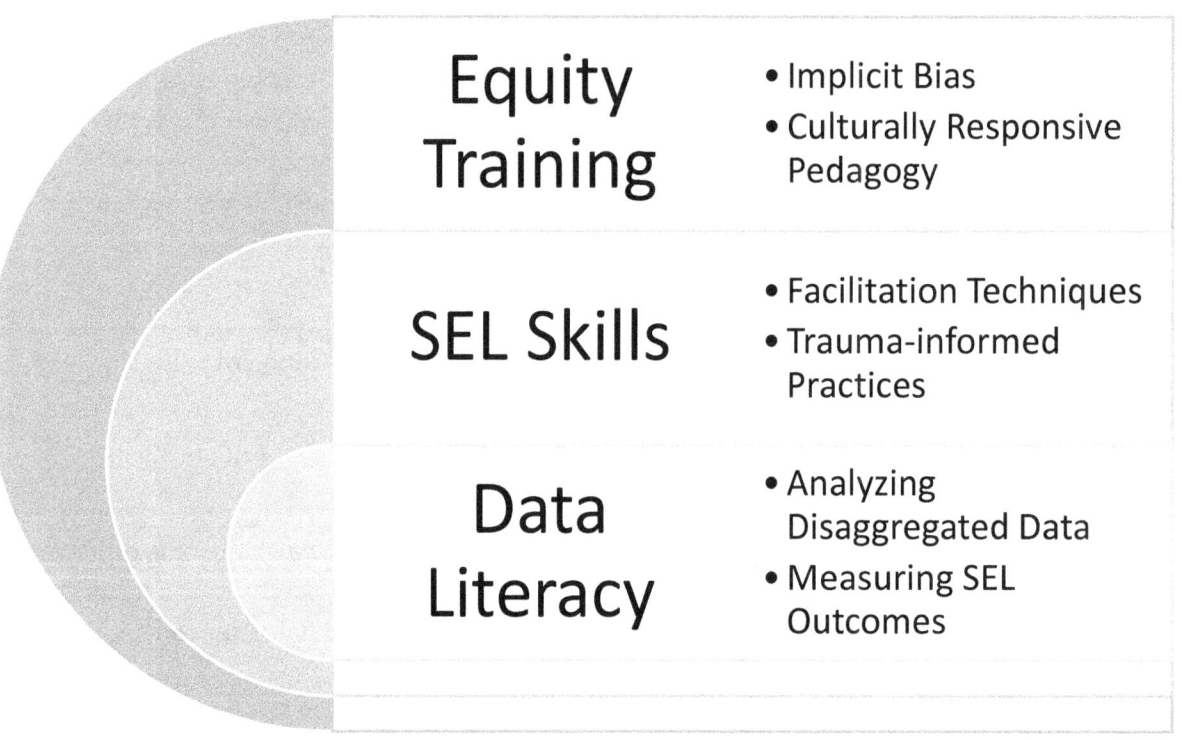

7.4 Reflection & Planning

Throughout Chapter 7, we've examined how **social-emotional learning (SEL)** and **equity** can—and must—be woven into a Multi-Tiered System of Supports (MTSS). From schoolwide structures in Tier 1, to targeted small-group and family engagement in Tier 2, and intensive, wraparound approaches in Tier 3, integrating SEL and culturally responsive practices ensures that every learner receives relevant, inclusive support (Gay, 2018). This concluding section offers guiding questions, action steps, and resources for reflecting on your current efforts and shaping a strategic plan to strengthen SEL and equity across all tiers.

Figure 7.4 illustrates the continuous improvement cycle for embedding SEL and equity in MTSS.

Figure 7.4 Cycle of Continuous Improvement

- **Plan:** Set goals for SEL and Equity
- **Do:** Implment Strategies
- **Study:** Analyze Outcomes and gather Feedback
- **Act:** Refine Practcies Based on Findings

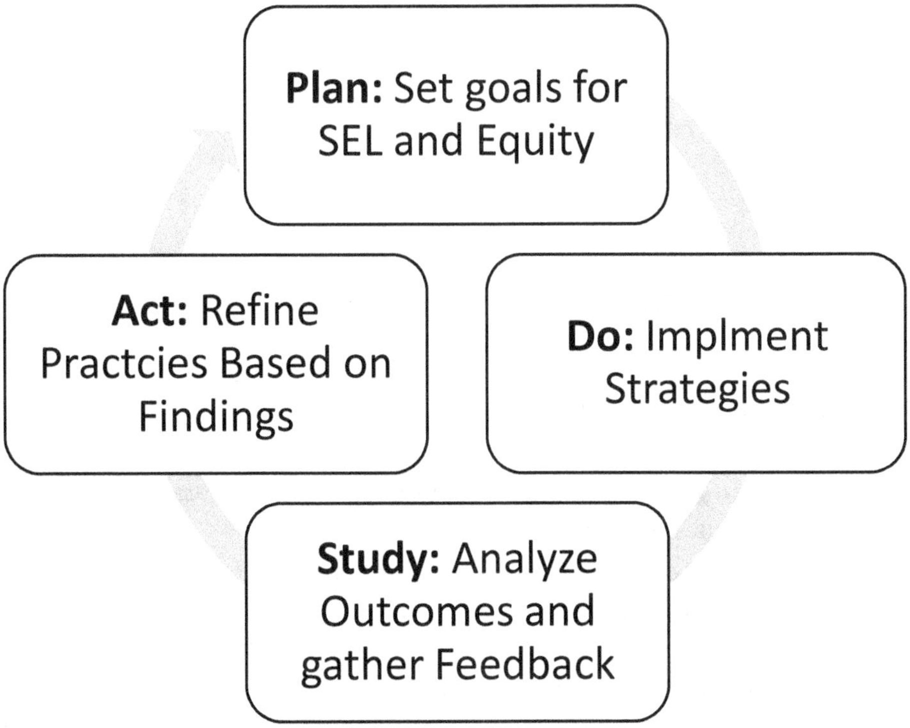

Reflecting on Your SEL and Equity Integration

1. **Assessing Current Practices**
   - **Instructional Content and Materials:** Do your lesson plans, textbooks, and classroom discussions consistently reflect diverse cultural and linguistic perspectives (Ladson-Billings, 1995)?
   - **Data Disaggregation:** How often do you analyze academic, behavioral, and SEL data by student subgroups to identify potential gaps or biases (Fergus, 2017)?
   - **Staff Capacity and Mindsets:** Are teachers and support staff trained to deliver culturally responsive SEL strategies? Do they possess the tools to engage diverse learners effectively (Marzano, 2017)?
2. **Identifying Key Gaps**
   - **Tier-Specific Shortfalls:** Is there a mismatch between your Tier 1 SEL supports and the needs of historically marginalized students? Are targeted (Tier 2) or intensive (Tier 3) interventions culturally aligned and trauma-informed (SAMHSA, 2014)?
   - **Policy and Procedure Review:** Which schoolwide or district-level guidelines might inadvertently perpetuate inequities—such as rigid discipline policies, insufficient language accommodations, or scheduling barriers (McIntosh & Goodman, 2016)?
3. **Examining Family and Community Engagement**
   - **Access and Communication:** Are school materials translated into families' home languages, and do families receive SEL updates or progress reports in a culturally respectful manner (Gay, 2018)?
   - **Shared Decision-Making:** How might you expand opportunities for families to co-create interventions, serve as parent advocates, or shape school policy and budget decisions (Ishimaru, 2019)?

Action Steps for Embedding SEL and Equity in MTSS

1. **Collaborative Team-Building**
   - **Equity and SEL Champions:** Identify staff members passionate about these areas to form an internal leadership team. They can lead professional development, curate resources, and model best practices for colleagues (DuFour & Fullan, 2013).
   - **Student and Family Representatives:** Invite students and parents into your decision-making teams to ensure their perspectives guide your SEL and equity initiatives (Fergus, 2017).
2. **Professional Development Plan**
   - **Ongoing Learning Cycles:** Rather than a one-time workshop, design a series of training sessions on cultural responsiveness, SEL facilitation, and bias recognition. Include follow-up coaching, peer observations, and reflection activities (Gay, 2018).

- **Focus on Data Literacy:** Train teachers and administrators to interpret disaggregated data, develop culturally relevant interventions, and measure SEL outcomes over time (Greenberg, Domitrovich, Weissberg, & Durlak, 2017).

3. **Resource and Budget Alignment**
   - **Prioritize Equity Funding:** Allocate portions of school or district budgets to support culturally responsive materials (e.g., multilingual texts, staff training on trauma-informed care) and robust SEL programs (SAMHSA, 2014).
   - **Community Partnerships:** Collaborate with local nonprofits, cultural centers, and mental health agencies to broaden wraparound services for students who need beyond-the-classroom support (Esparza Brown & Sanford, 2011).

4. **Policy and Practice Revisions**
   - **Equitable Discipline Policies:** Shift from punitive or zero-tolerance approaches to restorative and relational practices that keep students in class and build positive connections (Gregory & Evans, 2020).
   - **Culturally Responsive Curriculum Framework:** Establish a review process to ensure that new instructional materials and assessments respect and celebrate cultural diversity (Gay, 2018).

Resources and Tools for Sustaining Progress

1. **SEL and Equity Self-Assessments**
   - **School- or District-Level Rubrics:** Instruments like the "Culturally Responsive School Assessment" or the CASEL "School Guide" can help measure progress in implementing SEL and equity (CASEL, n.d.).
   - **Classroom Observation Checklists:** Develop or adopt tools that highlight culturally responsive teaching moves (e.g., inclusive questioning, representation in examples, welcoming climate).

2. **Continuous Feedback Loops**
   - **Plan-Do-Study-Act (PDSA) Cycles:** Embed SEL and equity goals into your data cycles. Revisit them regularly, celebrate wins, and refine strategies where needed (Bryk, Gomez, Grunow, & LeMahieu, 2015).
   - **Schoolwide Reflection Events:** Host annual or semiannual forums where students, families, and staff come together to review data, share stories, and co-develop next steps (Ishimaru, 2019).

3. **Networking and Collaboration**
   - **Professional Learning Communities (PLCs):** Leverage PLC sessions for deeper dives into culturally responsive teaching and SEL resources, featuring teacher-led mini-workshops or shared lesson-planning (DuFour & Fullan, 2013).
   - **Regional or Online Networks:** Connect with educators, advocacy groups, or research institutions that specialize in cultural competence, trauma-informed care, or advanced SEL interventions (Greenberg et al., 2017).

Looking Ahead

By intentionally integrating **SEL** and **equity** across your MTSS framework, you create a holistic learning environment where **every** student can flourish academically and personally. The work, however, does not stop with planning; it involves **continuous iteration**, community collaboration, and celebrating growth at each step. As you move forward, keep revisiting your data, refining your approaches, and listening to the voices of students and families most impacted by the system. Through this relentless commitment, you'll deepen a culture of **inclusion**, **respect**, and **excellence**—truly meeting the **whole child** at every tier of support.

Chapter 8: Professional Development and Stakeholder Engagement

8.1 Building Staff Capacity

An **effective Multi-Tiered System of Supports (MTSS)** depends on the collective expertise, commitment, and resilience of teachers, administrators, and support staff. While high-quality instructional materials and well-defined procedures are crucial, it is the **people** who ultimately bring the system to life in classrooms, hallways, and beyond (DuFour & Fullan, 2013). This section addresses strategies for **building staff capacity** through meaningful professional development (PD), ongoing coaching, and a collaborative culture that sustains MTSS efforts over the long term.

Designing Effective MTSS-Focused PD Cycles

1. **Needs Assessment and Goal Setting**
   - **Differentiated PD:** Just as students benefit from tiered supports, educators also require learning experiences tailored to their skill levels, roles, and content areas (Guskey, 2002). Begin by surveying staff on their familiarity with core MTSS components—such as data-based decision-making or culturally responsive teaching—and use the results to set clear, schoolwide PD goals.
   - **Link to School Improvement Plans:** Align all training with broader school or district priorities (e.g., improving reading proficiency, reducing discipline referrals). This ensures that PD is seen as relevant and immediately applicable (Marzano, 2017).
2. **Varied Formats for Engagement**
   - **Workshops and Seminars:** Large-group trainings can introduce key concepts, frameworks, or new intervention protocols. To make these sessions more interactive, use case studies, group tasks, and reflection prompts (Fisher, Frey, & Hattie, 2021).
   - **Job-Embedded Coaching:** Pair teachers with experienced coaches or mentors who can observe lessons, model strategies, and provide feedback in real-time (Bean & Ippolito, 2016). Coaching fosters a deeper, sustained impact than standalone workshops.
   - **Professional Learning Communities (PLCs):** PLCs offer ongoing, collaborative spaces for teachers and support staff to share data, reflect on instructional approaches, and exchange best practices (DuFour & Fullan, 2013).
3. **Balanced Focus: Academics, Behavior, and SEL**
   - **Cross-Disciplinary PD:** Encourage sessions where academic, behavioral, and social-emotional support specialists co-facilitate, modeling how these domains intersect within a multi-tiered framework (Greenberg, Domitrovich, Weissberg, & Durlak, 2017).

- **Equity and Cultural Responsiveness:** Integrate training on bias recognition, trauma-informed care, and linguistically diverse instructional strategies to ensure MTSS serves all students effectively (Gay, 2018).

Figure 8.1 outlines the continuous cycle of designing and refining MTSS-focused professional development.

Figure 8.1 Designing Effective MTSS-Focused PD Cycles

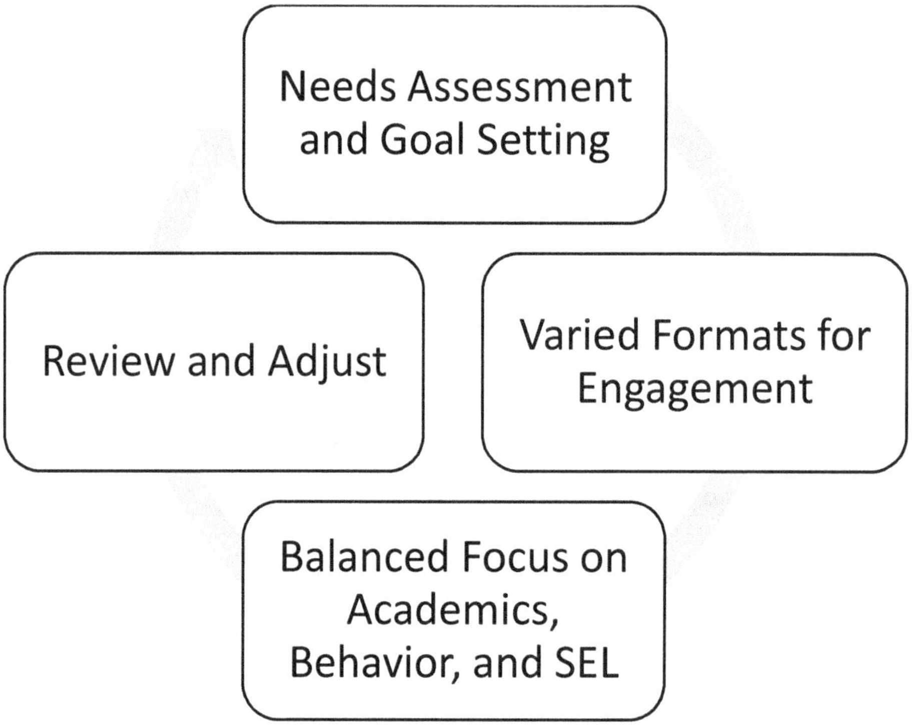

- Needs Assessment and Goal Setting
- Review and Adjust
- Varied Formats for Engagement
- Balanced Focus on Academics, Behavior, and SEL

Coaching and Peer Observation Models

1. **Instructional Coaching Structures**
   - **Full-Release or Hybrid Coaches:** Some schools employ full-time coaches, while others train master teachers to serve as part-time mentors. Either model can be effective if there is clarity in roles, responsibilities, and time allocation (Bean & Ippolito, 2016).
   - **Focus on Feedback Cycles:** Effective coaching emphasizes structured observations followed by reflective conversations and goal-setting. Teachers benefit from seeing specific examples of what went well and where adjustments are needed (DuFour & Fullan, 2013).
2. **Peer Observations and Learning Walks**
   - **Collaborative Culture:** Invite teachers to observe one another's classes, using agreed-upon protocols and reflection tools that highlight MTSS implementation—such as universal screening usage, small-group interventions, or SEL integration (McIntosh & Goodman, 2016).

- **Strengths-Based Feedback:** Rather than solely focusing on deficits, teams identify effective practices and discuss how to replicate them across different classrooms or grade levels (Marzano, 2017).

Ongoing Training in Data Literacy and Intervention Strategies

1. **Data Literacy for All Staff**
   - **User-Friendly Data Tools:** Ensure that teachers, counselors, and paraprofessionals have access to clear, concise data reports. Offer mini-PD sessions on navigating spreadsheets, digital dashboards, or online screening platforms (Buffum, Mattos, & Weber, 2010).
   - **Interpreting Trends and Making Adjustments:** Coaches or instructional leads can model how to analyze screening results, identify patterns (e.g., skill deficits in reading fluency or math computation), and select appropriate Tier 2 or Tier 3 interventions (Burns & Gibbons, 2012).
2. **Evidence-Based Intervention Techniques**
   - **Research-Informed Practices:** Provide deep dives into academic interventions (e.g., phonics-based programs, explicit math instruction) and behavioral/SEL strategies (e.g., Check-In/Check-Out systems, restorative conversations). Use simulations or case studies to illustrate how to apply these methods in real classrooms (Fuchs, Fuchs, & Vaughn, 2014).
   - **Scenario-Based Workshops:** Host sessions where teachers role-play delivering small-group interventions or conducting progress monitoring. Peer feedback helps refine these skills before they are applied with students (Durlak, Weissberg, Dymnicki, Taylor, & Schellinger, 2011).

Reflection & Planning

1. **Assess Current PD Approaches**
   - Do existing training sessions align with MTSS principles, or do they operate in isolation (e.g., solely academic-focused, minimal discussion of behavior or SEL)?
   - Are staff encouraged to set personal PD goals related to their roles in MTSS implementation?
2. **Expand Coaching Opportunities**
   - Who in your building or district can serve as coaches or mentors?
   - How can you integrate peer observation schedules without overburdening teachers?
3. **Target Data Skills and Intervention Proficiency**
   - Do all staff—including paraprofessionals and new teachers—feel confident analyzing universal screening results and selecting the right interventions?
   - Which intervention or SEL strategies might require deeper training or refresher sessions?

Cultivating **staff capacity** goes beyond a one-time workshop or a single coaching cycle. By embedding professional learning within everyday practice—through collaborative PD, meaningful coaching, and a relentless focus on **academics, behavior, and SEL**—schools create a culture that supports the **continuous improvement** at the heart of MTSS. In **Section 8.2**, we'll address **engaging families and community** as pivotal partners in the success of students and the sustainability of multi-tiered support systems.

8.2 Engaging Families and Community

Families and local communities are **indispensable partners** in a Multi-Tiered System of Supports (MTSS). They bring unique insights about students' backgrounds, cultural values, and personal strengths—insights that complement and enrich the academic, behavioral, and social-emotional interventions offered by schools (Ishimaru, 2019). This section focuses on practical strategies for engaging families and community organizations, ensuring that MTSS is **holistic** and **culturally responsive**, and that every student benefits from a web of support extending beyond the school walls.

Strategies for Family Outreach, Education, and Participation

1. **Building Trust and Reciprocity**
   - **Welcoming School Climate:** Greet families in their home languages, display student artwork that represents various cultures, and offer accessible meeting times or virtual options to accommodate working schedules (Gay, 2018).
   - **Two-Way Communication:** Move beyond automated messages or one-sided newsletters. Create opportunities—such as family nights, focus groups, or bilingual parent cafés—where parents and guardians can share their goals, concerns, and expertise (Fergus, 2017).
2. **Providing Clear and Actionable Information**
   - **Demystifying MTSS:** Offer user-friendly explanations of tiered interventions, screening data, and progress monitoring practices. Ensure families understand how the school identifies students who need extra support (McIntosh & Goodman, 2016).
   - **Culturally Responsive Materials:** Translate intervention plans and progress reports. Involve community liaisons or bilingual staff who can clarify next steps for parents with limited English proficiency (Esparza Brown & Sanford, 2011).
3. **Empowering Families as Co-Educators**
   - **At-Home Reinforcement:** Provide simple, at-home activities or conversation starters that align with Tier 1 classroom goals (e.g., reading fluency, behavior expectations, SEL skill-building). Encourage parents to share feedback on their child's progress (Greenberg, Domitrovich, Weissberg, & Durlak, 2017).
   - **Co-Planning Interventions:** When a student enters Tier 2 or Tier 3, invite families to help shape goals, select culturally relevant strategies, and establish consistent routines at home and school (Gay, 2018).

Partnering with Community Organizations and Mental Health Providers

1. **Expanding Wraparound Services**
   - **Local Non-Profits and Cultural Centers:** Collaborate with organizations offering after-school tutoring, mentorship programs, or family counseling. Students receiving Tier 2 or Tier 3 interventions may benefit from specialized services outside of school (Fergus, 2017).
   - **Mental Health Partnerships:** For students with significant emotional or behavioral needs, link families to community-based counseling or therapy services. School-based mental health professionals can coordinate care and track progress to ensure continuity (SAMHSA, 2014).
2. **Shared Learning Opportunities**
   - **Community Workshops and Resource Fairs:** Co-host events with libraries, faith-based organizations, or cultural associations to teach families about MTSS, SEL, and ways to support learning at home (Ishimaru, 2019).
   - **Blended Funding and Grants:** Seek joint grants or partner-driven funding to support bilingual programs, family engagement liaisons, or culturally tailored summer learning opportunities (McIntosh & Goodman, 2016).
3. **Sustaining Long-Term Partnerships**
   - **Regular Communication and Feedback:** Maintain consistent check-ins with community collaborators—e.g., monthly or quarterly—to review student outcomes, address emerging needs, and refine shared goals (DuFour & Fullan, 2013).
   - **Reciprocal Benefits:** As schools champion local events and highlight community expertise, organizations can increase visibility and outreach, creating a virtuous cycle of mutual support (Gay, 2018).

Fostering Collaborative Culture

1. **Family Leadership Roles**
   - **Advisory Councils and Task Forces:** Invite parents and community members to serve on leadership teams that shape MTSS policies, review data trends, and allocate resources equitably (Ishimaru, 2019).
   - **Peer Mentorship:** Encourage experienced families—especially those who have navigated Tier 2 or Tier 3 interventions—to support newcomers, offering guidance and reassurance throughout the process (Greenberg et al., 2017).
2. **Bridging Cultural and Linguistic Gaps**

- **Interpreters and Cultural Liaisons:** Designate staff or volunteers who can serve as interpreters for meetings, phone calls, or conferences, ensuring language barriers do not hinder participation (Esparza Brown & Sanford, 2011).
- **Cultural Protocols and Celebrations:** Learn about families' holiday traditions, communication norms, and decision-making styles. Incorporate these into school events to affirm belonging and respect (Gay, 2018).

3. **Celebrating Shared Success**
    - **School-Community Showcases:** Host events highlighting student achievements that result from collaborative efforts. Publicly acknowledge families, partners, and staff who contributed to each success story (Fisher, Frey, & Hattie, 2021).
    - **Storytelling and Testimonials:** Feature student and family voices—through newsletters, assemblies, or social media—to build awareness and inspire others to embrace partnerships that enhance MTSS outcomes (Fergus, 2017).

Reflection & Planning

1. **Current Family Engagement Structures**
    - Are parents/guardians typically informed **after** decisions are made, or are they involved from the start in shaping interventions and school policies?
    - Which communication methods (e.g., phone calls, text messages, online portals, home visits) have been most effective for engaging diverse families?
2. **Community Resource Map**
    - What local organizations, businesses, or cultural centers could potentially partner with your school to extend learning, counseling, or enrichment?
    - Are there existing partnerships that could be strengthened or expanded?
3. **Leadership and Sustainability**
    - How can your leadership team systematically involve families and community members in MTSS data reviews, strategic planning, and professional development?
    - Which roles or structures (e.g., parent liaisons, advisory councils) need to be formalized to sustain family and community engagement over time?

Engaging families and community members is **essential** to an MTSS framework that truly meets the needs of all students. By building trust, offering transparent communication, and collaborating with local partners, schools extend their reach and capacity. In **Section 8.3**, we will explore how these collaborative efforts bolster a culture of shared responsibility—where every stakeholder feels empowered to contribute to student success.

8.3 Fostering a Collaborative Culture

A **collaborative culture** is the bedrock of sustainable MTSS implementation. When staff, families, and community partners share ownership of student success, a school transcends traditional silos to become a **learning community** in which all stakeholders—teachers, administrators, support staff, students, and families—play active roles (DuFour & Fullan, 2013). This section explores key principles for fostering a culture of shared responsibility, emphasizing collaboration across disciplines, leadership development, and continuous communication.

Cross-Disciplinary Collaboration (General Ed, Special Ed, Administration)

1. **Unified Vision and Language**
   - **Shared MTSS Framework:** Ensure all stakeholders have a consistent understanding of MTSS tiers, data protocols, and intervention strategies. A common language around "universal supports," "targeted supports," and "intensive supports" helps streamline communication (McIntosh & Goodman, 2016).
   - **Aligned Goals:** Collaboratively set annual improvement targets—such as raising reading proficiency or reducing behavior referrals. Collective buy-in motivates every department and grade level to row in the same direction (Marzano, 2017).
2. **Regular Meeting Structures**
   - **Integrated MTSS Teams:** Include general and special educators, counselors, instructional coaches, and administrators in monthly or biweekly problem-solving sessions. Discuss universal screenings, Tier 2 placements, and progress data from multiple perspectives (Buffum, Mattos, & Weber, 2010).
   - **PLC and Department Dialogues:** Within established PLCs or department meetings, dedicate time to cross-disciplinary planning—ensuring academic, behavioral, and social-emotional initiatives remain synchronized (DuFour & Fullan, 2013).
3. **Respect for Diverse Expertise**
   - **Leveraging Strengths:** A reading specialist might guide Tier 2 literacy interventions while a school psychologist designs behavioral strategies. Recognize each professional's unique vantage point to develop the most effective student plans (Fuchs, Fuchs, & Vaughn, 2014).
   - **Collective Efficacy:** Celebrate when collaborative efforts yield positive student outcomes—reinforcing the mindset that no single person must carry the weight alone (Hattie & Zierer, 2018).

Teacher Leadership and Shared Responsibility

1. **Empowering Teacher Leaders**
   - **Facilitators and Coaches:** Identify teachers who excel in specific MTSS areas—data analysis, SEL integration, culturally responsive pedagogy—and encourage them to mentor peers or lead professional learning sessions (Bean & Ippolito, 2016).
   - **Rotating Roles:** Rotate facilitation of MTSS or grade-level meetings so multiple educators develop leadership skills. This practice fosters ownership and commitment across the entire staff (Guskey, 2002).

2. **Distributed Decision-Making**
   - **Problem-Solving Protocols:** Use structured protocols that invite all voices. Whether reviewing screening data or brainstorming Tier 2 supports, a teacher, paraeducator, or counselor can bring valuable insights to the table (Fisher, Frey, & Hattie, 2021).
   - **Transparent Processes:** Communicate how decisions are reached (e.g., through consensus or voting) and document rationales. Clarity in decision-making builds trust and reduces misunderstandings (DuFour & Fullan, 2013).

3. **Professional Growth Pathways**
   - **Data Teams and Action Research:** Encourage teachers to conduct action research—investigating questions about intervention fidelity or SEL impact—and share findings with colleagues (Burns & Gibbons, 2012).
   - **Career Ladders:** Provide avenues for teachers to become lead MTSS facilitators or instructional coaches, allowing them to advance professionally without leaving the classroom (Gay, 2018).

Shared Responsibility for Student Success

1. **Collective Accountability**
   - **Schoolwide Data Walls:** Display aggregate progress monitoring results (respecting student privacy) to keep the focus on meeting schoolwide goals—like improved reading fluency or reduced discipline referrals. Invite staff to discuss trends and brainstorm solutions (Greenberg, Domitrovich, Weissberg, & Durlak, 2017).
   - **Public Commitments:** Have each team articulate how they will contribute—for instance, the English department committing to weekly progress checks for reading fluency, or the counseling department pledging monthly SEL mini-lessons (Fergus, 2017).

2. **Student-Centered Focus**
   - **Individual Success Plans:** Instead of labeling students as "Tier 2 kids" or "behavior problems," approach every case with the question, "How can we collectively support this student's growth?" (Sugai & Horner, 2009).

- **Continuous Reflection:** After each universal screening cycle or intervention block, ask: "Where have we succeeded? Who still needs support?" and "How can we adapt?" (Deno, 2016).
3. **Community and Family Involvement**
    - **Open-Door Policies:** Encourage classroom visits, invite community leaders as guest speakers, and hold family workshops so external stakeholders can see MTSS in action and offer input (Ishimaru, 2019).
    - **Celebrating Shared Wins:** When progress is made—be it attendance improvements or SEL milestones—publicly acknowledge the roles of families, mentors, coaches, and teachers who made it happen (Fisher et al., 2021).

Reflection & Planning

1. **Assessing Collaborative Practices**
    - Does your school frequently bring general ed, special ed, and administrative staff together to review data and plan interventions?
    - How are teacher leaders identified and supported to guide MTSS initiatives?
2. **Cultivating Shared Ownership**
    - What systems are in place to ensure everyone, from paraeducators to department heads, feels responsible for student progress?
    - Are families and community organizations consistently included in decision-making processes?
3. **Sustaining a Learning Community**
    - Is there a structure (e.g., monthly "Pulse Meetings," quarterly data summits) to ensure continuous communication around MTSS priorities?
    - How do you celebrate successes (e.g., improved reading levels, reduced discipline incidents) in a way that fuels ongoing collaboration?

A **collaborative culture** is the heartbeat of MTSS. When educators, families, and the wider community work in unison, problem-solving becomes more creative, interventions become more aligned, and students experience a support network that stretches far beyond the classroom. In **Section 8.4**, we will explore how to craft **comprehensive professional learning plans** and devise **communication strategies** that bring all stakeholders on board, further enhancing schoolwide MTSS practices.

8.4 Reflection & Planning

Effective professional development (PD) and robust stakeholder engagement lie at the heart of every thriving Multi-Tiered System of Supports (MTSS). Chapters 8.1 through 8.3 have explored how to build staff capacity, engage families and the community, and foster a collaborative culture that sustains and enriches MTSS practices.

This concluding section provides guiding questions and action steps to help you assess your current approaches, identify areas for growth, and plan strategically for the future.

Reflecting on Chapter 8

1. **Staff Capacity (Section 8.1)**
   - **PD Cycles and Coaching**: Are your professional learning experiences job-embedded, ongoing, and aligned with core MTSS goals (DuFour & Fullan, 2013)?
   - **Data Literacy and Intervention Skills**: Do all staff—teachers, paraprofessionals, administrators—understand how to interpret screening results and implement evidence-based interventions (Burns & Gibbons, 2012)?
2. **Family and Community Engagement (Section 8.2)**
   - **Trust and Reciprocity**: Do families have equitable opportunities to co-create intervention plans, offer feedback, and access culturally appropriate resources (Ishimaru, 2019)?
   - **Community Partnerships**: Which local nonprofits, mental health agencies, or cultural centers are vital partners, and how often do you collaborate to strengthen Tier 1–3 supports (Gay, 2018)?
3. **Collaborative Culture (Section 8.3)**
   - **Shared Responsibility**: Are teacher leaders, counselors, administrators, and community members consistently working together to analyze data, refine interventions, and celebrate successes (McIntosh & Goodman, 2016)?
   - **Ongoing Communication**: Do established structures—grade-level teams, PLCs, monthly MTSS check-ins—promote transparency, cross-disciplinary problem-solving, and collective decision-making (Fergus, 2017)?

Action Steps for Comprehensive Professional Learning

1. **Annual or Semester-Wide PD Planning**
   - **Set Clear Targets**: Identify priority areas (e.g., Tier 2 interventions, culturally responsive teaching, SEL integration) and design PD sessions across the school year that scaffold these skills (Marzano, 2017).
   - **Flexibility and Responsiveness**: Periodically survey staff to gauge evolving needs. Adjust the PD calendar accordingly, offering targeted mini-sessions or coaching cycles for emerging challenges (Fisher, Frey, & Hattie, 2021).
2. **Coaching Networks and Peer Mentoring**
   - **Instructional Coaching Models**: Provide explicit training and time for coaches to collaborate with teachers on data analysis, intervention planning, and classroom implementation (Bean & Ippolito, 2016).

- **Peer Mentoring**: Establish informal "buddy systems" or structured triads where educators observe each other's lessons, focus on improving a specific MTSS practice, and offer supportive feedback (DuFour & Fullan, 2013).

3. **Professional Learning Communities (PLCs)**
    - **Data-Driven Conversations**: Embed regular data reviews (e.g., screening outcomes, Tier 2 progress) into PLC meetings. Use problem-solving protocols to identify solutions, track fidelity, and measure impact (Buffum, Mattos, & Weber, 2010).
    - **Cross-Department Collaboration**: Rotate meeting groups so that math teachers learn from counselors, reading specialists learn from special educators, and so on—reinforcing the interconnected nature of academic, behavioral, and SEL supports (Fuchs, Fuchs, & Vaughn, 2014).

Strategies for Effective Stakeholder Communication

1. **Unified Messaging**
    - **Schoolwide Communication Plan**: Outline key messages about MTSS, SEL, equity, and how families can participate. Maintain consistent language and visuals in newsletters, websites, and events (McIntosh & Goodman, 2016).
    - **Ongoing Touchpoints**: Use a mix of channels—social media, text updates, in-person forums—to keep families and partners informed about progress, successes, and upcoming training opportunities (Gay, 2018).
2. **Accessible and Inclusive**
    - **Language and Cultural Considerations**: Translate critical materials, including Tier 2 or Tier 3 intervention plans, into families' home languages. Offer interpreters at parent-teacher conferences and community meetings (Esparza Brown & Sanford, 2011).
    - **Showcase Student Growth**: Highlight personal stories or data snapshots that demonstrate how MTSS interventions benefit real students—fostering understanding, excitement, and mutual investment (Greenberg, Domitrovich, Weissberg, & Durlak, 2017).
3. **Celebration and Transparency**
    - **Public Recognition of Collaborations**: Invite community leaders or family representatives to speak at assemblies or board meetings about the positive impacts of their involvement. Acknowledge staff who model excellent collaboration or coaching (Fergus, 2017).
    - **Regular Check-Ins**: Host short, recurring sessions (e.g., monthly or quarterly) to discuss progress, refine goals, and keep momentum around professional learning and stakeholder engagement (DuFour & Fullan, 2013).

Reflection & Planning

1. **PD Implementation Fidelity**
   - How are you monitoring the follow-through of newly learned strategies in classrooms and within interventions?
   - Are teachers and staff supported with the time, coaching, and feedback necessary to sustain new practices?
2. **Equitable Stakeholder Engagement**
   - Which families or community groups are underrepresented or disengaged?
   - How can you adapt outreach methods to ensure everyone's voice is heard and valued?
3. **Long-Term Vision**
   - Does your leadership team have a clear plan for evolving PD priorities as MTSS matures (e.g., introducing advanced data analytics or deeper SEL integration)?
   - What structures (e.g., annual retreats, strategic planning days) will you use to reassess and recalibrate your MTSS-related PD and engagement efforts?

By **aligning professional development** with clear goals, **empowering stakeholders** through meaningful engagement, and **institutionalizing collaborative norms**, schools can sustain and expand the successes of their MTSS. In **Chapter 9**, we will delve into **technology, tools, and resources** that can further streamline MTSS implementation, making data analysis, documentation, and ongoing communication more efficient and user-friendly.

Chapter 9: Technology, Tools, and Resources

9.1 Leveraging EdTech in MTSS

Technology has the power to **streamline** and **enhance** every phase of a Multi-Tiered System of Supports (MTSS)—from universal screening to individualized interventions. By thoughtfully integrating educational technology (EdTech), schools can efficiently gather and interpret data, customize learning experiences, and maintain consistent communication with all stakeholders (McIntosh & Goodman, 2016). This section highlights how to choose and implement digital platforms that support **academic, behavioral,** and **social-emotional** outcomes within a multi-tiered framework.

Digital Platforms for Screening, Progress Monitoring, and Data Analysis

1. **User-Friendly Data Dashboards**
   - **Centralized Student Profiles:** Look for systems that consolidate a student's academic, behavioral, and SEL data in one place. This saves time and reduces the risk of missing critical patterns across domains (Burns & Gibbons, 2012).
   - **Real-Time Updates:** Dashboards that auto-sync with screening tools or gradebooks give teachers, counselors, and administrators the latest information, prompting timely interventions (Buffum, Mattos, & Weber, 2010).
   - **Disaggregation Capabilities:** Ensure platforms allow you to filter data by demographics (e.g., race/ethnicity, language status) to spot disproportionalities early and maintain equitable practices (Fergus, 2017).
2. **Online Screening and Progress Monitoring Tools**
   - **Adaptive Assessments:** Some digital assessments (e.g., i-Ready, MAP Growth) automatically adjust question difficulty based on the student's responses, providing a personalized snapshot of skill levels (Fuchs, Fuchs, & Vaughn, 2014).
   - **Automatic Graphing and Reporting:** Many tools generate easy-to-read charts for tracking fluency gains, behavior frequency, or SEL milestones—visuals that make data-driven decisions more efficient (Marzano, 2017).
   - **Alerts and Notifications:** Systems that flag students who are consistently below benchmarks or show a dip in progress help staff respond swiftly with targeted supports (McIntosh & Goodman, 2016).

Figure 9.1 highlights essential functionalities of digital platforms that enhance MTSS processes.

Figure 9.1 Digital Platforms for MTSS

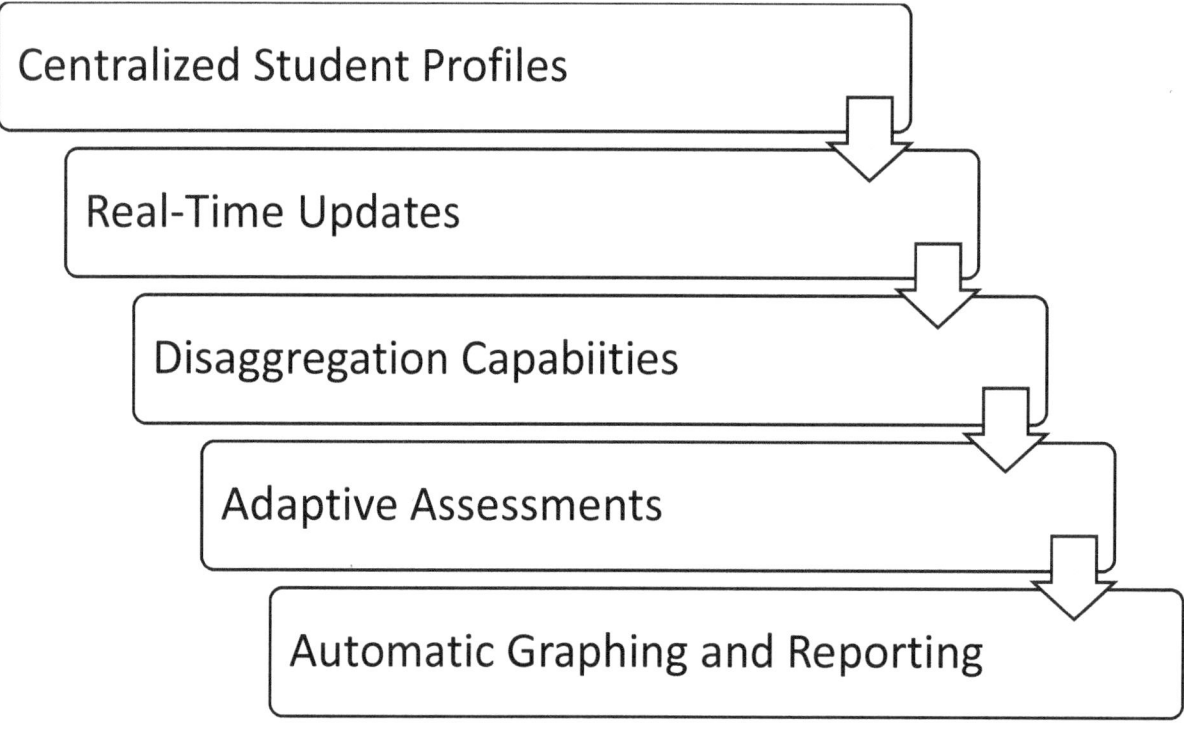

Online Intervention Tools and Personalized Learning Software

1. **Evidence-Based Digital Curricula**
   - **Adaptive Learning Paths:** Programs that adapt in real-time to student responses can keep each learner working at an optimal "just-right" level, reinforcing foundational skills or introducing new challenges as needed (Fisher, Frey, & Hattie, 2021).
   - **Multimodal Content:** Interactive videos, simulations, and gamified exercises often engage students who struggle with traditional approaches—especially in reading, math, and SEL skill-building (Greenberg, Domitrovich, Weissberg, & Durlak, 2017).
2. **Behavioral and SEL Applications**
   - **Check-In/Check-Out Tracking:** Digital platforms can replace paper-based point sheets, sending instant updates to students, mentors, or caregivers on goal progress (Sugai & Horner, 2009).
   - **Mindfulness and Emotional Regulation Apps:** Tools offering guided meditation, breathing exercises, or SEL lessons can complement Tier 1 or Tier 2 supports, reinforcing self-awareness and stress management beyond the classroom (Gay, 2018).
3. **Differentiation and Accessibility**

- **Language Supports and Text-to-Speech:** For English learners or students with reading challenges, built-in translations or read-aloud features help maintain engagement and comprehension (Esparza Brown & Sanford, 2011).
- **Accommodations for Disabilities:** Customizable font sizes, color overlays, or alternative input methods can empower students with visual, auditory, or motor impairments to fully participate (U.S. Department of Education, 2006).

Figure 9.2 categorizes key online tools that support personalized and equitable learning in MTSS.

Figure 9.2 Online Intervention Tools for Personalized Learning

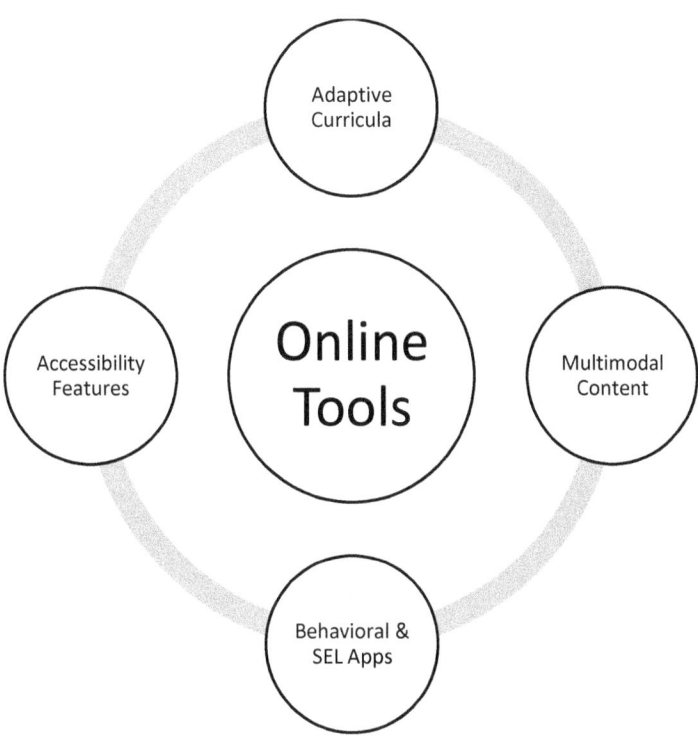

Practical Tips for Successful EdTech Integration

1. **Align Tools with MTSS Goals**
    - **Needs Assessment:** Before adopting a new platform, identify the specific problems you aim to solve—be it faster data retrieval, targeted SEL practice, or real-time progress monitoring (Burns & Gibbons, 2012).
    - **Fidelity Checks:** Provide staff training, create usage guidelines (e.g., frequency of screenings), and assess whether the tool is used consistently as intended (DuFour & Fullan, 2013).
2. **Professional Development and Ongoing Support**
    - **Technical and Instructional Training:** Teachers and interventionists need guidance not only on **how** to operate a tool but also on **why** it benefits MTSS (Fergus, 2017).

- **EdTech Coaches or Champions:** Designate tech-savvy staff to model classroom usage, troubleshoot technical issues, and help colleagues integrate digital interventions into their lesson plans (Bean & Ippolito, 2016).
3. **Privacy and Data Security**
    - **FERPA Compliance:** Ensure that any platform storing student information meets legal privacy standards and that staff understand protocols for data sharing and safeguarding (U.S. Department of Education, 2006).
    - **Family Communication:** If using apps that parents can access, provide clear instructions on data interpretation, so families can track progress and reinforce learning at home (Gay, 2018).

Figure 9.3 outlines prioritized strategies for effectively integrating EdTech into MTSS frameworks.

Figure 9.3 Practical Tips for EdTech Integration

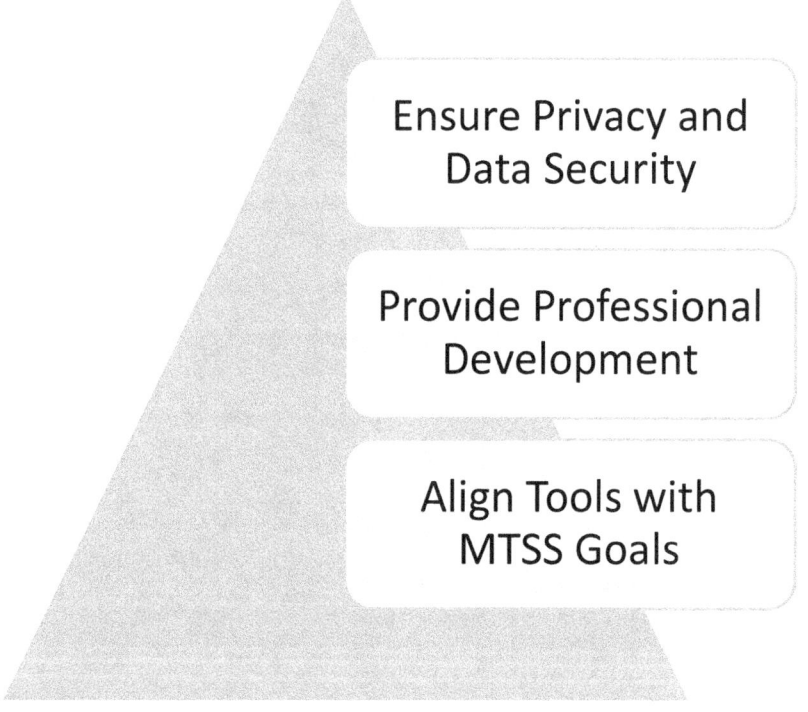

Reflection & Planning

1. **Current Technology Usage**
    - Are you effectively using digital tools for screening and progress monitoring, or do staff rely mostly on manual methods?
    - How easily can teachers and intervention teams access and analyze student data (academic, behavioral, SEL) in a timely manner?
2. **Selection Criteria for EdTech**

- Which features (e.g., adaptive assessments, bilingual supports, analytics) are most crucial for your MTSS goals?
- Have you engaged teachers, families, and students in evaluating potential tools for ease of use, cultural responsiveness, or compatibility with existing systems?

3. **Sustainability and Support**
    - What PD structures ensure staff remain confident in using digital interventions?
    - How do you budget for subscription fees, device replacements, or software updates over the long term?

Well-chosen EdTech can **streamline** MTSS processes—making data collection more efficient, personalizing student interventions, and opening channels for **real-time** collaboration among educators, families, and students. In **Section 9.2**, we will explore methods for **efficient documentation and reporting**, highlighting how digital platforms and systematic approaches keep stakeholders informed and ensure fidelity throughout the tiers of support.

9.2 Efficient Documentation and Reporting

A significant benefit of integrating technology into a Multi-Tiered System of Supports (MTSS) is the potential to **streamline documentation and reporting**. Comprehensive, accurate records help educators track interventions, monitor student growth, and communicate effectively with families and stakeholders—all while maintaining compliance with legal and ethical guidelines (U.S. Department of Education, 2006). This section explores methods to make documentation efficient and meaningful, emphasizing how to organize data, share reports, and ensure fidelity in a way that supports all tiers of MTSS.

Templates and Checklists for Tracking Student Interventions

1. **Standardized Intervention Logs**
    - **Core Fields and Consistency:** Create uniform templates for documenting date, time, skill focus, and student response. When every teacher or interventionist uses the same format, data becomes more comparable and easier to review (Burns & Gibbons, 2012).
    - **Tier-Specific Sections:** Differentiate logs for Tier 1 (universal supports), Tier 2 (targeted small groups), and Tier 3 (intensive, individualized interventions). This clarity reduces confusion about who is responsible for each action step (McIntosh & Goodman, 2016).
2. **Digital Checklists and Time Stamps**
    - **Immediate Recording:** Encourage staff to log interventions immediately—using mobile devices or laptops—to minimize the risk of forgetting key details. Some apps even require a digital signature or time stamp for accountability (Marzano, 2017).

- **Prompts for Reflection:** Build reflection prompts into the checklist (e.g., "What worked well today?" "Next steps?") so teachers can quickly note any adjustments needed for the following session (DuFour & Fullan, 2013).
3. **Compliance and Legal Considerations**
    - **Special Education Documentation:** If interventions overlap with an Individualized Education Program (IEP) or 504 Plan, ensure logs note alignment with IEP goals or accommodations. This helps demonstrate the continuum of support provided (U.S. Department of Education, 2006).
    - **Privacy Protections:** Develop clear guidelines for storing logs—whether on secure digital platforms or locked cabinets—to keep student information confidential (FERPA compliance) (Burns & Gibbons, 2012).

Figure 9.4 highlights tools and techniques that streamline documentation and reporting within MTSS.

Figure 9.4 Efficient Documentation and Reporting

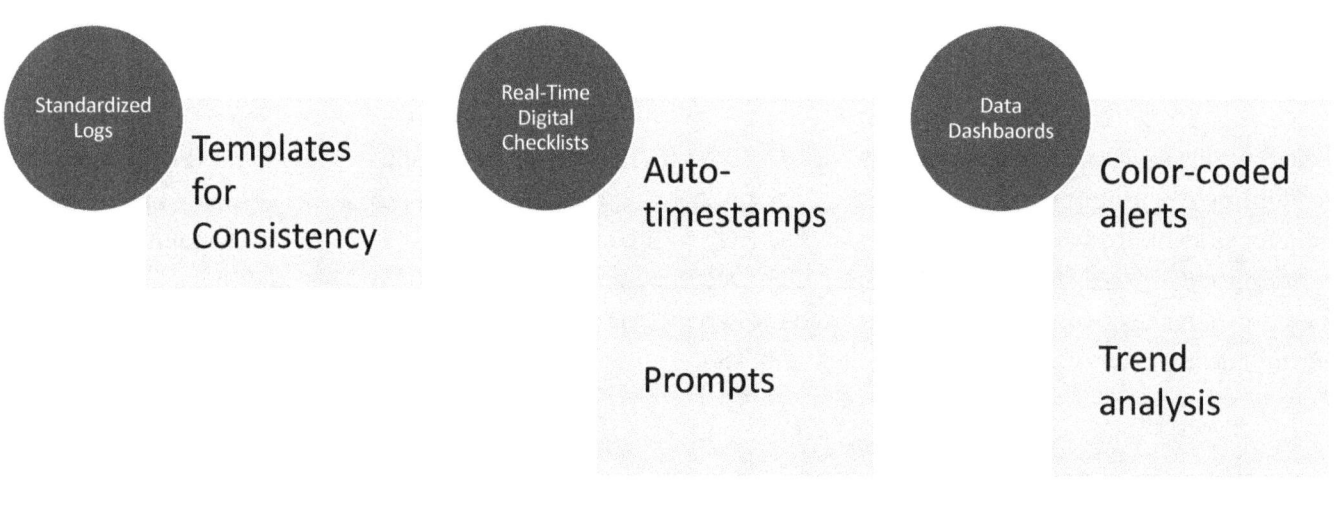

Using Dashboards and Data Visualization to Drive Decisions

1. **Real-Time Data Summaries**
    - **Color-Coded Alerts:** Some platforms flag students who fall below a certain threshold (e.g., reading fluency, behavior incidents) with color-coded indicators, prompting teams to intervene swiftly (Fergus, 2017).

- **Trend Analysis:** Graphs that display short-term and long-term progress help educators see if interventions are making a difference or if strategies need refinement (Fuchs, Fuchs, & Vaughn, 2014).

2. **Multi-Level Access**
    - **Role-Based Permissions:** Administrators might need districtwide overviews, while teachers or counselors require class-level data. Configure dashboards so users only see the level of detail relevant to their role (Buffum, Mattos, & Weber, 2010).
    - **Family-Friendly Views:** Some systems offer parent portals where families can track their child's assignments, attendance, and progress. Provide training or user guides to help them interpret the data accurately (Gay, 2018).
3. **Data Meetings and Collaboration**
    - **Structured Review Protocols:** During MTSS team meetings or PLCs, project the dashboard for real-time discussion of screening results, Tier 2 group outcomes, or individual student progress (DuFour & Fullan, 2013).
    - **Action-Oriented Results:** End each data review with documented next steps—whether adjusting group composition, assigning a different intervention, or scheduling a parent conference (McIntosh & Goodman, 2016).

Enhancing Communication and Transparency

1. **Regular Reporting Cycles**
    - **Short, Clear Reports:** Issue brief updates (weekly, biweekly, or monthly) to keep staff, families, and community partners in the loop. Highlight what interventions occurred, how the student responded, and upcoming goals (Greenberg, Domitrovich, Weissberg, & Durlak, 2017).
    - **Virtual Platforms:** Leverage learning management systems or secure messaging apps to distribute reports. Consistent communication fosters trust and proactive problem-solving with families (Fisher, Frey, & Hattie, 2021).
2. **Parent and Guardian Engagement**
    - **Data Literacy Sessions:** Host workshops or send video tutorials showing how to read progress graphs, interpret screening results, and collaborate on next steps (Esparza Brown & Sanford, 2011).
    - **Language Accessibility:** Provide translations of reports, dashboards, and instructions. Encourage bilingual staff or community volunteers to help families navigate student data and intervention plans (Gay, 2018).
3. **Professional Learning on Documentation Practices**
    - **Coaching on Reporting**: Provide mini-PD sessions where teachers practice writing succinct intervention summaries, focusing on clarity and actionable insights for stakeholders (Bean & Ippolito, 2016).
    - **Peer Feedback**: Invite staff to exchange sample reports, offering suggestions on how to strengthen communication or highlight student strengths more effectively (Fergus, 2017).

Reflection & Planning

1. **Current Documentation Habits**
   - Do staff have consistent templates for recording interventions, or does everyone use a different approach?
   - What is the turnaround time between an intervention session and documentation? Does this lag affect data reliability?
2. **Tools and Platforms**
   - Is your school or district utilizing dashboards effectively, or are you still piecing together data from multiple sources?
   - Which visualizations (graphs, color codes, alerts) would make your intervention decisions more efficient?
3. **Stakeholder Communication**
   - How easily can families or community partners access student progress data, and do they understand how to act on it?
   - Are teachers and staff comfortable explaining data trends to parents in plain language that fosters collaboration?

Through **efficient documentation and reporting**, schools create a transparent, data-driven environment where **every** stakeholder can follow a student's MTSS journey—from universal supports to the most intensive interventions. In **Section 9.3**, we will delve into **curating high-quality resources**—including evidence-based intervention programs, toolkits, and communities of practice—to ensure that staff have the best possible materials and support at their fingertips.

9.3 Curating High-Quality Resources

From instructional programs to professional communities of practice, **the right resources** can significantly enhance and sustain a Multi-Tiered System of Supports (MTSS). Whether you're seeking evidence-based curricula, intervention toolkits, or communities where educators exchange best practices, a thoughtful approach to **resource curation** ensures that staff, students, and families all benefit from reliable, research-backed materials. This section explores **how** to identify and evaluate high-quality MTSS resources, providing examples of **go-to repositories** and strategies to foster an ongoing culture of learning and improvement.

Identifying and Vetting Evidence-Based Programs

1. **Alignment with Tiered Supports**
    - **Tier-Specific Criteria:** Before selecting a resource (e.g., a reading intervention program), clarify whether it's most effective as a **universal**, **targeted**, or **intensive** support. Resources intended for Tier 3 may be too intensive for Tier 1, and vice versa (Fuchs, Fuchs, & Vaughn, 2014).
    - **Learning Targets and Student Needs:** Cross-check each program's objectives (e.g., phonemic awareness, math computation, SEL skill-building) with the specific gaps identified by screening or progress monitoring data. A resource is only valuable if it addresses **actual** student challenges (Marzano, 2017).
2. **Reputable Databases and Clearinghouses**
    - **What Works Clearinghouse (WWC):** Maintained by the U.S. Department of Education's Institute of Education Sciences, WWC reviews research on programs and interventions to identify those with proven effectiveness (Burns & Gibbons, 2012).
    - **National Center on Intensive Intervention (NCII):** Offers tools charts and practice guides specifically designed for intensive academic and behavioral interventions, helping teams pinpoint appropriate Tier 3 strategies (McIntosh & Goodman, 2016).
    - **Evidence for ESSA:** Curated by John Hopkins University, this platform categorizes programs based on ESSA (Every Student Succeeds Act) evidence tiers, aiding educators in meeting federal compliance and quality standards (Fergus, 2017).
3. **Cultural and Linguistic Responsiveness**
    - **Diverse Populations:** Evaluate whether a program includes examples and representations that reflect the cultural identities and experiences of your student body (Gay, 2018).
    - **Language Supports:** For English learners, check if interventions offer scaffolds, translations, or bilingual materials. Programs that seamlessly integrate language development can enhance both academic and linguistic progress (Esparza Brown & Sanford, 2011).

Figure 9.6 illustrates the process of vetting high-quality resources for MTSS.

Figure 9.5 High-Quality Resource Vetting Criteria

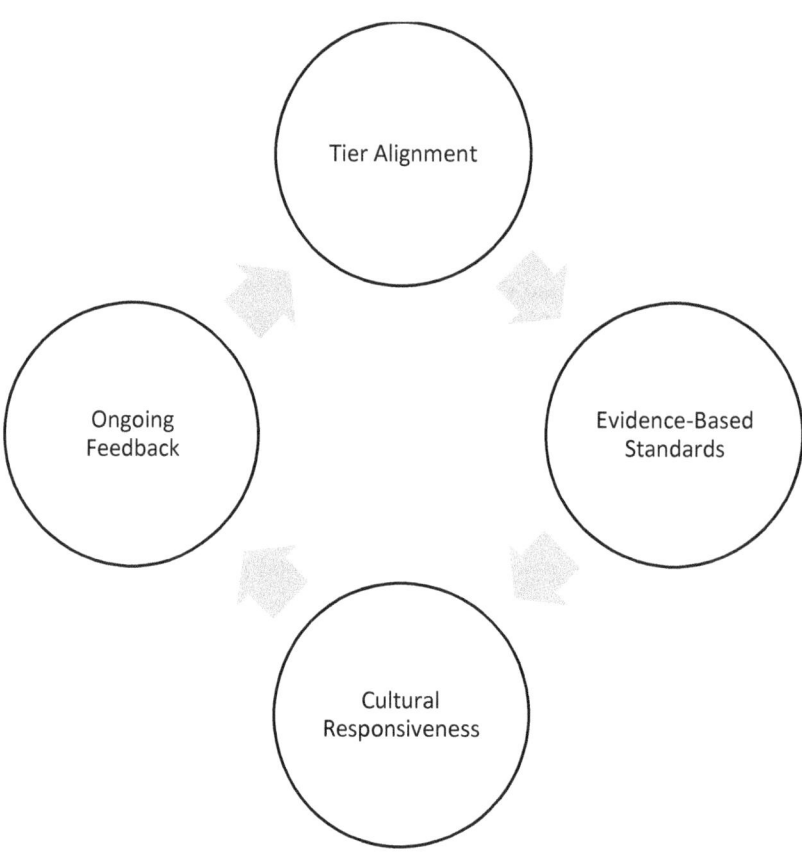

Resource Hubs, Toolkits, and Communities of Practice

1. **District-Level Resource Libraries**
    - **Centralized Portals:** Many districts compile vetted resources—assessments, lesson plans, intervention guides—in an internal digital library or Google Drive folder. This ensures staff can quickly locate materials aligned with district policies and standards (Buffum, Mattos, & Weber, 2010).
    - **Shared Procurement:** When multiple schools collaborate to purchase or license high-quality interventions, costs are reduced, and fidelity is often easier to maintain across the district (Burns & Gibbons, 2012).
2. **Professional Organizations and Online Forums**

- **Subject-Specific Networks:** Groups like the International Literacy Association or the National Council of Teachers of Mathematics frequently publish research-based toolkits and host discussion boards where educators exchange MTSS strategies (Fisher, Frey, & Hattie, 2021).
- **Social Media and EdTech Platforms:** LinkedIn groups, Twitter chats (e.g., #EduTwitter), or specialized forums on sites like Edutopia can connect staff with educators worldwide who share resources, lesson ideas, and problem-solving tips (Greenberg, Domitrovich, Weissberg, & Durlak, 2017).

3. **Conferences and Workshops**
    - **In-Person or Virtual:** Attending conferences dedicated to MTSS, Response to Intervention (RTI), or Positive Behavioral Interventions and Supports (PBIS) allows teams to learn from national experts and gather fresh, evidence-based resources (Sugai & Horner, 2009).
    - **Train-the-Trainer Models:** Schools can send a small group of staff to specialized workshops, who then return to lead in-house professional development—spreading new insights and tools across all tiers (Fergus, 2017).

Cultivating an Ongoing Resource Culture

1. **Resource Vetting Committees**
    - **Cross-Functional Teams:** Establish small teams (teachers, specialists, administrators) responsible for evaluating and recommending new programs or tools. Committees can conduct pilot studies, collect staff feedback, and finalize selections (DuFour & Fullan, 2013).
    - **Fidelity and Review Cycles:** Check each resource's implementation fidelity over time. If data shows minimal impact or alignment issues, revisit the decision and consider alternatives (Marzano, 2017).
2. **Staff-Led Sharing Sessions**
    - **Resource Showcases:** During staff meetings or professional learning community (PLC) gatherings, invite educators to demo how they used a particular toolkit or app to boost student engagement. Hearing peers' success stories builds internal buy-in (McIntosh & Goodman, 2016).
    - **"Bright Spots" Tracking:** Keep a running list of especially effective lessons, videos, or websites that address recurring student needs (e.g., fraction fluency, conflict resolution). Organizing these "bright spots" for quick access fosters a spirit of collaboration (Fisher et al., 2021).
3. **Student and Family Feedback**
    - **User Experience Surveys:** Periodically ask students how they perceive the usefulness or relevance of new learning software or SEL activities. Parents can also share whether they notice improvements at home (Gay, 2018).
    - **Language and Access Considerations:** Translate resource guides for families, ensuring all can meaningfully engage with at-home supports. Tools that are accessible to both English learners and their families can increase consistency between school and home (Esparza Brown & Sanford, 2011).

Reflection & Planning

1. **Current Resource Landscape**
    - Are your teachers relying on a scattered assortment of interventions, or do they have a centralized library of vetted programs?
    - How regularly do you update this library to retire outdated resources and add new, evidence-based materials?
2. **Quality Assurance**
    - Do you have a protocol or checklist for vetting the cultural and linguistic responsiveness of each new resource?
    - Are staff encouraged to run small pilots before fully adopting a new curriculum or software?
3. **Nurturing a Resource-Sharing Culture**
    - How can staff learn from one another's successes and challenges with specific programs or tools?
    - Are families and students given avenues to provide feedback or suggest resources that align with their interests or cultural backgrounds?

By **curating high-quality, evidence-based** resources and encouraging a culture of shared learning, schools ensure that **every** student benefits from interventions tailored to their academic, behavioral, and social-emotional needs. In **Section 9.4**, we will pivot toward **Reflection & Planning**, examining how to conduct resource audits, make data-driven refinements, and continuously evolve your MTSS toolkit over time.

9.4 Reflection & Planning

Chapters 9.1 through 9.3 detailed how technology, streamlined documentation, and evidence-based resources can bolster a Multi-Tiered System of Supports (MTSS). This final section offers **reflective prompts** and **action steps** to help you evaluate your current use of tools, platforms, and interventions—ensuring that they align seamlessly with your school or district's overarching MTSS vision. By taking a purposeful, data-driven approach, you can sustain the growth and innovation necessary to support **all** learners effectively.

Reflecting on Sections 9.1–9.3

1. **EdTech Integration (Section 9.1)**
    - **Relevance and Alignment:** Have you carefully selected digital platforms (screening tools, dashboards, or adaptive apps) that serve the goals of each MTSS tier?

- **Training and Support:** Do staff receive ongoing professional development to maximize the benefits of new technology, and do they have a clear point of contact for troubleshooting (Bean & Ippolito, 2016)?
2. **Documentation and Reporting (Section 9.2)**
    - **Consistency and Accuracy:** Are educators using standardized logs, templates, or checklists to record interventions and student progress? Does this documentation feed into a single data system (Burns & Gibbons, 2012)?
    - **Stakeholder Communication:** Do families and students understand how to interpret progress reports or dashboard data, and are these resources culturally and linguistically accessible (Gay, 2018)?
3. **High-Quality Resource Curation (Section 9.3)**
    - **Evidence-Based Selections:** Does your resource library include proven interventions appropriate for Tier 1 (universal), Tier 2 (targeted), and Tier 3 (intensive) needs (Fuchs, Fuchs, & Vaughn, 2014)?
    - **Ongoing Vetting and Feedback:** Is there a process for regularly assessing whether a program remains effective, culturally responsive, and aligned with student needs (Esparza Brown & Sanford, 2011)?

Technology and Resource Audit

1. **Evaluate Current Platforms**
    - **Overlap or Gaps:** Are there multiple tools serving the same purpose, or critical areas (e.g., SEL progress monitoring) lacking a digital solution?
    - **Fidelity of Use:** Conduct brief staff surveys or observations to gauge how consistently teachers and support staff apply these tools (McIntosh & Goodman, 2016).
2. **Assess Data Accessibility**
    - **Ease of Navigation:** Can teachers, coaches, and administrators quickly retrieve data across academic, behavioral, and social-emotional domains?
    - **Summative vs. Real-Time:** Determine whether your system emphasizes retrospective data (e.g., end-of-quarter) or offers immediate insights that foster rapid intervention adjustments (Fergus, 2017).
3. **Resource Mapping**
    - **Identify Redundancies:** Check if different grade levels or departments are purchasing separate programs that could be unified or replaced by one robust option (Buffum, Mattos, & Weber, 2010).
    - **Address Equity and Accessibility:** Ensure that each resource, digital or otherwise, accommodates diverse learners, including English learners and students with disabilities (Gay, 2018).

Making Data-Driven Refinements

1. **Pilot and Review Process**
   - **Short-Term Trials:** When considering a new intervention or platform, run a small pilot with a select group of teachers or grade levels. Collect data on usage, student outcomes, and user satisfaction (Burns & Gibbons, 2012).
   - **Decision Points:** Establish criteria for full-scale adoption versus discontinuation. If a pilot shows minimal impact, revise your approach or evaluate alternative solutions (Fisher, Frey, & Hattie, 2021).
2. **Collaborative Analysis**
   - **Team Discussions:** Use PLC or MTSS team meetings to interpret pilot data together, ensuring a range of perspectives (e.g., reading specialist, school psychologist, general education teachers) (DuFour & Fullan, 2013).
   - **Transparent Reporting:** Share findings with families and community partners—particularly if the resource or tool will change how student progress is monitored or how interventions are delivered (Greenberg, Domitrovich, Weissberg, & Durlak, 2017).
3. **Sustainability Considerations**
   - **Budget Forecasting:** Plan how you'll finance licensing, renewals, or expansions. If a tool proves invaluable, build its cost into future budget cycles or explore grants (Fergus, 2017).
   - **Professional Development:** Provide ongoing coaching and refresher sessions. Even the best tools can fail if staff don't feel confident or supported (Marzano, 2017).

Fostering a Future-Focused Mindset

1. **Continuous Improvement**
   - **Annual Tech Summits:** Consider an annual "EdTech & Resources Review Day" where teams showcase new platforms, highlight data from successful pilots, and retire outdated tools (McIntosh & Goodman, 2016).
   - **District-Wide Collaboration:** If you're part of a larger system, share successes or challenges across schools. A district-level perspective can lead to more coherent resource adoption and equity in student supports (Buffum et al., 2010).
2. **Innovation and Responsiveness**
   - **Listening to Voices:** Encourage teachers, parents, and students to propose new ideas or improvements. Crowdsource insights on how to refine the digital ecosystem to meet evolving needs (Gay, 2018).
   - **Anticipating Emerging Trends:** Stay current with research on SEL assessments, AI-driven learning tools, and culturally responsive interventions. Evaluate their alignment with your MTSS approach before making major changes (Greenberg et al., 2017).
3. **Celebrating Milestones**

- **Staff Acknowledgments:** Recognize educators who pioneer effective use of new tools or resources—such as significantly improving reading benchmarks or reducing discipline referrals with a targeted intervention (Fisher et al., 2021).
- **Community Showcases:** Host events or online galleries where families see the impacts of digital dashboards, SEL apps, or curated curricula on real student progress (Esparza Brown & Sanford, 2011).

Conclusion of Chapter 9

By thoughtfully integrating **technology**, establishing **efficient documentation** systems, and **curating high-quality resources**, schools enable **effective** and **equitable** MTSS implementation. These elements form the operational backbone of tiered supports—maximizing limited time, streamlining data-driven decisions, and ensuring that every student has access to engaging, culturally responsive interventions.

In **Chapter 10**, we will delve into **continuous improvement and sustainability**, examining how schools can move from pilot phases to long-term success stories—scaling MTSS practices across grade levels, buildings, and entire districts. With the right tools and an unwavering commitment to reflection and growth, your MTSS journey can remain flexible, inclusive, and profoundly impactful for all learners.

Chapter 10: Continuous Improvement and Sustainability

10.1 Developing a Continuous Improvement Mindset

A Multi-Tiered System of Supports (MTSS) is not a one-time rollout—it is an **ongoing process** that demands frequent reflection, responsive adaptations, and a collective commitment to success (DuFour & Fullan, 2013). Continuous improvement ensures that your MTSS framework remains relevant and effective, evolving alongside student needs, staff capacity, and emerging research. In this section, we delve into why a **Plan-Do-Study-Act (PDSA)** cycle is essential for sustaining MTSS and how schools can embed these iterative practices into daily routines.

Figure 10.1 illustrates the PDSA cycle as a continuous improvement framework for MTSS.

Figure 10.1 Plan-Do-Study-Act (PDSA) Cycle for MTSS

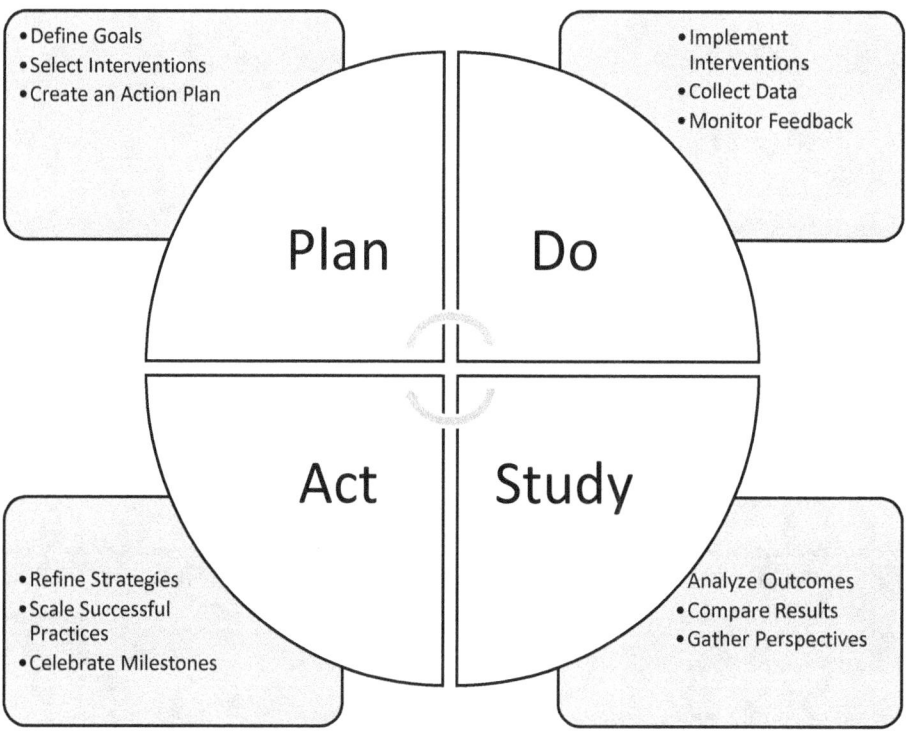

Plan-Do-Study-Act (PDSA) Cycles for MTSS Teams

1. **Plan**
   - **Define Specific Goals:** Whether you're aiming to increase math proficiency by 10% or reduce office discipline referrals by half, set clear, measurable objectives (Doran, 1981).
   - **Identify Interventions and Resources:** Select evidence-based strategies that align with your MTSS tiers. Consider how much time, funding, and personnel each intervention requires (Burns & Gibbons, 2012).
   - **Create an Action Plan:** Outline the who, what, when, where, and why of each strategy. Decide which data points (e.g., screening scores, progress monitoring logs) will indicate success (Fuchs, Fuchs, & Vaughn, 2014).
2. **Do**
   - **Implement with Fidelity:** Ensure that teachers and support staff have the training, materials, and time to deliver interventions as intended (McIntosh & Goodman, 2016).
   - **Collect Ongoing Data:** Record baseline metrics and track student performance regularly. Use digital dashboards, logs, or spreadsheets for consistent documentation (Marzano, 2017).
   - **Monitor Staff and Student Feedback:** Encourage teams to note challenges (e.g., scheduling conflicts, student engagement issues) and successes (DuFour & Fullan, 2013).
3. **Study**
   - **Analyze Outcomes:** Convene MTSS or professional learning community (PLC) meetings to review progress data, discussing what trends emerge and why (Buffum, Mattos, & Weber, 2010).
   - **Compare Results to Goals:** If you aimed for a 10% reading fluency increase, did your data confirm that growth? If not, dig into potential root causes—such as mismatched interventions or fidelity gaps (Fergus, 2017).
   - **Gather Multiple Perspectives:** Invite input from teachers, specialists, administrators, and possibly students or families—everyone who can shed light on what's working and what needs refinement (Gay, 2018).
4. **Act**
   - **Refine or Scale Up:** If your interventions demonstrate positive impacts, consider expanding them across grade levels or departments. Provide additional coaching or resources to maintain momentum (Greenberg, Domitrovich, Weissberg, & Durlak, 2017).
   - **Revisit the Plan:** When data shows insufficient progress, adjust your approach—whether it's increasing the intervention's frequency, switching tools, or incorporating new professional development (Fisher, Frey, & Hattie, 2021).
   - **Celebrate Milestones:** Recognize quick wins and positive student gains, reinforcing a culture where iterative improvement feels both rewarding and necessary (Hattie & Zierer, 2018).

Iterative Goal-Setting and Adjustment

1. **Short-Term vs. Long-Term Goals**
   - **Monthly or Quarterly Targets:** Define mini-benchmarks that keep staff focused on near-term achievements (e.g., screening completion rates, Tier 2 group formation) (McIntosh & Goodman, 2016).
   - **Annual or Multi-Year Vision:** Align these shorter goals with broader district or school aims, ensuring daily actions contribute to long-range outcomes (Marzano, 2017).
2. **Data-Driven Flexibility**
   - **Frequent Progress Monitoring:** Regularly review indicators (e.g., reading fluency, SEL survey results). If data trends indicate a change in student needs, pivot quickly instead of waiting until the end of a term (Burns & Gibbons, 2012).
   - **Responsive Resource Allocation:** When a new challenge arises—such as a sudden dip in math performance—reallocate coaching hours or invest in targeted materials that address the specific gap (Fergus, 2017).
3. **Ongoing Reflection and Collaboration**
   - **Cross-Functional Dialogues:** Encourage teachers, counselors, special educators, and administration to engage in open conversations about tier placement, interventions, and fidelity. Collective ownership propels consistent improvement (DuFour & Fullan, 2013).
   - **Incorporating Stakeholder Voice:** Periodically solicit feedback from parents, students, and community members about how MTSS is working for them. Their insights can guide refinements in both academic and SEL interventions (Gay, 2018).

Figure 10.2 highlights the interconnected elements of iterative goal-setting within MTSS.

Figure 10.2 Iterative Goal-Setting Framework

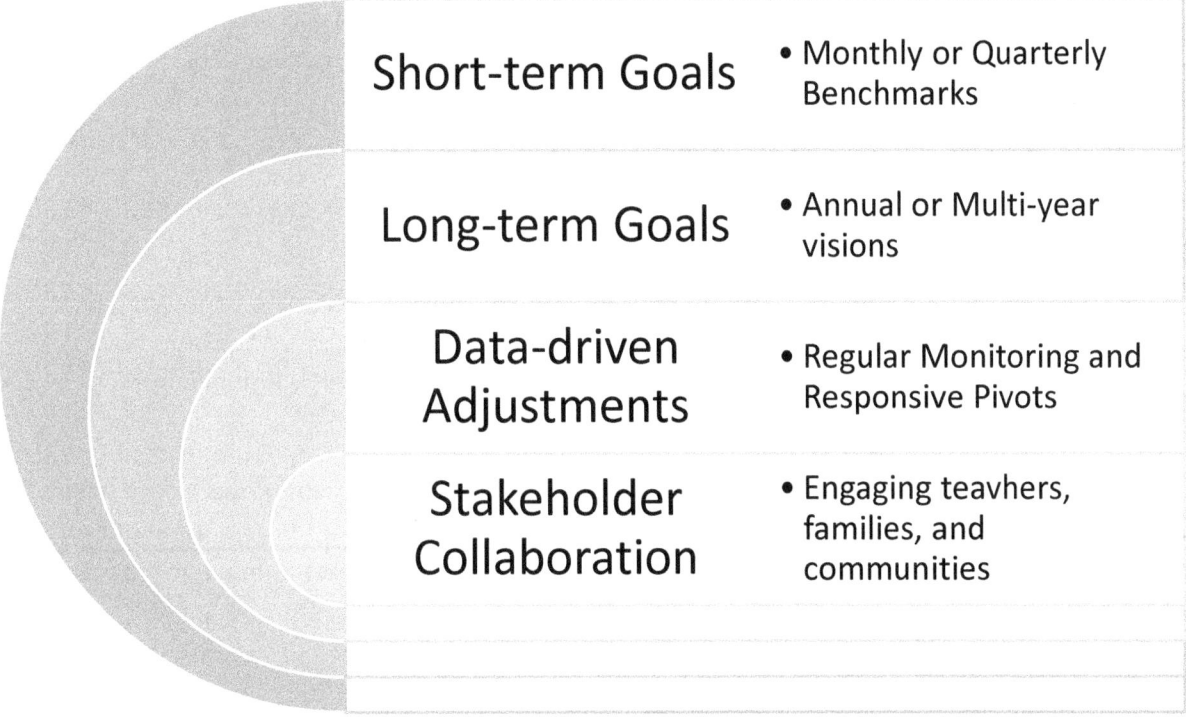

Examples of PDSA in Action

1. **Academic Focus**
   - **Reading Fluency Initiative:** *Plan* to improve fluency by adopting a new Tier 2 reading tool for at-risk 2nd graders. *Do* train teachers, then deliver the intervention thrice weekly for six weeks. *Study* results by analyzing reading logs and progress monitoring data. *Act* by adjusting group sizes or tool usage if gains fall short (Fuchs et al., 2014).
2. **Behavioral and SEL Focus**
   - **Schoolwide Respect Campaign:** *Plan* to reduce discipline referrals by 25% via new Tier 1 strategies (e.g., posters, daily SEL lessons). *Do* implement weekly respect-themed activities and track referral frequency. *Study* how teachers perceive changes in student interactions. *Act* by amplifying or adjusting strategies if certain grade levels aren't seeing improvement (McIntosh & Goodman, 2016).

Reflection & Planning

1. **Current Improvement Cycles**
   - Are your MTSS teams already following a regular schedule to review data and refine strategies?
   - How structured are these meetings—does each session result in clear action steps?
2. **Measuring Success**
   - What key performance indicators (KPIs) reflect progress in academic, behavioral, and social-emotional domains?
   - Are these KPIs disaggregated by demographics to ensure equity?
3. **Sustaining a Continuous Improvement Culture**
   - Do staff and stakeholders view "failures" or missed benchmarks as learning opportunities instead of dead ends?
   - How are successful practices documented and shared across grade levels or buildings?

By embedding a **continuous improvement mindset**, schools can keep their MTSS frameworks responsive and future-focused, evolving in tandem with changing student populations and educational research. In **Section 10.2**, we'll examine how to **scale MTSS across the district**, ensuring fidelity and consistency as multiple schools or grade spans adopt tiered supports at once.

10.2 Scaling MTSS Across the District

Implementing Multi-Tiered Systems of Supports (MTSS) at a single school can be challenging enough—but **scaling** those efforts districtwide introduces additional layers of coordination, communication, and resource allocation (McIntosh & Goodman, 2016). For districts seeking to replicate a successful MTSS model across multiple campuses, careful **planning**, robust **professional development**, and consistent **fidelity checks** become paramount. In this section, we explore strategies for **phased implementation**, sustaining **fidelity at scale**, and sharing both **success stories** and **lessons learned** to motivate continuous improvement.

Phased Implementation Strategies for Multiple Sites

1. **Pilot and Refine**
   - **Start Small:** Select one or two "early adopter" schools to pilot the MTSS framework. Use these sites to refine protocols for data collection, Tier 2 interventions, and professional development (DuFour & Fullan, 2013).
   - **Document Lessons Learned:** Keep detailed records of successes and hurdles—such as scheduling issues, staff training needs, or resource gaps—so you can address them before expanding to more campuses (Burns & Gibbons, 2012).

2. **Tiered Rollout**
   - **One Component at a Time:** Rather than implementing all MTSS elements simultaneously, districts might phase in universal screening and progress monitoring first, followed by targeted interventions, and finally advanced Tier 3 practices (Fuchs, Fuchs, & Vaughn, 2014).
   - **Building Capacity:** Give schools time to develop internal expertise—often through designated MTSS leads or instructional coaches—before adding the next layer of implementation (Fergus, 2017).
3. **Differentiated Support for Each Campus**
   - **Site-Based Autonomy:** Allow each school to adapt MTSS processes to its unique context (e.g., student demographics, existing programs), as long as core fidelity standards are maintained (Gay, 2018).
   - **Centralized Resources and Training:** Offer districtwide professional development on screening tools, data platforms, and evidence-based interventions. Then let schools choose how to integrate these resources effectively (Marzano, 2017).

Figure 10.3 outlines the phased approach to scaling MTSS across multiple sites.

Figure 10.3 Phased Implementation Strategies

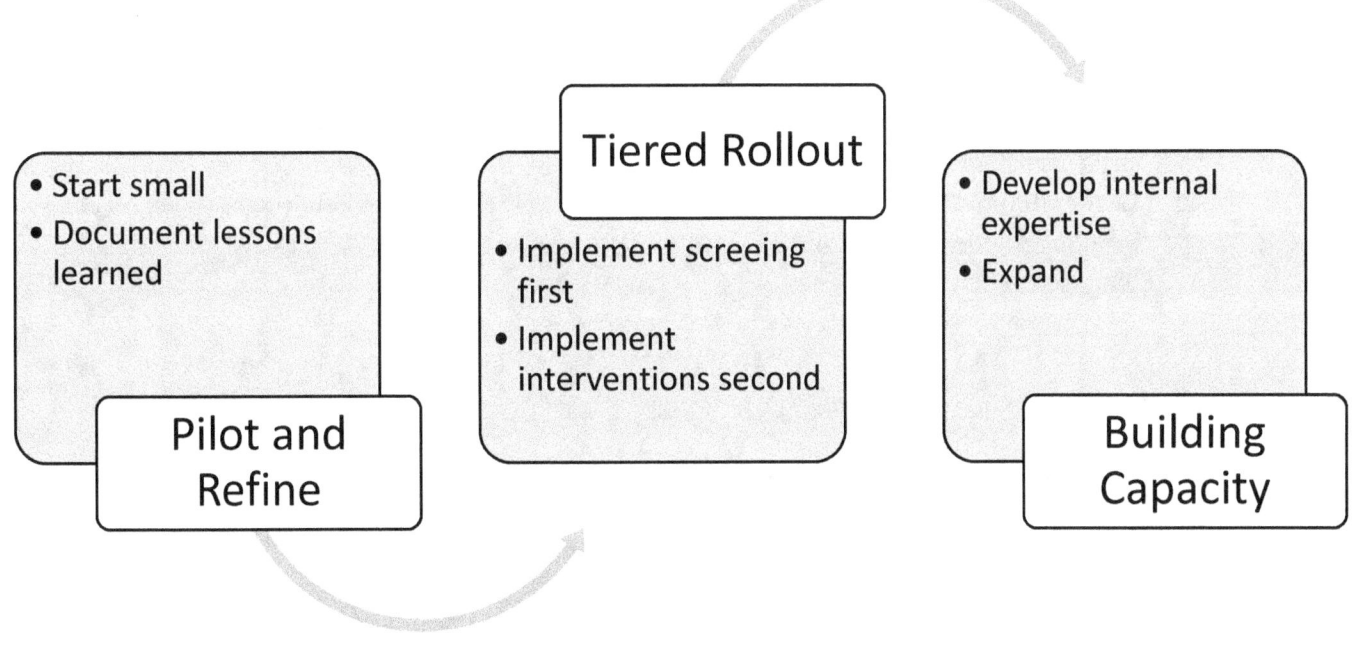

Maintaining Fidelity at Scale

1. **Common District Framework**
   - **Standardized Protocols:** Ensure all schools follow the same definitions, tiers, and data reporting protocols. Consistent language around "Tier 2," "screening thresholds," and "progress monitoring schedules" reduces confusion (Buffum, Mattos, & Weber, 2010).
   - **Centralized Data Systems:** A unified data platform enables district leaders to compare trends across schools, spotting potential inequities or bright spots in performance (McIntosh & Goodman, 2016).
2. **Regular Site Visits and Coaching**
   - **Fidelity Checks:** District-level MTSS coordinators or instructional coaches can conduct observations, review student data, and provide feedback to each campus, ensuring interventions match their intended design (Burns & Gibbons, 2012).
   - **Implementation Rubrics:** Tools like PBIS or RTI fidelity checklists help measure whether each school is adhering to essential MTSS components—like universal screening frequency or using evidence-based practices (Fisher, Frey, & Hattie, 2021).
3. **Professional Learning Networks**
   - **Cross-School Collaboration:** Host districtwide MTSS meetings where teams from different schools exchange lessons learned, share successful interventions, and problem-solve common challenges (DuFour & Fullan, 2013).
   - **Leadership Cohorts:** Group school principals or MTSS leads into cohorts that meet regularly, fostering peer mentorship and a shared sense of accountability for district-level outcomes (Fergus, 2017).

Sharing Success Stories and Lessons Learned

1. **District-Wide Data Dashboards**
   - **Highlight Growth Metrics:** Display reading/math gains, reduced discipline referrals, or SEL improvements across schools. Celebrating success at the district level builds momentum for continuous improvement (Greenberg, Domitrovich, Weissberg, & Durlak, 2017).
   - **Equity Focus:** Disaggregate data to show progress among different student subgroups. This transparency can spark conversations on how to close gaps districtwide (Gay, 2018).
2. **Case Studies and Best Practices**
   - **Exemplar Schools:** Spotlight campuses that excel in specific MTSS areas (e.g., Tier 2 reading interventions or SEL integration). Document their strategies, resources used, and implementation timelines (McIntosh & Goodman, 2016).

- **Peer-Led Workshops:** Invite successful school teams to facilitate mini-conferences or in-service sessions, ensuring practical insights are shared directly from those who have "lived" the process (Fisher et al., 2021).

3. **Celebrating Milestones**
   - **Showcase Events:** Host an annual district MTSS symposium where schools present data, highlight innovations, and invite family or community feedback (DuFour & Fullan, 2013).
   - **Recognition Programs:** Acknowledge staff who champion MTSS core principles—like data-driven decision-making or culturally responsive practices. Public accolades reinforce the district's values (Fergus, 2017).

Reflection & Planning

1. **Current State of District-Wide MTSS**
   - How many schools in your district have a robust MTSS framework vs. those in the early stages?
   - Are universal definitions and protocols in place, or does each school interpret MTSS differently?
2. **Scalability and Resource Allocation**
   - Do you have enough coaches, specialists, or budget to support a districtwide rollout?
   - What professional development is essential for schools lagging behind, and how can you sustain training over time?
3. **Long-Term Sustainment**
   - Are district policies (e.g., strategic plans, budgeting cycles) aligned with MTSS priorities?
   - How will you maintain an ongoing cycle of fidelity checks, data reviews, and staff capacity building once MTSS is in place across all sites?

Scaling MTSS across a district offers **tremendous** benefits for students, teachers, and families—ensuring that every campus has a cohesive, data-driven system of supports. Yet it also requires **careful orchestration**, collaborative leadership, and a strong commitment to **fidelity** at every step (McIntosh & Goodman, 2016). In **Section 10.3**, we will explore **funding and resource management** approaches that help sustain MTSS efforts over the long haul, from local budget allocations to leveraging state and federal grants.

10.3 Funding and Resource Management

Building and sustaining a robust Multi-Tiered System of Supports (MTSS) requires **thoughtful planning** around how to **allocate finances**, **personnel**, and **materials** (McIntosh & Goodman, 2016). Whether you are piloting MTSS at a single school or rolling it out across an entire district, securing and strategically managing resources ensures that every tier—from universal (Tier 1) to intensive (Tier 3)—is supported with **high-quality interventions**, **professional development**, and **technology**. This section explores **budgeting**, **grants**,

community partnerships, and **ongoing evaluation** to help leaders maintain the momentum and impact of MTSS over the long term.

Budgeting for MTSS (Local, State, and Federal Funding Sources)

1. **Local Budget Allocations**
   - **School and District Priorities:** Incorporate MTSS expenditures (e.g., screening tools, intervention materials, coaching positions) directly into annual budgets and improvement plans, signaling that tiered supports are a non-negotiable priority (Marzano, 2017).
   - **Site-Based Flexibility:** Allow principals and MTSS teams to make case-by-case decisions—such as hiring part-time interventionists or purchasing specialized software—based on each school's student needs (Burns & Gibbons, 2012).
2. **State and Federal Grants**
   - **Title I and IDEA Funds:** Schools serving high-need populations can leverage Title I resources for early intervention and professional development. Meanwhile, Individuals with Disabilities Education Act (IDEA) funds may help provide Tier 3 supports for students with disabilities (U.S. Department of Education, 2006).
   - **Competitive Grants:** Many districts apply for state-level or philanthropic grants focusing on reading achievement, SEL, or technology integration. Demonstrating an established MTSS framework and clear data-driven goals often strengthens grant applications (Fergus, 2017).
3. **Earmarking Professional Development**
   - **PD-Heavy Investments:** Professional learning is a linchpin of MTSS success. Budget specifically for ongoing coaching, training workshops, and conference attendance to keep staff up to date on best practices (DuFour & Fullan, 2013).
   - **Cost-Benefit Analysis:** Evaluate the return on investment (ROI) from each PD initiative. If reading proficiency or SEL indicators improve significantly, it may justify expanding or extending certain training programs (Buffum, Mattos, & Weber, 2010).

Grant Writing and Community Partnerships

1. **Tailoring Proposals**
   - **Needs-Based Narratives:** When crafting grant applications, clearly articulate how MTSS addresses local challenges (e.g., high absenteeism, low reading scores, discipline disparities) and provide strong evidence of your plan for ongoing data review (Fuchs, Fuchs, & Vaughn, 2014).
   - **Measurable Outcomes:** Funders want tangible results—like increased proficiency rates, decreased referral numbers, or improved school climate survey data. Link these outcomes to the tiered interventions you plan to implement (McIntosh & Goodman, 2016).
2. **Leveraging Community Resources**

- **Nonprofits and Local Agencies:** Partner with organizations offering after-school tutoring, mental health services, or family engagement events. Such alliances can reduce district costs while broadening wraparound supports (Greenberg, Domitrovich, Weissberg, & Durlak, 2017).
- **In-Kind Contributions:** Sometimes, community partners provide volunteer hours, meeting spaces, or free resources. Track and acknowledge these contributions, as they help sustain MTSS efforts without straining budgets (Gay, 2018).

3. **Building Long-Term Relationships**
    - **Shared Ownership:** Involve funders and community partners in data reviews and strategic planning sessions, so they can see progress and contribute feedback. This transparency fosters trust and renews investment (Fisher, Frey, & Hattie, 2021).
    - **Recognition and Reciprocity:** Publicly celebrate partnerships—through school events, newsletters, or social media—highlighting how external support bolsters student growth (Fergus, 2017).

Maintaining Fidelity Over Time

1. **Ongoing Data Review and Adjustments**
    - **Regular Audits:** Compare spending (e.g., intervention materials, coaching time) with student outcomes. If certain investments show low ROI, redirect funds to more effective strategies (Burns & Gibbons, 2012).
    - **Continuous Improvement Mindset:** Integrate financial reviews into your Plan-Do-Study-Act (PDSA) cycles, ensuring resource allocation remains flexible and responsive to evolving needs (DuFour & Fullan, 2013).
2. **Sustaining Intervention Quality**
    - **Resource Upkeep:** Plan for software renewals, hardware updates, and professional development refreshers. Neglecting these recurring costs can erode fidelity (Marzano, 2017).
    - **Staff Retention:** Address any turnover issues by embedding MTSS responsibilities into job descriptions and offering robust induction programs for new hires—so knowledge and practices don't leave with departing staff (McIntosh & Goodman, 2016).
3. **Equitable Resource Distribution**
    - **Priority to High-Need Sites:** Schools with higher at-risk populations or less experienced staff may require additional coaching hours, Tier 2 specialists, or universal screening materials (Gay, 2018).
    - **Transparency and Communication:** When allocating funds or support personnel, explain the data-driven rationale (e.g., a steep rise in behavior referrals) to foster understanding and buy-in across the district (Fergus, 2017).

Reflection & Planning

1. **Funding Gaps and Opportunities**
   - Are you maximizing all potential revenue streams—Title I, IDEA, local grants, philanthropic partnerships—to fund MTSS priorities?
   - Which new or underutilized grants could address emergent needs, such as SEL or culturally responsive interventions?
2. **Resource Tracking and ROI**
   - Is there a formal process (e.g., quarterly reviews) for comparing spending on interventions with student outcome data?
   - Who oversees this process, and how are adjustments communicated to staff and stakeholders?
3. **Long-Range Sustainability**
   - How will you maintain continuity if key staff members who champion MTSS retire or relocate?
   - Which district policies or strategic goals explicitly integrate and protect MTSS budget lines?

By embedding **funding and resource management** into your MTSS strategy, you ensure that tiered supports not only launch successfully but also thrive over time. Thoughtful budgeting, strategic partnerships, and continuous data-driven refinements keep interventions accessible, equitable, and impactful for all learners. In **Section 10.4**, we will wrap up our exploration of **continuous improvement and sustainability**, offering a final checklist and roadmap to help you maintain momentum as your MTSS journey evolves.

10.4 Reflection & Planning – Next Steps for Your MTSS Journey

Throughout Chapter 10, we have explored how to maintain and scale your Multi-Tiered System of Supports (MTSS) through **continuous improvement cycles, districtwide implementation**, and **strategic resource management**. This concluding section offers a **final sustainability checklist** and a **forward-looking roadmap** to help you refine your MTSS practices, protect them against common pitfalls, and guide new generations of educators and students toward successful, equitable outcomes.

Sustainability Checklist: From Pilot to District-Wide Adoption

1. **Fidelity and Data Review**
   - **Regular Monitoring:** Have you embedded frequent check-ins (e.g., monthly or quarterly) to evaluate Tier 1, Tier 2, and Tier 3 interventions for fidelity and effectiveness (McIntosh & Goodman, 2016)?

- **Continuous Improvement Mindset:** Do staff view setbacks or unexpected data as opportunities to iterate and improve, rather than reasons to abandon MTSS (DuFour & Fullan, 2013)?

2. **Resource and Funding Security**
    - **Budgetary Commitments:** Are core aspects of MTSS (e.g., screening tools, coaching positions, PD) written into school or district budgets to ensure stability (Buffum, Mattos, & Weber, 2010)?
    - **Grant and Community Partnerships:** Are you actively exploring or maintaining external funding streams or collaborations (e.g., nonprofits, mental health agencies) that enhance wraparound services (Greenberg, Domitrovich, Weissberg, & Durlak, 2017)?
3. **Leadership and Capacity Building**
    - **Distributed Leadership:** Are MTSS responsibilities—data analysis, fidelity checks, professional development—shared among a broad leadership team to prevent reliance on a single "champion" (Fergus, 2017)?
    - **Succession Planning:** In the event key staff (administrators, coaches) retire or leave, do you have a strategy for on-boarding and mentoring new leaders, preserving institutional knowledge (Burns & Gibbons, 2012)?
4. **Equity and Culturally Responsive Practices**
    - **Data Disaggregation:** Are you consistently examining outcomes by race, language proficiency, gender, or socioeconomic status to identify and address any emerging gaps (Gay, 2018)?
    - **Inclusive Family Engagement:** Do families have meaningful opportunities to share insights on interventions, data trends, and next steps, regardless of language or cultural background (Esparza Brown & Sanford, 2011)?

A Roadmap for Long-Term Success

1. **Phase Out the "Pilot" Mentality**
    - **Institutionalize MTSS:** Move from seeing MTSS as an "initiative" to an integral part of your district's identity. Incorporate tiered supports into job descriptions, professional evaluations, and strategic plans (Marzano, 2017).
    - **Scale Thoughtfully:** As more schools join the effort, ensure each site receives adequate training, coaching, and resources. Overextension without sufficient support can dilute fidelity (Fisher, Frey, & Hattie, 2021).
2. **Anchor in Policy and Leadership Structures**
    - **Board-Level Commitment:** Seek endorsements or resolutions from your school board emphasizing MTSS as a core strategy for student success (DuFour & Fullan, 2013).
    - **Ongoing Leadership Development:** Offer leadership pathways (e.g., MTSS lead teacher, district MTSS coordinator) and robust professional development that maintains momentum across staff transitions (McIntosh & Goodman, 2016).
3. **Stay Agile and Future-Focused**

- **Emerging Research and Tools:** Monitor new evidence-based interventions, EdTech platforms, and SEL frameworks. Adapt your MTSS approach as promising solutions or changing student needs arise (Fuchs, Fuchs, & Vaughn, 2014).
- **Innovation Through Collaboration:** Encourage cross-school or cross-district communities of practice, where educators share creative solutions to challenges, preventing stagnation (Greenberg et al., 2017).

Celebrating Milestones and Looking Ahead

1. **School and Community Recognition**
   - **Positive Storytelling:** Highlight improved student outcomes (e.g., reading proficiency, reduced discipline referrals, SEL gains) in newsletters, social media, or local media outlets. Public acknowledgment helps sustain enthusiasm (Gay, 2018).
   - **Staff and Stakeholder Honors:** Consider annual awards or certificates for teachers, counselors, administrators, and family or community partners who have made exceptional contributions to MTSS (Fergus, 2017).
2. **Cultivating a Legacy**
   - **Mentorship Programs:** Encourage experienced MTSS implementers to mentor new hires or newly involved community members, fostering continuity and a collective sense of purpose (Burns & Gibbons, 2012).
   - **Reflect and Renew:** Schedule an annual "MTSS Summit" where data insights, successes, and new initiatives are presented districtwide, reaffirming commitment and inspiring fresh ideas (DuFour & Fullan, 2013).
3. **Next Steps for Your MTSS Journey**
   - **Self-Assessment:** Revisit the reflection and planning tools throughout this book—scoring your current fidelity, stakeholder engagement, and sustainability efforts.
   - **Adapting as Needed:** Tailor each tool, from universal screeners to Tier 3 interventions, to your evolving student population, building on the strong foundation you've established (Marzano, 2017).

Conclusion of Chapter 10

A **continuous improvement ethos** ensures that your MTSS journey never stalls. By weaving **equity**, **collaboration**, and **evidence-based practices** into the fabric of your district, you create a lasting impact on student achievement, social-emotional well-being, and school culture. This concludes the main chapters of the MTSS Blueprint. In **Chapter 11**, we will share **real-world case studies** and **success stories**, offering concrete examples of how schools and districts have transformed their MTSS visions into daily reality.

Chapter 11: Case Studies and Success Stories

11.1 Real-World Examples of MTSS Implementation

Learning about the **theory and framework** of a Multi-Tiered System of Supports (MTSS) is essential—but **seeing** how these principles unfold in real schools and districts brings the model to life. This section spotlights **three success stories**: one at the elementary level, one at the secondary level, and one reflecting district-wide transformation. Each example highlights **key strategies**, **challenges**, and **lessons learned**, illustrating how MTSS can adapt to different contexts while maintaining core fidelity and impact.

Elementary School Success Story

1. **Context and Challenges**
   - **School Demographics:** A K–5 campus serving a diverse, high-poverty neighborhood. Many students enter with limited literacy skills and varied English language proficiency levels (Esparza Brown & Sanford, 2011).
   - **Initial Pain Points:** Chronic absenteeism, inconsistent behavior referrals, and a reading achievement gap highlighted a need for a **coordinated** approach to academic and behavioral supports (Fergus, 2017).
2. **Key MTSS Strategies**
   - **Structured Literacy Focus:** Using a research-based phonics program for Tier 1 reading instruction, combined with weekly progress monitoring for at-risk students (Fuchs, Fuchs, & Vaughn, 2014).
   - **Behavioral Check-In/Check-Out (CICO):** For students flagged by teachers or data for repeated minor infractions, a daily mentor check-in system reduced discipline referrals by reinforcing positive behavior (McIntosh & Goodman, 2016).
   - **Culturally Responsive Family Nights:** Monthly events inviting parents to learn reading strategies and SEL activities in their home languages, fostering trust and reinforcing skills at home (Gay, 2018).
3. **Results and Lessons Learned**
   - **Data Highlights:** Reading proficiency among third graders rose from 52% to 69% in two years, with particularly strong gains among English learners. Behavior referrals decreased by 30% in the same period.
   - **Scaling Success:** The school's literacy and behavior frameworks served as a pilot for the district. Dedicated professional development and coaching were vital to sustaining fidelity (Buffum, Mattos, & Weber, 2010).

Secondary School Success Story

1. **Context and Challenges**
   - **School Demographics:** A 6–12 campus with high suspension rates, significant achievement gaps, and students disengaged in traditional instructional models (Fergus, 2017).
   - **Initial Pain Points:** Teachers reported limited time for differentiation, and the counseling team struggled to keep up with increasing mental health needs. Students voiced concerns about belonging and cultural representation.
2. **Key MTSS Strategies**
   - **Block Scheduling for Tiered Interventions:** The school revised its master schedule to include "WIN" (What I Need) periods, offering Tier 2 small-group tutoring or counseling sessions multiple times a week (DuFour & Fullan, 2013).
   - **Trauma-Informed SEL Curriculum:** A universal SEL program taught stress management, relationship skills, and cultural humility during homeroom. Tier 2 and Tier 3 counseling addressed more significant issues (Greenberg, Domitrovich, Weissberg, & Durlak, 2017).
   - **Teacher-Led Data Teams:** Departments met biweekly to analyze formative assessments, identify students needing Tier 2 re-teaching, and plan next steps (Fisher, Frey, & Hattie, 2021).
3. **Results and Lessons Learned**
   - **Data Highlights:** Over two years, ninth-grade math pass rates rose by 15%, while overall discipline referrals dropped by 40%. Students cited the SEL program and "WIN" blocks as critical supports.
   - **Challenges:** Staff turnover initially hampered fidelity. Providing structured onboarding for new teachers was pivotal to keeping Tier 2 and Tier 3 interventions consistent (Burns & Gibbons, 2012).

District-Wide Transformation

1. **Context and Challenges**
   - **District Demographics:** A medium-sized district of 15 schools, serving a diverse student body with varying levels of academic preparedness and socio-emotional needs (Gay, 2018).
   - **Initial Pain Points:** Each school had its own approach to intervention, causing confusion for mobile students and difficulty in scaling resources. District leaders sought a unified data system and consistent tier definitions (Marzano, 2017).
2. **Key MTSS Strategies**
   - **Unified Screening and Data Platforms:** The district adopted one universal screening tool for reading, math, and behavior, feeding into a centralized digital dashboard. This allowed district leaders to compare trends across schools (McIntosh & Goodman, 2016).
   - **Districtwide MTSS Leadership Teams:** Each school formed an MTSS team, meeting monthly to review data, set goals, and share best practices. A district coordinator facilitated cross-site collaboration (DuFour & Fullan, 2013).

- **Professional Development Cohorts:** Teacher leaders and administrators participated in year-long MTSS coaching academies—building internal capacity to lead interventions, track data, and guide peers (Fergus, 2017).
3. **Results and Lessons Learned**
    - **Data Highlights:** Three years after implementation, reading proficiency districtwide improved from 62% to 75%. Behavioral incidents requiring administrative intervention dropped by 35%.
    - **Fidelity at Scale:** Centralized protocols and robust coaching overcame initial inconsistencies. Yet, the district continues to refine scheduling, resource allocation, and Tier 3 processes as student populations evolve (Fuchs et al., 2014).

Reflection & Planning

1. **Adapting Lessons to Your Context**
    - Which successes from these case studies resonate with your school's or district's challenges—literacy initiatives, SEL integration, or cross-building alignment?
    - How might you replicate their strategies (e.g., a literacy pilot, "WIN" periods, unified data dashboards) on a smaller or larger scale?
2. **Overcoming Common Barriers**
    - Did teacher turnover, scheduling constraints, or varied leadership stances hinder fidelity in any of the examples? How can you proactively address those issues?
    - Are there existing collaborative structures (e.g., grade-level teams, district committees) that can serve as anchors for your MTSS rollout?
3. **Leveraging These Stories for Buy-In**
    - How can sharing these real-world examples inspire staff, families, or community stakeholders to embrace MTSS?
    - Could inviting educators from successful sites to present at your school or district catalyze a renewed sense of commitment?

By examining **real-world MTSS implementations**, we see how schools and districts creatively adapt tiered supports to their specific needs while maintaining fidelity. Lessons learned about scheduling, data usage, professional development, and cultural responsiveness can serve as **blueprints** for your own journey. In **Section 11.2**, we will delve into **common pitfalls** and how to address them—ensuring that your MTSS efforts stay on course despite inevitable challenges.

11.2 Lessons Learned and Common Pitfalls

Every Multi-Tiered System of Supports (MTSS) journey is unique, but certain **common challenges** tend to emerge across schools and districts. Drawing from the case studies in Section 11.1—and broader research—this section outlines frequent **pitfalls** schools encounter and the **lessons learned** about how to address or preempt these obstacles. By proactively anticipating these issues, you can maintain **fidelity**, **motivation**, and **sustainability** at each tier of support.

Pitfall 1: Inconsistent Application of Tiers and Interventions

1. **Description**
   - **Vague Tier Definitions:** When schools lack clear criteria for transitioning students from Tier 1 to Tier 2 or Tier 3, confusion arises about who qualifies for additional supports (Fuchs, Fuchs, & Vaughn, 2014).
   - **Random or "One-Size-Fits-All" Approaches:** Interventions may be inconsistently delivered if teachers are unsure which resources align with each tier.
2. **Lesson Learned**
   - **Establish Districtwide Protocols:** Ensure **universal** screening thresholds and tier definitions are standardized. Provide easy-to-understand flowcharts or decision rules for staff (McIntosh & Goodman, 2016).
   - **Regular Training & Refreshers:** Offer ongoing PD or coaching so newer staff fully grasp the rationale behind each tier, while veteran staff stay aligned with evolving practices (DuFour & Fullan, 2013).

Pitfall 2: Data Overload or Underuse

1. **Description**
   - **Excessive Assessments:** Some schools administer too many screeners, overwhelming both staff and students without actionable insights (Burns & Gibbons, 2012).
   - **Underuse of Existing Data:** Conversely, some schools collect data but fail to analyze it promptly or use it to drive Tier 2/Tier 3 decisions (Fergus, 2017).
2. **Lesson Learned**
   - **Streamline Assessments:** Focus on high-quality universal screeners and progress monitoring tools that yield relevant, timely data. Eliminate redundant tests to free up instructional time (Marzano, 2017).

- **Data-Driven Decision-Making:** Build protected meeting times (e.g., monthly MTSS team sessions) to review data, identify trends, and plan interventions swiftly (Fisher, Frey, & Hattie, 2021).

Pitfall 3: Lack of Fidelity and Follow-Through

1. **Description**
   - **Implementation Drift:** Even well-chosen interventions can fail if educators modify them excessively or skip essential components (Buffum, Mattos, & Weber, 2010).
   - **"Set It and Forget It" Mentality:** Schools may treat interventions as fixed solutions, neglecting periodic fidelity checks or mid-course corrections.
2. **Lesson Learned**
   - **Coaching and Observation Cycles:** Regular classroom observations or intervention group walkthroughs help verify that strategies are delivered as intended (Burns & Gibbons, 2012).
   - **Fidelity Checklists and Peer Feedback:** Simple rubrics can clarify essential intervention elements—encouraging staff to self-assess and refine continuously (McIntosh & Goodman, 2016).

Pitfall 4: Insufficient Collaboration and Stakeholder Engagement

1. **Description**
   - **Teacher Isolation:** Without structures (e.g., PLCs, data teams) that encourage joint problem-solving, educators may feel overwhelmed or uncertain about how to support struggling students (DuFour & Fullan, 2013).
   - **Limited Family Involvement:** Families might be informed too late in the process or provided minimal context about interventions, hampering at-home reinforcement (Gay, 2018).
2. **Lesson Learned**
   - **Formal Collaborative Frameworks:** Schedule recurring data reviews and co-planning sessions among teachers, counselors, and administrators. Invite specialists (e.g., reading coaches, behavior analysts) as needed (Fuchs et al., 2014).
   - **Robust Family and Community Outreach:** Provide user-friendly progress reports, host informational meetings in multiple languages, and invite families to co-create Tier 2 or Tier 3 plans (Esparza Brown & Sanford, 2011).

Pitfall 5: Ignoring Cultural Responsiveness and Equity

1. **Description**
   - **Disproportionate Referrals:** When implicit biases go unchecked, certain student groups (e.g., English learners, students of color, low-income families) may be overrepresented in Tier 2 or Tier 3 interventions (Fergus, 2017).
   - **Misaligned Interventions:** Relying solely on mainstream or monolingual strategies can alienate students who need culturally and linguistically relevant approaches (Gay, 2018).
2. **Lesson Learned**
   - **Equity Audits and Data Disaggregation:** Routinely examine outcomes by race, language status, socioeconomic indicators, and more. Address patterns that suggest systemic barriers (Greenberg, Domitrovich, Weissberg, & Durlak, 2017).
   - **Culturally Responsive Practices:** Embed diverse literature, SEL themes, and bilingual supports in Tier 1. For Tier 2 and Tier 3, tailor interventions to honor linguistic and cultural strengths (Esparza Brown & Sanford, 2011).

Additional Pitfalls and Considerations

- **Teacher Turnover:** High turnover can disrupt MTSS consistency. Provide **robust on-boarding** and mentoring for new staff (Fisher et al., 2021).
- **Overemphasis on Academics, Underemphasis on SEL or Behavior:** Balancing academic interventions with social-emotional or behavioral supports is crucial—neglecting one domain often undermines overall progress (McIntosh & Goodman, 2016).
- **Resource Constraints:** Budget limitations or insufficient staff can hinder fidelity. Districts must creatively leverage grants, community partnerships, and cross-campus collaboration to maintain momentum (Burns & Gibbons, 2012).

Reflection & Planning

1. **Identify Potential Pitfalls**
   - Which of these pitfalls—fidelity, data overload, lack of collaboration, cultural responsiveness—seem most likely to hinder your MTSS progress?
   - How can you proactively mitigate these issues? (e.g., introducing simpler data systems, scheduling routine fidelity checks, implementing targeted PD)
2. **Establish a Pitfall Response Plan**
   - **Fidelity Action Steps:** Train a small group of coaches to regularly observe Tier 2 sessions, offering constructive feedback.

- **Collaboration Boosters:** Launch a monthly cross-departmental meeting that includes data review, next-step planning, and sharing of bright spots.
3. **Tracking and Addressing Equity**
    - **Disaggregate Your Data:** Are you consistently using screening tools that consider language proficiency?
    - **Staff and Family Engagement:** How can you co-develop culturally responsive strategies with families, focusing on two-way communication and shared decision-making?

By learning from **common pitfalls** and leveraging the lessons gleaned from other schools' experiences, you can fortify your MTSS framework against routine challenges. This approach keeps the **focus on students**, ensuring your system remains both flexible and steadfast in delivering timely, equitable supports. In **Section 11.3**, we will summarize **practical strategies** for applying these lessons across various contexts, offering a final reflection on how to adapt MTSS principles to ever-changing school environments.

11.3 Reflection & Planning – Applying Lessons Across Contexts

Having explored **real-world MTSS implementations** (Section 11.1) and dissected **common pitfalls and lessons** (Section 11.2), we now consider how to **translate** these insights to your unique school or district. Every context—whether urban, rural, large, or small—carries its own challenges and strengths. By intentionally **adapting** the successes and strategies from other settings, you can craft an MTSS framework that remains **faithful** to core principles while **responsive** to local needs. This concluding section offers prompts and action steps to guide you in **customizing** and **operationalizing** MTSS in any environment.

1. Tailoring Lessons to Your School's Demographics and Needs

1. **Comparative Analysis**
    - **Student Profiles:** Is your student population similar in socioeconomic status, language diversity, or mobility to the elementary, secondary, or districtwide examples shared earlier (Esparza Brown & Sanford, 2011)?
    - **Parallel Concerns:** Do you face similar academic gaps (e.g., early literacy, ninth-grade algebra proficiency) or SEL/behavior issues (e.g., discipline referrals, truancy) that were successfully addressed in the case studies (Fuchs, Fuchs, & Vaughn, 2014)?
2. **Localized Adaptation**
    - **Cultural Responsiveness:** Even proven interventions must be attuned to local languages, cultural values, and community histories. Engage families and community members to align strategies with students' lived experiences (Gay, 2018).

- **Resource Alignment:** If you have fewer staff or limited funding, implement a **scaled-down** pilot—perhaps focusing on one grade level or a select group of students—before expanding (Burns & Gibbons, 2012).

2. Building on Strategies That Yield "Quick Wins"

1. **Focused Pilots**
    - **Incremental Approach:** Rather than launching multiple new interventions at once, pick one or two high-impact strategies (e.g., small-group reading supports, Check-In/Check-Out for behavior) to pilot. Gather data, adjust as needed, and celebrate early successes (DuFour & Fullan, 2013).
    - **Shared Ownership:** Involve teachers, counselors, and administrators from the start, clarifying each person's role and how the chosen pilot fits into broader MTSS goals (McIntosh & Goodman, 2016).
2. **Document and Celebrate Success**
    - **Data Transparency:** Maintain simple progress-tracking spreadsheets or digital dashboards to visualize improvements. Even modest gains (e.g., +5% in reading fluency) can galvanize staff morale (Marzano, 2017).
    - **Public Acknowledgment:** Recognize educators who champion the pilot, share success stories in staff meetings, and invite families to witness positive changes firsthand (Fergus, 2017).

3. Evolving with Your Changing Student Population

1. **Continuous Data Cycles**
    - **Regular Check-Ins:** Conduct monthly or quarterly reviews of screening data, progress monitoring logs, and SEL or behavioral metrics. Ensure your data reflects **equity considerations** (e.g., disaggregated by race, language status) (Gay, 2018).
    - **Responsive Interventions:** If new trends emerge—such as an uptick in a particular grade's reading gaps—adjust or expand Tier 2 supports accordingly. MTSS thrives on nimbleness and ongoing collaboration (Greenberg, Domitrovich, Weissberg, & Durlak, 2017).
2. **Adaptation for Shifting Contexts**
    - **Staff Turnover:** Provide robust onboarding for new teachers or specialists so they understand the MTSS framework and can maintain continuity of interventions (Fisher, Frey, & Hattie, 2021).
    - **Demographic Changes:** As community demographics evolve, refresh interventions to remain culturally and linguistically aligned. Seek input from families and local organizations to keep Tier 1 universal supports relevant (Esparza Brown & Sanford, 2011).

4. Sustaining Momentum Through Reflection and Collaboration

1. **Ongoing Professional Development**
   - **Coaching and Learning Communities:** Use in-house experts or external trainers to lead sessions on new tools, data analysis techniques, and advanced intervention methods (Buffum, Mattos, & Weber, 2010).
   - **Networking Beyond Your School:** Consider cross-district PLCs or state-level conferences to learn from others who face similar challenges or have pioneered innovative solutions (DuFour & Fullan, 2013).
2. **Leadership Structures for Continuous Improvement**
   - **Distributed Responsibilities:** Assign clear roles (data manager, intervention lead, SEL coordinator) so that no single individual shoulders the entire MTSS effort (Burns & Gibbons, 2012).
   - **Frequent Fidelity Checks:** Regular, low-stakes observations or peer reviews keep interventions on track. Encourage teachers to reflect on how changes in student data might prompt adjustments to Tier 2 or Tier 3 practices (McIntosh & Goodman, 2016).

Reflection & Planning

1. **Customizing Strategies from Others' Successes**
   - Which one or two interventions or structures from the case studies align most closely with your existing frameworks and staff expertise?
   - How will you adapt these approaches to fit your scheduling, staffing, and cultural context?
2. **Preventing Pitfalls in Your Context**
   - Based on Section 11.2, which pitfalls (e.g., data overload, lack of fidelity) are you most prone to?
   - What immediate steps can you take to address or preempt these issues (e.g., standardizing data collection, scheduling routine fidelity meetings)?
3. **Keeping Pace with Change**
   - As students' needs evolve, how can you maintain an agile response through short data cycles and open communication channels?
   - Which community partners, families, or external experts can help you refine MTSS in an ongoing manner?

By **reflecting** on your local context, **adapting** proven MTSS strategies, and remaining open to **continuous learning**, you can shape an approach that serves your students' evolving academic, social-emotional, and behavioral needs. In **Chapter 12**, we'll synthesize the entire MTSS Blueprint—tying together the frameworks, case studies, and reflections into a **comprehensive roadmap** for success. Here, you will have the opportunity to **create a personalized MTSS plan** tailored to your unique school or district trajectory.

Chapter 12: Your MTSS Blueprint in Action

12.1 Creating Your Personalized MTSS Roadmap

After exploring the foundational concepts, data-driven strategies, tiered interventions, and real-world success stories throughout this Blueprint, you now stand on the threshold of **action**. Section 12.1 focuses on **building a customized MTSS roadmap** that draws from all previous chapters—ensuring a step-by-step, context-specific plan for your school or district. This roadmap should reflect your **unique demographics**, **resource landscape**, and **shared goals**, while adhering to the core principles of **fidelity**, **equity**, and **continuous improvement** (McIntosh & Goodman, 2016).

1. Pulling Together Reflection and Planning Components

1. **Review Key Takeaways**
   - **Chapter Highlights:** Revisit your notes from earlier chapters—particularly the reflections in Chapters 1–4 (core concepts), 5–7 (tiered interventions), and 8–11 (professional development, stakeholder engagement, case studies). Identify the most relevant strategies for your local context (Fuchs, Fuchs, & Vaughn, 2014).
   - **Common Themes:** Did you spot recurring needs for, say, advanced reading interventions, SEL supports, or cross-functional data teams? Make a list of these priorities (Marzano, 2017).
2. **Synthesize Existing Data**
   - **Baseline Metrics:** Gather current screening data (e.g., reading benchmarks, behavior referrals, SEL surveys), along with recent progress monitoring results to establish your starting point (Burns & Gibbons, 2012).
   - **Equity Check:** Ensure you've disaggregated data by demographics—race, language status, socioeconomic status—to identify any disproportionality in achievement or discipline (Fergus, 2017).
3. **Set Clear Goals and Outcomes**
   - **Tier-Specific Aims:** For Tier 1, you might aim to boost reading proficiency by 10%. For Tier 2, perhaps reduce chronic absenteeism by 15%. For Tier 3, decrease the frequency of individual crisis referrals by half (Buffum, Mattos, & Weber, 2010).
   - **SMART Framework:** Goals should be Specific, Measurable, Achievable, Relevant, and Time-Bound (Doran, 1981). Example: "Increase third-grade reading fluency from 60% to 75% at or above benchmark by the end of the academic year."

2. Implementation Timeline and Checkpoints

1. **Phase In Your Initiatives**
   - **Early Adopter Pilots:** Start with one or two grade levels or departments that show readiness to adopt new screening tools or interventions. This allows you to refine your approach before districtwide expansion (DuFour & Fullan, 2013).
   - **Staggered Rollout:** Rather than launching Tier 2 and Tier 3 simultaneously, ensure Tier 1 fidelity first. Gradually layer on targeted and intensive supports as staff capacity grows (Fisher, Frey, & Hattie, 2021).
2. **Quarterly or Semester Milestones**
   - **Short-Term Targets:** Example: By the end of Quarter 1, 100% of staff have completed MTSS refresher PD on Tier 1 universal screening.
   - **Data Review Schedules:** Plan monthly or bi-monthly MTSS team meetings to assess screening data, Tier 2 group progress, and any emerging needs (McIntosh & Goodman, 2016).
3. **Annual Evaluation and Reflection**
   - **Summative Data Analysis:** At year's end, compare actual growth or reductions (e.g., discipline referrals, SEL skill measures) against the SMART goals. Document successes, challenges, and unexpected findings (Greenberg, Domitrovich, Weissberg, & Durlak, 2017).
   - **Revision of Goals:** Use these insights to reset or adjust goals for the following academic year—demonstrating a true commitment to **continuous improvement** (Marzano, 2017).

Figure 12.1 outlines an example MTSS implementation timeline with quarterly milestones.

Figure 12.1 MTSS Implementation Timeline

Q1: MTSS Refresher PD and Pilot Rollout

Q2: Tier 1 Fidelity Chack and Tier 2 Expansion

Q3: Mid-year Data Review and Tier 3 Refinement

Q4: Annual Evaliation and Goal Setting for Next Year

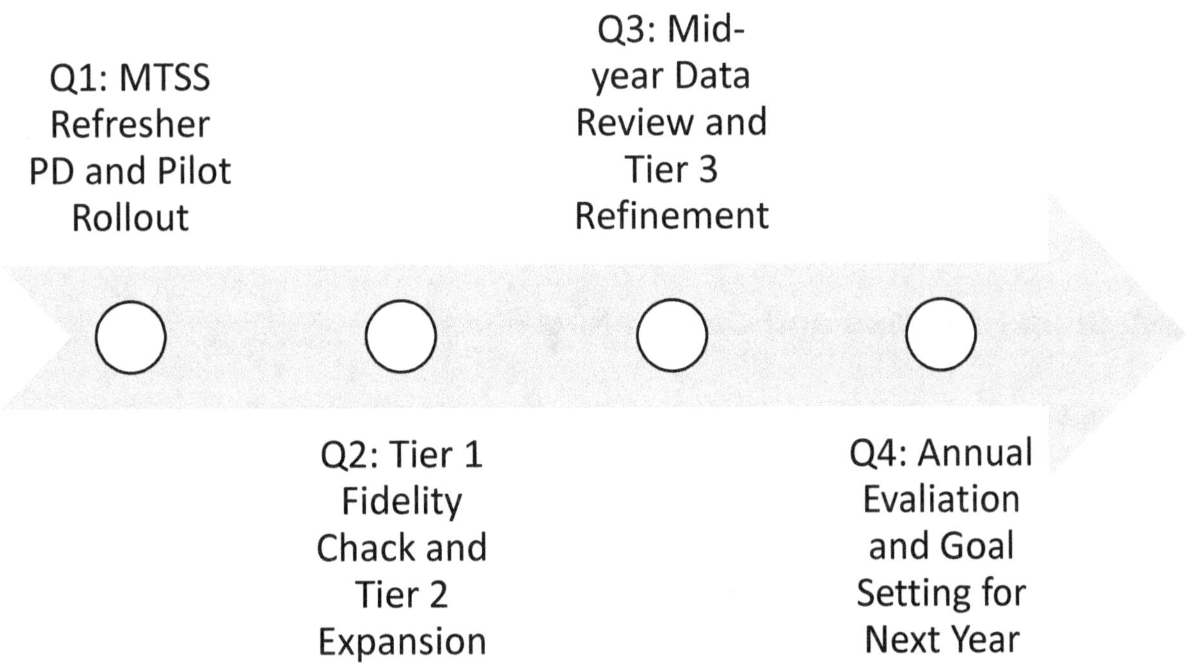

3. Structures and Checkpoints for Accountability

1. **Leadership and Team Roles**
   - **Core MTSS Team:** Consisting of administrators, counselors, general educators, special educators, and family representatives. Clarify each member's responsibilities (e.g., data collection, intervention fidelity checks) (Burns & Gibbons, 2012).
   - **Subcommittees or Grade-Level Leads:** Each grade or department can manage Tier 2/3 scheduling, progress monitoring, and communication with families—reporting back to the core MTSS team (McIntosh & Goodman, 2016).
2. **Documentation Protocols**
   - **Unified Data Platform:** Store logs of Tier 2 and Tier 3 interventions, screening scores, and progress data in a secure, centralized system—making data analysis more efficient (Fergus, 2017).
   - **Fidelity Rubrics:** Use checklists or observation forms to ensure staff deliver interventions with consistency. Peer observations or coaching cycles reinforce accountability (DuFour & Fullan, 2013).
3. **Ongoing Professional Development**
   - **Training Cycles:** Offer mini-PD sessions on the interventions staff are using this quarter (e.g., new reading software, SEL modules) to maintain momentum and clarify best practices (Gay, 2018).
   - **EdTech and Data Mastery:** Provide coaching on digital dashboards or screening platforms so teachers comfortably interpret real-time data, adjusting interventions promptly (Fuchs et al., 2014).

4. Sustaining Progress and Celebrating Wins

1. **Culture of Recognition**
   - **Public Acknowledgments:** Share stories in staff meetings, newsletters, or social media about teacher-led breakthroughs in reading fluency or a dramatic improvement in a student's behavior (Fisher et al., 2021).
   - **Student Involvement:** When students witness their own growth, they become more invested. Showcase achievement gains or SEL milestones in assemblies, highlighting each learner's efforts (Greenberg et al., 2017).
2. **Adapt as You Grow**

- **Scalability:** If one school or grade-level sees consistent positive results, replicate that model elsewhere. This fosters districtwide synergy and a sense of collective success (McIntosh & Goodman, 2016).
    - **Community Partnerships:** As your MTSS evolves, maintain ties with local nonprofits, mental health agencies, or family advocacy groups that can augment wraparound supports (Gay, 2018).
3. **Reflect and Reset Annually**
    - **Year-End Data Summits:** Bring staff, families, and community partners together to review major findings, celebrate gains, and plan refinements. Solidify or revise your roadmap for the next academic year (Marzano, 2017).
    - **Building Institutional Knowledge:** Document each year's improvements and continuing gaps in a living "MTSS Handbook," so new leaders or teachers can seamlessly carry forward (Buffum et al., 2010).

Reflection & Planning

1. **Crafting Your Roadmap**
    - Which data points (e.g., academic, SEL, behavior) will you track to define and measure success?
    - Are your initial goals ambitious yet realistic, given staff capacity and resources?
2. **Implementation Timeline**
    - How will you divide responsibilities among the core MTSS team, grade-level leads, and specialists?
    - What milestones will indicate progress at the 3-, 6-, and 12-month marks?
3. **Ongoing Adaptation**
    - When you encounter unexpected obstacles, do you have a structure (e.g., monthly PLC data reviews) to pivot quickly?
    - Which communication methods—staff meetings, newsletters, social media—will keep families and stakeholders consistently informed and engaged?

By consolidating **all** your reflection and planning notes—from universal supports to intensive interventions, from family engagement to data management—you create a **living roadmap** that guides your MTSS forward. In the subsequent sections of **Chapter 12**, we'll discuss **accountability measures**, **final reflections**, and how to **synthesize every element** of this Blueprint into a cohesive, actionable plan.

12.2 Establishing Accountability Measures

Even the most well-crafted MTSS roadmap relies on **clear, consistent accountability** to bring it from vision to tangible results. Accountability measures ensure that **everyone** involved—leaders, teachers, counselors, families, and community partners—knows their role, tracks progress, and strives toward the same goals (DuFour & Fullan, 2013). This section details how to **design** accountability structures, **monitor** fidelity, and **celebrate** both quick wins and long-term successes, anchoring your MTSS plan in ongoing collaboration and data transparency.

1. Setting Up Review Processes and Feedback Loops

1. **Scheduled Data Reviews**
   - **Recurring Team Meetings:** Establish monthly or bi-monthly MTSS team sessions dedicated to evaluating progress monitoring data (academic, behavior, and SEL). Regular check-ins foster continuous improvement and prevent issues from escalating (McIntosh & Goodman, 2016).
   - **Grade-Level/Department Insights:** Incorporate smaller, more frequent reviews within PLCs or department meetings, allowing teachers to share student performance trends, intervention outcomes, and next-step strategies (DuFour & Fullan, 2013).
2. **Fidelity Observations and Coaching**
   - **Structured Walkthroughs:** Administrators or instructional coaches observe interventions in action—tracking whether strategies are delivered with the essential components intact (Burns & Gibbons, 2012).
   - **Peer Feedback:** Encourage teachers or specialists to conduct brief, non-evaluative peer observations, fostering a culture of shared learning and mutual accountability (Fisher, Frey, & Hattie, 2021).
3. **Transparent Documentation**
   - **One-Stop Data Platform:** Consolidate logs of Tier 2/3 interventions, screening results, and teacher reflections into a unified digital tool (Buffum, Mattos, & Weber, 2010).
   - **Accessible Reporting:** Provide staff and families with concise, jargon-free summaries that highlight each student's growth or areas needing further support (Gay, 2018).

2. Celebrating Quick Wins and Milestones

1. **Acknowledge Incremental Gains**
   - **Short-Term Achievements:** Whether a student gains 5 words-per-minute in reading fluency or a class reduces behavior incidents by 20%, highlighting these small victories sustains motivation (Fergus, 2017).
   - **Public Recognition:** Share anecdotes in newsletters or at staff meetings. Students and families often appreciate seeing their efforts recognized in a community forum (Esparza Brown & Sanford, 2011).
2. **Staff and Leadership Appreciation**

- **Teacher Spotlights:** Shine a light on educators who excel in Tier 2 interventions, SEL facilitation, or data analysis. Positive reinforcement validates their efforts and inspires peers to follow suit (Marzano, 2017).
 - **Ongoing Mentorship:** Pair these "exemplar" staff members with colleagues seeking guidance. Peer-driven mentorship builds capacity and deepens a culture of collaboration (Burns & Gibbons, 2012).
3. **Student-Centered Celebrations**
 - **Growth Tracking:** Involve students in graphing or charting their own progress, making them active participants in their success. When they see tangible gains, they're more likely to persist (Greenberg, Domitrovich, Weissberg, & Durlak, 2017).
 - **Reflective Celebrations:** Close out each quarter or semester by inviting students to share personal challenges they've overcome through Tier 2 or Tier 3 support, reinforcing self-efficacy (Fisher et al., 2021).

3. Sustaining Accountability Over Time

1. **Longitudinal Data Views**
 - **Year-to-Year Comparisons:** Track progress over multiple academic years to identify patterns—such as consistent improvement in early literacy or repeated dips in middle school math (Marzano, 2017).
 - **Equity Audit:** Continue disaggregating data by race, language status, socioeconomic indicators, and more—ensuring that gains are shared across all subgroups (Gay, 2018).
2. **Fidelity and Adaptation**
 - **Mid-Cycle Adjustments:** If data shows insufficient progress or a mismatch between student need and the selected intervention, pivot quickly. Swift adaptation prevents minor issues from becoming systemic (Fuchs, Fuchs, & Vaughn, 2014).
 - **Community Input:** Encourage ongoing feedback from families and local organizations, especially when demographic shifts or external factors affect student engagement (Esparza Brown & Sanford, 2011).
3. **Dedicated Accountability Roles**
 - **MTSS Coordinator or Lead:** A point person (or team) ensures each stakeholder group knows deadlines for data submission, fidelity checks, and reporting. This role orchestrates the multi-tiered puzzle (Buffum et al., 2010).
 - **Shared Responsibility:** Keep in mind that accountability is not about blame—it's about unity of purpose. Every teacher, staff member, and administrator should feel empowered to contribute to students' growth (DuFour & Fullan, 2013).

Reflection & Planning

1. **Mapping Accountability Structures**
   - Which teams or committees already handle data reviews, and how can you align their efforts with MTSS accountability?
   - Does each tier (1, 2, and 3) have designated staff overseeing fidelity and progress checks?
2. **Focusing on Milestones**
   - Are you scheduling monthly or quarterly celebrations of progress (no matter how small)?
   - Which communication methods—like newsletters or staff bulletins—keep the broader community aware of MTSS milestones?
3. **Maintaining Long-Term Commitment**
   - How do you plan to archive data and findings so future teachers and administrators can continue the work seamlessly?
   - If staff turnover occurs, do you have processes in place (e.g., mentorship, PD modules) that sustain institutional memory around MTSS practices?

By weaving **robust accountability measures** into your MTSS roadmap, you foster a culture of **collective ownership** for student outcomes. Systematic data reviews, regular fidelity checks, and a spirit of celebration not only keep staff focused on goals but also validate their dedication to helping every learner thrive. In **Section 12.3**, we'll share **final thoughts and emerging trends** in MTSS—offering a glimpse of future directions and innovative practices to consider as you refine your multi-tiered support system.

12.3 Final Thoughts and Future Directions

A Multi-Tiered System of Supports (MTSS) is more than a collection of strategies or programs—it is a **mindset** rooted in **equity**, **collaboration**, and **continuous learning**. Throughout this Blueprint, we have explored how to design tiered interventions, leverage data effectively, engage families and communities, and nurture an enduring culture of shared responsibility. Section 12.3 looks **beyond** immediate goals—inviting you to consider **emerging trends** and **ongoing opportunities** that can further refine and future-proof your MTSS framework.

1. Evolving Research and Emerging Trends in MTSS

1. **Advanced Data Analytics**
   - **Predictive Modeling:** As technology grows more sophisticated, some districts use predictive analytics to forecast which students are most likely to struggle, allowing for earlier or more targeted interventions (McIntosh & Goodman, 2016).

- **Machine Learning:** Experimental applications of AI can personalize interventions in real time, adjusting lesson difficulty or content as students demonstrate mastery or confusion (Fisher, Frey, & Hattie, 2021).

2. **Holistic SEL and Mental Health Integration**
   - **Trauma-Informed Practices:** Research underscores the importance of recognizing trauma's impact on learning and behavior. Embedding trauma-sensitive approaches into Tier 1 can proactively support more students (Greenberg, Domitrovich, Weissberg, & Durlak, 2017).
   - **School-Based Mental Health Services:** Partnerships with local clinics or telehealth providers can expand Tier 3 support for students needing intensive counseling or therapy, reducing barriers to outside referrals (Gay, 2018).

3. **Micro-Credentials and Personalized PD**
   - **Teacher-Centered Learning Pathways:** Instead of one-size-fits-all workshops, teachers can earn digital badges or micro-credentials in targeted MTSS skills—like culturally responsive reading interventions or SEL facilitation (Fergus, 2017).
   - **Virtual Collaboration:** Online platforms allow educators from different schools—or even different states—to share data dashboards, compare interventions, and problem-solve collaboratively (Burns & Gibbons, 2012).

2. Long-Term Vision for Your School/District

1. **Institutionalizing Equity**
   - **Policy Alignment:** When school boards and district leadership embed MTSS principles into official policies, strategic plans, and budgets, they underscore its importance for **all** students (Buffum, Mattos, & Weber, 2010).
   - **Sustained Data Disaggregation:** Continually examining outcomes by race, language, and other subgroups fosters a districtwide culture of **equitable** resource allocation and **culturally responsive** interventions (Gay, 2018).

2. **Scaling Beyond Academics**
   - **Career and College Readiness:** MTSS frameworks can expand to support not just academic benchmarks, but also pathways to postsecondary success—incorporating career exploration or advanced course supports (Marzano, 2017).
   - **Community Partnerships:** As your MTSS matures, deepen relationships with local businesses, nonprofits, and higher education institutions—bringing real-world projects, internships, or community service into your Tier 1 universal experiences (Esparza Brown & Sanford, 2011).

3. **MTSS as a Lifelong Skill-Building Model**
   - **Transferrable Mindsets:** Students who learn to self-monitor progress, seek help when needed, and set personalized goals carry these mindsets into future academic and career endeavors (Fuchs, Fuchs, & Vaughn, 2014).
   - **Continuous Reflection for Staff:** Educators' practice of ongoing data review, peer coaching, and adaptation can evolve into a lifelong professional stance—improving teaching efficacy and job satisfaction (DuFour & Fullan, 2013).

3. Next Steps for Your MTSS Journey

1. **Commit to Iteration**
   - **Annual MTSS Summits:** Host forums where staff, families, and community members analyze year-end data, reflect on challenges, and propose refinements—ensuring a shared sense of purpose (Greenberg et al., 2017).
   - **Regional Collaborations:** Join or form consortia with neighboring districts, sharing best practices, professional learning opportunities, and resource vetting to avoid reinventing the wheel (Fisher et al., 2021).
2. **Empower Emerging Leaders**
   - **Distributed Roles:** Encourage teachers, counselors, and support staff to become MTSS leads, data coaches, or family liaisons—cementing your system's resilience beyond a single champion (Burns & Gibbons, 2012).
   - **Succession Planning:** Create pathways for younger or newer staff to learn from experienced colleagues, inheriting the knowledge and passion that sustains your MTSS legacy (McIntosh & Goodman, 2016).
3. **Keep Students at the Center**
   - **Co-Design with Students:** Invite student representatives to contribute ideas about how to refine Tier 1 lessons or Tier 2 mentorship programs. Their firsthand experience can illuminate blind spots (Fergus, 2017).
   - **Celebrate Student Growth:** Highlight stories of transformation—whether academic, behavioral, or social-emotional—to remind the community why MTSS matters (Gay, 2018).

Reflection & Planning

1. **Aligning with Future Trends**
   - Are you open to exploring new data tools or AI-driven interventions if they align with your school's capacity and privacy standards?
   - How can you ensure SEL, mental health, and equity remain integral as your MTSS framework matures?
2. **Institutionalizing Your Gains**
   - What policies, job descriptions, and budget lines can permanently embed MTSS roles and resources in your district's structure?
   - Have you identified or created leadership cohorts to champion MTSS beyond current staff?
3. **Long-Term Aspirations**
   - As you achieve early or intermediate MTSS goals, where do you envision your school or district five years from now?

- How might your evolving student demographics or shifts in educational technology shape the next phase of your MTSS?

Embracing **continuous improvement**, nurturing **equitable practices**, and enabling **collective ownership** will keep your MTSS thriving. By staying curious, celebrating progress, and remaining adaptable to fresh insights, you ensure that every student, teacher, and stakeholder experiences the deep and lasting benefits of a holistic, data-informed, and community-driven approach to education.

12.4 Integrating Continuous Feedback and Iterative Refinement

As you embark on implementing your personalized Multi-Tiered System of Supports (MTSS) roadmap, maintaining momentum requires **continuous feedback** and **iterative refinement**. This section delves into establishing mechanisms for ongoing evaluation, fostering a culture of adaptability, and ensuring that your MTSS framework evolves in response to emerging needs and insights. By embedding these practices, your MTSS implementation remains **dynamic**, **responsive**, and **sustainable**, ultimately enhancing outcomes for all students.

1. Establishing Feedback Mechanisms

A. Multiple Feedback Channels

1. **Staff Feedback**
   - **Regular Surveys and Questionnaires:** Distribute anonymous surveys quarterly to gather insights on the effectiveness of interventions, professional development, and overall MTSS implementation. Utilize platforms like Google Forms or SurveyMonkey for ease of distribution and analysis (DuFour & Fullan, 2013).
   - **Focus Groups and Interviews:** Conduct biannual focus groups with teachers, counselors, and administrators to delve deeper into qualitative feedback. These sessions can uncover nuanced challenges and successes that surveys might miss (Fergus, 2017).
2. **Student Feedback**
   - **Student Voice Initiatives:** Implement regular check-ins, such as student councils or suggestion boxes, where students can express their experiences with MTSS interventions. Tools like online forums or digital surveys can facilitate broader participation (Greenberg, Domitrovich, Weissberg, & Durlak, 2017).
   - **Reflective Journals:** Encourage students to maintain journals reflecting on their academic and social-emotional growth, providing valuable insights into the personal impact of MTSS supports (Fuchs, Fuchs, & Vaughn, 2014).
3. **Family and Community Feedback**

- **Parent-Teacher Conferences:** Incorporate MTSS progress discussions into regular parent-teacher meetings, allowing families to provide feedback and collaborate on student support plans (Gay, 2018).
- **Community Forums:** Host annual or semi-annual forums inviting community members, local organizations, and stakeholders to share their perspectives and suggestions for enhancing MTSS practices (Esparza Brown & Sanford, 2011).

B. Utilizing Technology for Feedback Collection

1. **Digital Platforms:** Leverage Learning Management Systems (LMS) or dedicated feedback tools to streamline the collection and analysis of feedback from all stakeholders.
2. **Data Integration:** Ensure that feedback data is integrated into your central MTSS data dashboard, enabling real-time monitoring and responsive action (Marzano, 2017).

Figure 12.2 outlines the continuous cycle of feedback and refinement in MTSS.

Figure 12.2 Feedback and Iterative Refinement Cycle

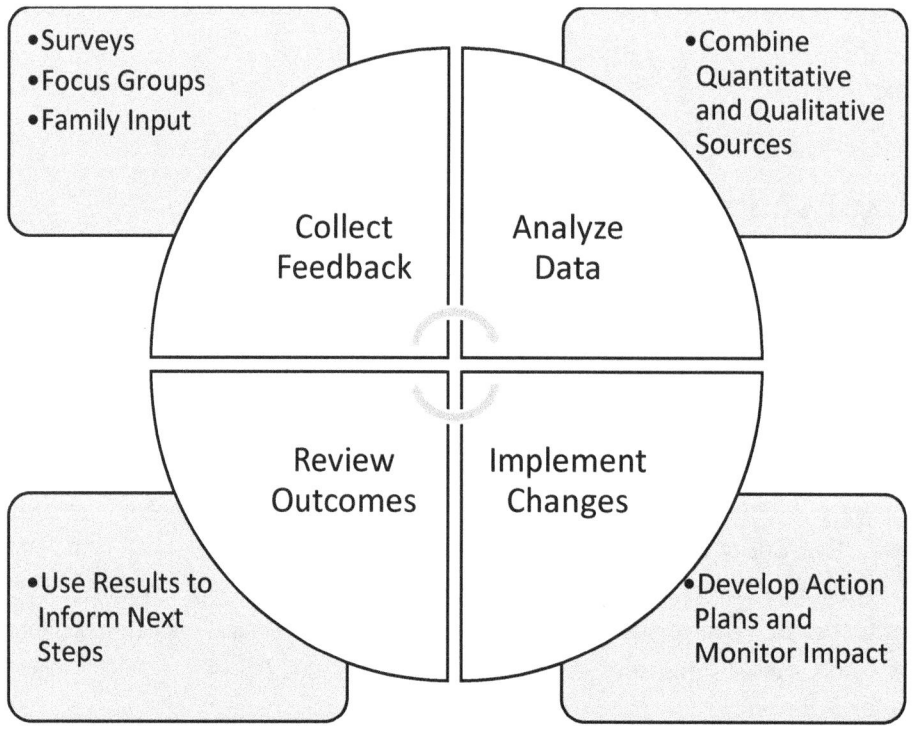

2. Analyzing and Acting on Feedback

A. Systematic Data Review

1. **Triangulation of Data Sources:** Combine quantitative data (e.g., test scores, behavior incidents) with qualitative feedback (e.g., survey responses, focus group insights) to gain a comprehensive understanding of MTSS effectiveness (Buffum, Mattos, & Weber, 2010).
2. **Trend Identification:** Look for patterns or recurring themes in the feedback that indicate strengths to build upon or areas needing improvement (McIntosh & Goodman, 2016).

B. Actionable Insights and Strategic Adjustments

1. **Prioritizing Issues:** Identify the most critical areas for improvement based on impact and feasibility. Focus on high-priority issues that align with your MTSS goals and resource availability (Fisher, Frey, & Hattie, 2021).
2. **Implementing Changes:** Develop targeted action plans to address identified issues. Assign responsibilities, set timelines, and allocate resources to ensure effective implementation (DuFour & Fullan, 2013).
3. **Monitoring Adjustments:** After implementing changes, closely monitor their impact through the established data review cycles. This ensures that adjustments lead to the desired outcomes and allows for further refinements if necessary (Marzano, 2017).

3. Fostering a Culture of Adaptability and Continuous Improvement

A. Promoting Growth Mindset

1. **Staff Development:** Encourage educators to view challenges as opportunities for growth. Provide training on resilience, adaptability, and innovative problem-solving techniques (Fergus, 2017).
2. **Celebrating Efforts:** Acknowledge and celebrate not just successes but also the efforts and creativity involved in overcoming obstacles (Fisher et al., 2021).

B. Institutionalizing Continuous Improvement Practices

1. **Regular Reflection Sessions:** Schedule dedicated times for MTSS teams to reflect on progress, discuss feedback, and brainstorm solutions. These can be part of existing Professional Learning Community (PLC) meetings or separate MTSS-focused gatherings (DuFour & Fullan, 2013).
2. **Iterative Planning Cycles:** Embrace the Plan-Do-Study-Act (PDSA) cycle as an ongoing framework for refining MTSS practices. Each cycle allows for testing new strategies, evaluating their effectiveness, and making informed adjustments (Doran, 1981).

C. Leadership Commitment

1. **Visible Support:** District and school leaders should consistently demonstrate their commitment to MTSS through active participation in meetings, resource allocation, and public endorsements of MTSS initiatives (Burns & Gibbons, 2012).
2. **Empowering Staff:** Provide opportunities for teachers and staff to take ownership of MTSS processes, fostering a sense of agency and accountability across all levels (McIntosh & Goodman, 2016).

4. Sustaining Momentum Through Innovation

A. Embracing New Technologies and Methodologies

1. **Stay Informed:** Keep abreast of the latest research and technological advancements in education, SEL, and behavioral supports to integrate innovative practices into your MTSS framework (Fuchs et al., 2014).
2. **Pilot Emerging Tools:** Experiment with new tools or interventions on a small scale before broader implementation, allowing for evidence-based integration into your MTSS system (Marzano, 2017).

B. Expanding MTSS Beyond Core Areas

1. **Career and College Readiness:** Incorporate supports that prepare students for postsecondary success, such as career counseling, college application assistance, and vocational training opportunities (Gay, 2018).
2. **Holistic Student Development:** Address diverse aspects of student well-being, including physical health, financial literacy, and digital citizenship, ensuring a comprehensive support system (Greenberg et al., 2017).

Reflection & Planning

1. **Evaluating Feedback Effectiveness**
   - How effectively are your current feedback mechanisms capturing diverse stakeholder perspectives?
   - Are there additional channels or methods you could employ to gather more comprehensive feedback?
2. **Adapting to New Insights**
   - What recent feedback has prompted you to rethink or adjust any aspect of your MTSS implementation?
   - How can you ensure that adjustments are data-driven and aligned with your overarching MTSS goals?
3. **Enhancing Continuous Improvement Practices**
   - Are your reflection and planning sessions structured to facilitate honest and productive dialogue?
   - What additional support or resources do staff need to engage fully in continuous improvement efforts?
4. **Innovating for the Future**
   - Which emerging trends or technologies could you explore to further enhance your MTSS framework?
   - How can you cultivate a mindset of innovation among your staff to keep MTSS practices fresh and effective?

By **integrating continuous feedback** and **embracing iterative refinement**, your MTSS framework remains robust, responsive, and resilient. These practices ensure that your system evolves in tandem with your students' needs, educational advancements, and community dynamics, fostering an environment where every learner can thrive. In **Section 12.5**, we will outline a comprehensive checklist and action steps to solidify your MTSS implementation, ensuring that all elements work harmoniously toward sustained success.

Glossary of Key Terms

A

- Academic Intervention: Targeted instructional strategies designed to address specific learning gaps identified through data analysis, typically implemented at Tier 2 or Tier 3 levels within the MTSS framework.
- Adaptability: The ability of an MTSS framework to adjust strategies and interventions in response to evolving student needs and emerging educational trends.
- Assessment: The systematic process of collecting, analyzing, and interpreting data to evaluate student performance and inform instructional decisions.

B

- Behavioral Check-In/Check-Out (CICO): A Tier 2 behavioral intervention where students regularly check in with a mentor or teacher at the beginning and end of the day to set goals and receive feedback, aimed at reinforcing positive behavior.
- Behavioral Supports: Strategies and interventions designed to promote positive behavior and address behavioral challenges within the school environment, often integrated into Tier 1 and Tier 2 supports.

C

- Culturally Responsive Teaching (CRT): An educational approach that recognizes and incorporates students' cultural backgrounds into the curriculum and instruction to enhance engagement and learning outcomes.
- Data Dashboard: A visual tool that consolidates and displays key data metrics related to academic performance, behavior, and social-emotional learning (SEL) to facilitate informed decision-making within MTSS.
- Disproportionality: The overrepresentation or underrepresentation of certain student groups (e.g., by race, language status, socioeconomic status) in Tier 2 or Tier 3 interventions, often indicative of systemic biases or inequities.

E

- Equity Audits: Systematic reviews of educational practices and outcomes to identify and address disparities affecting marginalized or underrepresented student groups, ensuring equitable access to supports within MTSS.
- Equity: The fair treatment, access, and opportunities for all students, taking into account their diverse backgrounds and needs to achieve similar outcomes.

F

- Fidelity of Implementation: The degree to which an intervention or program is delivered as intended by its design, ensuring its effectiveness and reliability within the MTSS framework.
- Feedback Loops: Continuous processes of collecting, analyzing, and responding to feedback from various stakeholders (e.g., staff, students, families) to refine and improve MTSS practices.

G

- Growth Mindset: The belief that abilities and intelligence can be developed through dedication and hard work, fostering resilience and a love for learning among students and staff.

H

- High-Fidelity Intervention: An intervention implemented with strict adherence to its original design and protocols, ensuring its effectiveness and consistency across different settings.

I

- Individualized Intervention Plan: A tailored support plan designed to meet the unique academic, behavioral, or social-emotional needs of a student, typically implemented at Tier 3 within MTSS.
- Inclusive Practices: Teaching strategies and school policies that accommodate and celebrate diverse student backgrounds, ensuring all students feel valued and supported.

L

- Leadership Development: Professional growth initiatives aimed at equipping school and district leaders with the skills and knowledge necessary to effectively implement and sustain MTSS frameworks.

M

- Multi-Tiered System of Supports (MTSS): An integrated framework that provides varying levels of academic, behavioral, and social-emotional support based on students' individual needs, typically structured across three tiers.
- Monitoring Progress: The ongoing process of tracking student performance and behavior to assess the effectiveness of interventions and make data-driven adjustments within MTSS.

P

- Plan-Do-Study-Act (PDSA) Cycle: An iterative four-step model used for continuous improvement, involving planning an intervention, implementing it, studying the results, and acting on the findings to refine practices.

- Positive Behavioral Interventions and Supports (PBIS): A proactive approach to establishing the behavioral supports and social culture needed for all students to achieve social, emotional, and academic success.
- Professional Learning Community (PLC): A group of educators that collaborates regularly to share expertise, analyze student data, and improve teaching practices to enhance student learning outcomes.

R

- Response to Intervention (RTI): A multi-tiered approach to early identification and support of students with learning and behavior needs, focusing primarily on academic interventions and progress monitoring.
- Rubric: A scoring guide used to evaluate the quality and fidelity of intervention implementation, ensuring consistency and accountability among staff.

S

- Social and Emotional Learning (SEL): The process through which students develop the skills to manage emotions, set positive goals, show empathy for others, establish positive relationships, and make responsible decisions.
- Stakeholder Engagement: The active involvement of all parties interested in or affected by MTSS implementation, including teachers, administrators, families, and community partners.

T

- Tiered Interventions: The structured levels of support provided within MTSS, ranging from universal (Tier 1) to targeted (Tier 2) and intensive (Tier 3) interventions based on student needs.
- Translational Practices: Strategies that ensure MTSS frameworks are effectively adapted and applied within the unique contexts of different schools and districts.

U

- Universal Screening: The process of evaluating all students to identify those who may need additional support, ensuring that interventions are based on comprehensive data.

V

- Vision Statement: A clear and inspiring declaration of the district's long-term goals and aspirations for student success through MTSS implementation.

W

- Workforce Development: Efforts to train and prepare educators and support staff with the necessary skills and knowledge to implement and sustain MTSS practices effectively.

References

- Buffum, A., Mattos, M., & Weber, C. (2010). *The why behind RTI.* Solution Tree Press.
- Burns, M. K., & Gibbons, K. (2012). *Implementing response-to-intervention in elementary and secondary schools: Procedures to assure scientific-based practices.* Routledge.
- Doran, G. T. (1981). There's a SMART way to write management's goals and objectives. *Management Review,* 70(11), 35–36.
- DuFour, R., & Fullan, M. (2013). *Cultures built to last: Systemic PLCs at work.* Solution Tree Press.
- Esparza Brown, J., & Sanford, A. (2011). RTI for English language learners: Appropriately using screening and progress monitoring tools to improve instructional outcomes. *National Center on Response to Intervention.*
- Fergus, E. (2017). *Solving disproportionality and achieving equity: A leader's guide to using data to change hearts and minds.* Corwin.
- Fisher, D., Frey, N., & Hattie, J. (2021). *The distance learning playbook: Teaching for engagement and impact in any setting.* Corwin.
- Fuchs, D., Fuchs, L. S., & Vaughn, S. (2014). What is intensive instruction and why is it important? *Teaching Exceptional Children,* 46(4), 13–18.
- Gay, G. (2018). *Culturally responsive teaching: Theory, research, and practice* (3rd ed.). Teachers College Press.
- Greenberg, M. T., Domitrovich, C. E., Weissberg, R. P., & Durlak, J. A. (2017). Social and emotional learning as a public health approach to education. *Future of Children,* 27(1), 13–32.
- Hattie, J., & Zierer, K. (2018). *10 mindframes for visible learning: Teaching for success.* Routledge.
- Marzano, R. J. (2017). *The new art and science of teaching: More than fifty new instructional strategies for academic success.* Solution Tree Press.
- McIntosh, K., & Goodman, S. (2016). *Integrated multi-tiered systems of support: Blending RTI and PBIS.* Guilford Press.
- U.S. Department of Education. (2006). *34 CFR Parts 300 and 301: Assistance to states for the education of children with disabilities and preschool grants for children with disabilities; final rule.* Federal Register.

About the Author

Anthony J. Fitzpatrick, Ed.D. is a highly accomplished educational leader with a robust career spanning over two decades in instructional leadership, curriculum development, and professional development. Dr. Fitzpatrick holds a Doctorate in Leadership with a focus on Instructional Leadership from the American College of Education, a Master of Education in School Leadership from Rowan University, and a Bachelor of Arts in History and Secondary Education, also from Rowan University.

Dr. Fitzpatrick currently serves as the Assistant Superintendent for Curriculum and Instruction for the Delsea Regional and Elk Township School Districts, where he oversees instructional innovation, grant management, professional development, and organizational leadership for a student population of approximately 2,000. His tenure has been marked by initiatives such as federal grant management, educator evaluation enhancements, and the implementation of diverse faculty hiring processes.

Previously, Dr. Fitzpatrick held leadership roles as a principal, supervisor of instruction, and Director of School Innovation at the New Jersey Department of Education. He is recognized for his expertise in professional learning, curriculum articulation, and equity-focused programming. He has also played pivotal roles in state-level initiatives, including the Future Ready New Jersey Certification Program and the AchieveNJ educator effectiveness initiative.

Beyond administration, Dr. Fitzpatrick has a strong background in professional development services, having served as Vice President of Professional Development Services at the American Institute for History Education, where he designed and led national training programs for educators.

Dr. Fitzpatrick is also a published author and sought-after presenter, contributing to the field through scholarly work and thought leadership on topics such as teacher self-efficacy, leadership, grant writing, advocacy, and effective instructional practices. His career demonstrates a consistent focus on improving educational outcomes and fostering an environment of growth and inclusivity for all learners.